The Habit

The Habit

SUSAN MORSE

OPEN ROAD
INTEGRATED MEDIA
NEW YORK

For MB, who never protested

CONTENTS

PREFACE

Nobody dies at the end of this book.

Try not to let this fact mislead you.

As far as my mother is concerned,

it's important to distinguish between what death actually is,

and what it isn't.

There's a body, and there's a soul. One dies, the other doesn't. Ever.

And then there's how I feel about this. Which is complicated.

1.
Correct

I USED TO be able to pick out Ma's parked car from all the way up the block. It's been over a year since she stopped driving, but I still expect to see that beat-up Camry's nose protruding from the line of neatly placed cars, sticking its tongue out at me in cheeky nonparallel defiance. (*There wasn't enough room on the street but, Susie, I simply CAN'T use the garage anymore. That dreadful pillar bashed into my car again this morning. It knocked off my side mirror! I may have been in a bit of a hurry, but we must tell them about that pillar. It's very poorly designed.*)

When I step out of my own law-abidingly parked minivan and head across the street to the lobby of her apartment building, I feel weightless and uneasy. I'm not here to take Ma to the doctor today. I have no shopping bags to plop with the doorman so I can make a quick getaway. No calculator—this is not one of our monthly sessions of despair untangling her impossible checkbook. The kids are in school, my husband's out of town, and nobody else needs me, so I'm here. Nothing to protect me but a rather gigantic chip on my shoulder, and my camera. I'm on a strictly social call. Social calls can be dangerous.

My mother is becoming a nun today. She's eighty-five, so I guess it's about time.

I'm pretty sure it's just a new attempt to secure my full, undivided attention.

I gave up trying to educate myself on Ma's religious pursuits when I reached the age of consent. The identifying aspects of her latest conversion are a bit of a blur (we're on number six, after all). I do know an Orthodox Christian church when I see one now—their cross is distinctive. It has the traditional upright beam with the crossbar most people know. But instead of a single horizontal, you get three: There's the classic beam about a third of the way down, as expected, and a smaller one at the top, which must be the plaque they posted above Jesus's head. I can't make any sense of that other odd little messed-up beam near the bottom. It's cockeyed; sort of dangling, as if an essential nail popped out and nobody had the nerve to fix it.

We're coping with all kinds of inconvenient new Orthodox differences, like Christmas, which Ma insists must be in January now, not December. And there's been an awful hullabaloo about who gets to be a saint. There was a schism in the eleventh century when a bunch of Christians disagreed about something, and they all excommunicated one another. Then the upstart Roman Catholic Church's crusaders grabbed a lot of priceless icons and relics in Constantinople and made off with them so they could hog all the glory in the West. The Orthodox are essentially Eastern, which is closer to where Jesus lived, and they refuse to acknowledge any of the new saints named by *heretic* Roman popes. Francis of Assisi is not legit. He's pleasant enough but *sadly misinformed*: a pope's man with a thing about birds. Ma's got her own Orthodox saints now: Nicholas, the murdered tsar; his extinguished wife and children; and lots of others, Greeks and Russians mostly, with long complicated names I'd rather not try to keep straight. Even if I could.

I'll have to shake myself into a more open-minded, friendly mood before I reach the tenth floor, because there will be other people up in Ma's apartment. A few of her old friends have rallied at the last minute. The bishop called yesterday on his way down from Toronto to announce that her in-home nun ceremony is finally a go. They call it *tonsure*. Younger, fitter candidates must be tonsured in church—I hear they lie prostrate on the floor for a large chunk of the service. Because of Ma's advanced age and general decrepitude, she gets a break.

There will be priests—but not the kind I'm used to. Not the Episcopalian kind who baptized me as an infant: their only distinguishing accessory an unassuming white collar tucked almost apologetically into the neckband of a plain black shirt. And not the Roman Catholic kind who came next, swathed in rich satin brocade. Today's priests on the tenth floor of Ma's building will be the kind who really sorted her out for good with a full immersion dunk in the River Jordan a few years ago. These guys are old school: serious Orthodox Christian dudes with gigantic crosses chained to their necks; long beards and ponytails; exotically draped Middle Eastern-type robes.

The elevator in Ma's building stalls on occasion, so I have the front desk's number on speed-dial in my cell phone. I could use a little interval suspended between floors today, on the off-chance my timing's not right—when I told Ma I'd skip the main event this morning and just arrive in time for the after-ceremony brunch, her lack of protest put me on guard. I've learned to dodge Ma's ceremonies, no matter how hard she tries to get me there. My attendance can be interpreted as spiritual hunger, and trigger a flood of instructional pamphlets in my mailbox with helpful notes in the margin and follow-up pop quizzes on the telephone.

The doors slide open. I take deep cleansing breaths on the long walk to the end of the hall, plaster on a smile for my bad-prodigal-daughter-who-missed-the-important-stuff entrance. An elaborate crucifix hangs reproachfully over Ma's peephole. On the other side of this door will be my mother, reborn. I turn the knob.

There are six people sprinkled around the living room. Walls lined with choice artwork and old family photographs do nothing to absorb the crackle of tension in the air. Ma is nowhere in sight.

I shake hands with Olivia and Babbie, huddled together in the corner looking slightly startled: dear old friends who live nearby in a retirement community. My friend Margaret's mother, Ellie, is also here. She's devoted to Ma, and seems sincerely relieved to see me for some reason.

Photini, Ma's Orthodox partner in crime, is perched near Ma's paint box and easel: prim on the fraying sofa in her usual kerchief and Amish-style denim pinafore. She and Ma met at a Byzantine icon workshop when they were both still infidels. (Ma's the one who decided they had to go Orthodox. She found the first church they tried in the Yellow Pages.) Photini introduces me first to a nondescript, mousy little man in faded blue jeans with a gentle smile whose name goes instantly in one burning ear and out the other. Next is a guy I mistakenly assume is the bishop. It turns out he's actually part of the entourage: a priest. He has the standard cassock-type thing over his significant belly, long hair tied back out of the way, and a huge frizzy white beard that is trying to take over the whole top half of his body. He's very excited when he hears my last name.

—You're the daughter with that husband! I *wanted* to meet you! I thought *I* was going to be an actor, too!

This kind of non sequitur can throw me. My life's been so disconnected from that show business world since we moved back East thirteen years ago. Days will go by without me even remembering what my husband does. When this fuzzy-faced, friendly hedgehog of a person erupts with a delighted riff about his early years in the theatre, I'm speechless—too self-conscious with our family eccentricities all out in the open like this. Everyone seems to be waiting for me to say something, and no socially acceptable response comes to mind: *How sensible of you to fall back on becoming a leader in an obscure religious sect instead; why didn't I think of that when I gave up acting?* Or: *Maybe if you'd had a shave and a haircut you could have had more range?*

Better to change the subject.

—Where's my mother?

Ellie lifts her eyebrows.

—She's in the bedroom having confession with the bishop.

—Oh, how was the service?

—It hasn't happened yet.

—Oh great, I say. I was *so* hoping I wouldn't miss anything.

Ellie looks skeptical. She has known me since I was three.

My cell phone rings: my brother, Felix, calling, safe in Vermont.

—How did it go?

—Still hasn't started. They seem to be running behind. You know Ma.

—Right. What's happening?

—I guess she's having an extra-long session in the bedroom with the bishop.

—In the *bedroom*?! What are they doing in the *bedroom*?

—Apparently, confession.

—Oh. Good for Ma. She's got a *lot* of stuff to cover, so don't hold your breath.

There are bagels for after the service, which Olivia tells me conspiratorially are her calculated donation in the spirit of ecumenism. It seems the need for unity, respect, and cooperation between the various Christian faiths is what was being debated when I arrived. Orthodox Christians aren't big on cooperation. The one thing I actually have looked up is the definition of that suspicious qualifying adjective: orthodox. We've all heard of Orthodox *Jews*—they're the ones with all the dietary restrictions. What's an Orthodox *Christian*?

Orthodox means *Traditional*, according to an online thesaurus, which is not offensive. It also means *Correct*, and this is where they lose me. It's not sporting to name your religion *Correct Christianity*. Ellie, who is not without her own opinions, tells me she desperately needed a way to change the subject while they were all waiting for Ma to emerge from the bedroom, because things were advancing to a confrontational head. Perhaps this explains why she looks so glad to see me.

Between Ellie's ecumenism and Olivia's bagels, I'm feeling a reassuring sensation of solidarity. Behind them on the wall (flanked by two nineteenth-century Italian sconces—old family treasures) is a gilt-framed canvas I covet: a still life of tart green apples so immediate they make your teeth hurt, painted by Ma during a typically fraught visit with us in Los Angeles before the kids were born and we moved here to Philadelphia. Ma's art is a confusing comfort to me; it's so compelling, it almost makes up for everything. I check the pass-through kitchen to see what needs doing. It's pretty tidy, but I know enough not to open any cupboards or drawers (there is alive stuff in there, and it might escape).

This business about confession shouldn't surprise me. Felix was only partly serious, but still: What if this is some kind of test? I thought the tonsure ceremony was a done deal, but who knows? What's really going on in that bedroom? She could be facing herself so sincerely that the bishop (or maybe even Ma herself) might decide she's just not cut out for this nun idea after all. What's everybody going to do then? Eat the bagels and go home?

I peer down the hall, past Ma's gallery dominated by all of our Main Line patrician ancestors I can't ever get straight. They are partly to blame for this mess we're in now: pale, inbred, and inscrutable in lace and starched collars. I watch the closed bedroom door. I wait.

2.
Special

MA IS EIGHTY-FIVE. She's struggling with a stomachache. We've been on the phone a lot, especially tonight, which happens to be the night before my birthday.

Ring. Ring.

—Hello?

—Susan?

—Yes. Hello, Doctor Maxwell.

My mother and her GP have been playing phone tag all week. She calls his office and offers unintelligible descriptions of her digestive affliction to the staff:

—*Tell the doctor that there has been considerable difficulty with elimination, resulting in great distress in the undercarriage, if you please.*

This is passed on to Maxwell, who doesn't seem to be grasping the urgency of the situation. I sense we are destined for a colon specialist of some kind, but I dread the process of choosing one. My mother has strict specifications, which she won't articulate. I have to guess.

Last month, she wanted a gynecologist. When I checked her HMO's approved list:

—*How about John Mathews at Stone Mills Hospital?*

—I won't go to one in Stone Mills; it has to be Abington and it has to be a woman.

—Okay, how about Alice Greenberg in Abington?

—No.

—Why? What do you know about her?

—I just know I don't want to see her.

—Ruth Rothschild?

—I don't want to see her, either.

—Ma. What's going on here?

—Nothing, I just don't—

—I've got one for you: Martha Sullivan. Nice Catholic-sounding name. That okay with you? Oh, never mind—someone named Ali Mohammed shares the office with her, we can't have that—

—Oh stop it. I have to be comfortable. This is my body and I have to feel all right about who I see.

This afternoon, I poked my nose in and called Maxwell's office myself. Maybe they've spoken to each other by now.

—Susan. Your mother has explained her symptoms to me, and I am deeply concerned.

—Okay.

Maxwell is my GP, too, and my husband's. This outburst is a little abrupt for him, which is alarming. Like most doctors for whom medicine is a calling as well as a career, he does his best to keep things human with a little personal talk before getting into the technical. When my mother is the subject, we usually have to first get through *Susan Susan Susan. I want to make sure you're taking care of yourself. That woman is incredibly headstrong, so first I want to know about YOU.*

Maxwell's as busy as any doctor, which makes it easy to excuse him for forgetting I've heard this lecture over and over. But tonight he cuts straight to the chase:

—Susan. She needs to go to the emergency room at Abington Hospital and be evaluated right away. Can you drive her there?

—Of course. (It would have been nice if they had spoken earlier

*in the week, when this could have been handled in a normal office
instead of the frigging ER. . . .)*

—Susan. Did you know she has blood in her stool?

—What?

—This is very serious, Susan. Your mother may have a bowel
obstruction. It could be a matter of Life and Death.

Ma sits erect on a bed in Abington's ER, managing somehow to look
elegant in her hospital gown. People often say we resemble each other,
which makes me uneasy and pleased at the same time. I wouldn't mind
aging as gracefully as she has, with her limber, trim figure and flashy,
close-cropped white hair. She's mostly been blessed with good physical
health—I've only had to take her to an emergency room once, eleven
years ago, when she slipped on some ice and broke a kneecap. We did
spend a lot of time together in an ICU in Florida when my father was
dying. Those two events aside, it occurs to me now that the only other
time we've been in a room in a hospital together would have to have
been forty-eight years ago almost to the day. The night I was born.

We've brought an overnight bag, and Ma's friend Bess has typed up
a list of her medications and supplements. But the intake nurse, Jeffrey,
wants to hear it from Ma.

—Do you have any allergies?

—Lots, says Ma.

—Like what? How about medications? Antibiotics?

—I am allergic to all antibiotics.

—All?

—Yes.

—How do you know? Did you take them all?

—No, I didn't have to. I took one or two and now I just know.

—Which one or two?

—I don't know.

—What doctor prescribed them?

—I don't remember; it was in Sarasota.

—What happened when you took them?

—I just felt—ah.

Ma gives a discreet little gasp, tilts her head, and looks pained.

I love my mother's description of her near-fatal brush with antibiotics. For years, I have been dreading the moment when some doctor tells her antibiotics are the only way to keep her alive and she refuses them because one time years ago in Florida, some drug nobody made a note of caused her to gasp a little and look pained. What if she is unconscious and they want me, with the Medical Power of Attorney, to approve the use of them? Do I allow it because I don't think her explanation has been valid enough, and possibly cause her accidental death? Or do I withhold them per her wishes, which could kill her for sure?

Which reminds me of Maxwell: a matter of Life and Death. And here we are.

Jeffrey ponders.

—Where are you from? he asks.

—I'm from Philadelphia.

—No, I mean originally—your accent is British, right?

—This is the way I was brought up to speak, by my family and my school, Shipley.

Ma's people were Philadelphia WASPs. They all had nicknames like Gaga, Aunt Tiny, Cousins Buckety and Hebe Dick. Ma's mother was born where her family summered on the Isle of Wight: a few miles off the southern coast of England, conveniently and strategically within very close range of Queen Victoria and Prince Albert's summer digs. That whole side of the family had faintly British accents going back many generations. My grandmother somehow managed to pass hers on to Ma and the rest of her children, despite the sketchy amount of time she actually lived with them. This mostly depended on how long my grandmother stayed married to their fathers and whether or not the courts deemed her fit to be left alone with her own children while she was carrying on with dwindled funds and whatever dashing but equally penniless new husband she had taken up with at the time.

Jeffrey releases Ma's blood pressure cuff.

—Shipley? We played against them in high school.

—Really? It's very different now. When I was there it was a girls' school. In the back of one of the alumni bulletins last year, there was a picture of three young women. . . .

(I have a feeling I know where this is going.)

—One of the women was an alumna. She was posing between her new wife and the female chaplain who had just performed their wedding. I wrote the headmistress that it simply *wouldn't do.*

I watch to see how Jeffrey will take this. Not a blink. Good for him.

They do an x-ray and there is no obstruction. They decide the cramping is due to the senna tea Ma took for constipation, and recommend she see a colorectal surgeon as soon as she can. We are free to leave.

On the ride home, we notice it is after midnight, and I point out it is now my birthday, which I had insisted I didn't want to spend with her this year.

Ma crows in delight:

—Right at the time of day you were born!

My birth was not an easy one. There were fifteen years and five miscarriages between Ma's first child (my brother, Felix) and her youngest (me). Two sisters between us survived, thanks to luck and whatever god-awful drugs they used back then to deal with our parents' unusual situation: Ma had that rare Rh-negative baby-killing blood, and Daddy's was Rh-positive. This incompatibility could have been seen as a sign of the greater obstacles they faced as a married couple, but it was particularly problematic when producing children. The babies in this situation tend to inherit their father's more common blood type, which is eventually lethal to the mother. So Ma's body had to automatically produce antibodies after Felix, her first Rh-positive child was born, in order to keep her blood cells intact. These antibodies would then kill off the rest of her Rh-positive babies one by one, her body deliberately rejecting its own offspring in order to save itself.

Ma's always told me she was sick as a dog during her pregnancy with me, and even wished at times that I'd get it over with and abandon ship like the other five miscarriages.

—*But you didn't. I couldn't understand why you were being so stubborn.*

By my birthday in 1959, the doctors were attempting a few new tricks. Since my mother's blood and its lethal antibodies would enter my system during delivery and kill me, they swept me away within hours of my birth for two complete transfusions and stuck me in an incubator for almost a week. I can still make out little scars between my fingers and toes from their incisions. I'm a miracle of science.

—*Actually, I had already guessed you were* Special *because of my veins.*

Ma had been a smoker for years, through all the other pregnancies and births. I guess no doctor in the 1940s or 1950s knew enough to point out that everyone involved might be better off if she'd quit. Still, just after Ma knew she was pregnant with me, she says, when she took a drag of a cigarette the veins on the backs of her hands immediately hurt *like the dickens.* So she stopped cold turkey. Her theory is that Someone was looking out for us, because I was *Special.*

Philadelphia, 1960

According to my mother, it was important for me *in particular* to survive this antibody thing. I've never been entirely clear as to why she thinks I was chosen to make it in 1959, or if such a thing is even possible—this *someone's* supposed plan is taking time to reveal itself. There's one thing we know for sure: My other siblings aren't geographically, physically, or emotionally available right now to drive Ma to the ER for a matter of Life and Death.

I went along with Ma's *Special Susie* theory for a spell. My Montessori school was seen by her as her finest discovery to date as a parent, following years of disappointment in the early education options for my older siblings. My brother and sisters saw the delight she took in my resulting supposed *brilliance* as favoritism. There was a four-year gap between my next oldest sibling and me; I was the prized, irritating baby who sucked up all the attention, and none of them could hide their disgust at seeing me trundled out to recite Shakespeare or sing "The First Noel" for the dinner guests at age three.

It didn't occur to me not to accept the petting and praise until the treatment began to rankle as a teenager. That's when I figured out that distance was optimal. Till then, along with all the religious conversions there had been an awful lot of school switches for one reason or another—not all of them, in fairness, due to my mother's whim—nine moves in total. By a twist of luck, I was shipped out to a Rhode Island boarding school in eleventh grade, followed by college in the Berkshires.

I felt liberated once I was away from home, but not quite liberated enough. My parents separated temporarily after I left, due to intense disagreements, which could have otherwise led to mass casualties (he thought she spent too much, she thought he drank too much—they were both right). I discovered the theatre, and they would each take turns coming to see me perform. Daddy would drive up with one change of underwear and a couple of bottles of vodka stashed in the trunk of his VW beetle. He was pretty self-sufficient, but Ma had a knack for picking the most academically stressful weekend possible and making peculiar demands:

—*My bus arrives at eleven tonight.*

—*I have a ninety-page paper due in the morning.*

—*That's all right. You can meet me at the bus and help me carry my suitcases to your dorm.*

—*But that's completely across campus! Why do you want to come to my dorm at eleven at night anyway? Can't you go to the hotel and meet me for breakfast?*

—*I can't afford a hotel because of your father. Find me a room in your dorm.*

—*Ma. There's only one empty room in my whole dorm. It's empty because the last person who slept there had a breakdown. They found him in the closet with a dry cleaner's bag over his head and now nobody wants to go near it.*

—*That will be fine. I'll need a pillow, though, and some sheets. And I see you have a French class the next day. I'll come with you to that.*

—*Oh my gosh. Please don't come to my class, nobody's parents ever do that. It's tiny and the professor is really boring.*

—*Nonsense. I'll be fascinated.*

(This was a class with only four students. We would sit around a small table with the professor, and he really was very, very boring. Ma came as promised, sat right next to him, and was snoring within the first ten minutes.)

Williamstown, 1980

After college, I made a beeline for Hell's Kitchen in Manhattan where I hoped to become an actress of the Chekhov/Shakespeare variety. I took great pleasure in breaking out of the conventional mold in which I'd been raised, and got an optimistic start in *Macbeth*, off-off-off Broadway in the Bowery. (I felt particularly drawn to the nutcase roles because they reminded me so much of my mother. Playing Lady Macbeth was like pulling on a comfy old bathrobe.)

My parents were polite but dubious about my career choice. My father had made it crystal clear that after college I'd be taking care of myself, so there wasn't much Ma could do, although she was worried about my dodgy new neighborhood. I'm still not sure if I liked living on the rougher side of town simply in order to reject my roots, or because Ma would be less likely to visit. She had always seemed disappointed in my boyfriends, and began looking for opportunities to introduce me to nice young men who lived on the East Side, with promising, solid but dull futures. My roommate and I didn't need an alarm clock because most mornings started at seven a.m. with a wake-up call from Ma, wanting to discuss my prospects:

—*How did you like that nice boy, Matt Thing?*

—*Who?*

—*You know, the one who went to Andover and Penn and drove you back to the city last weekend after you were here.*

—*Oh. Stupid.*

—*Susie!*

—*Really, he was. When we got to my corner, he took one look at the guys standing outside the deli and he said he couldn't let me out of the car in such a dangerous neighborhood. These people are my* FRIENDS, *Ma.*

Not long after I got to New York, I did manage to fall in love with David Morse, an actor who wandered in for a bowl of chowder at the bar I was tending on the corner of Fifty-first Street and Ninth Avenue. Barely any words were exchanged at our first meeting other than a brief discussion about the quality of the soup (David thought it was lacking in heft). I didn't think much about the encounter till the following week when he wandered in again, looking as if he sort of didn't know what he was doing there. The restaurant was deserted except for the cook in the back and me in the front—we weren't open yet, and when I asked David if I could help him, he asked if I'd like to go out some time.

Yes, I said, somewhat baffled (not just because I'd accepted a date with a complete stranger, but because he then nodded, turned abruptly, and walked back outside and down the street).

Our courtship took place over the bar. David would bring friends in to get their approval of me or something, and the friends would do most of the talking. I began to wonder if he ever planned to mention that date possibility again. I finally decided to bring it up myself, and by the second date, we were pretty much fused at the hip.

I almost ruined David's extremely cagey marriage proposal. He had just found out he was going to have to go to L.A. for an undetermined amount of time to play a doctor in a new hospital series called *St. Elsewhere.* This was exciting, but it felt worrisome to think of the geographical distance.

—*Have you ever thought about getting married?* he asked.

Sensing some degree of reluctance, I parried:

—*To who?*

This seemed to stump him. He paused for so long, I had to quickly rescue us both (not to mention our future children) by proposing more directly myself.

California, 1984

26

We went together to L.A., and it seemed that my metamorphic escape was complete. Philadelphia was virtually in another country, and Ma's early morning phone calls had to stop because of the time difference. I managed to act in occasional plays, but mostly got roles in small movies and guest appearances on sitcoms.

It's hard to look me up because I couldn't settle on a stage name. Before I met David, I was foolish enough to try my maiden name, von Moschzisker. This seemed to irritate people. The *z* is silent—if you ignore the *schz* and make it a *sh* sound you can come close to being able to pronounce the name unassisted, but still: Susan von Moschzisker? That girl didn't stand a chance.

My married name was not an option—the Screen Actors Guild had a Susan Morris, and they said they'd get us confused. When my agent put her foot down about von Moschzisker, I tried being Susan Wheeler Duff, using my two middle names. Even that seemed excessive, so I finally shortened it again, to Susan Wheeler. This turned out all right, although I kept worrying that people might check and think I was padding my résumé, claiming false credit for jobs that Susan von Moschzisker and Susan Wheeler Duff had done.

Just when Susan Wheeler began to hit her stride, our daughter, Eliza, arrived, swiftly followed by twin sons, Ben and Sam.

Twin sons came as a bit of a shock. By the time Ben and Sam were born, David's series was over and he was traveling more for work. I think I may have had a mild but undiagnosed case of post-partum depression or something—I was terrified of accidents and didn't want to be alone with the children. So I was uncharacteristically glad to see Ma when she came to meet the new babies. Ma's visits were usually not in response to an invitation, and mostly fraught with tension—she'd spend a lot of her stay trying to convert me to whatever her latest religion was. Or she'd hand us an itemized list on her way back to the airport of what should have been in the guest room:

- *A lamp by the bed*
- *Pleasant, interesting reading material*

- *A full-length mirror AND a small hand mirror to check the back of one's head in the bathroom*
- *A television or AT LEAST a radio. With a clock.*
- *A telephone, preferably with its own private line and answering machine*
- *Fresh water, flowers, and a bowl of fruit*
- *A mini-fridge to store extra food, in case the fruit is not to the guest's liking*

But that visit when the boys were infants was truly remarkable. Ma loves babies and seemed more than happy to pitch in. She did all the grocery shopping, held one twin and entertained Eliza while I nursed the other, and generally made herself so indispensable that when it was time for her to leave, I completely surprised myself by asking her to stay another week.

Sherman Oaks, 1992

It's important to give credit where it's due. All that kindness without the comfort of a mini-fridge.

It quickly became clear that having two acting parents was not ideal for children. I really loved mothering, and David was the bigger earner, so it seemed natural for me to give up auditioning for sitcoms and embrace my inner Susan Morse, especially after our Sherman

Oaks house was destroyed in the Northridge earthquake in 1994. We abruptly decided to move our headquarters to more solid, familiar territory in Philadelphia. This was David's idea, and I agreed, partly because Ma and Daddy had moved to Florida a few years before and were not showing any signs of returning. Eliza was five, and the boys were two. Adolescence was around the corner, we knew L.A. was risky for teenagers, and we just couldn't imagine them having their childhoods in New York. David loved my old stomping grounds in Stone Mills, a walking neighborhood on the outskirts of Philadelphia with good shops, near a rambling city park. I'd heard the insular, self-satisfied *Preppy Handbook* quality that used to bother me as a kid was changing, and I got the feeling we'd be in good company. A number of old friends had also spent their early professional lives in larger cities, where they'd had a chance to broaden their horizons a bit before returning to raise families in a child-friendly environment. The idea of embracing the best of my roots to establish the kind of happy family I felt I'd missed out on was a tempting challenge—a chance to "get it right."

Everything went as planned until a couple of years later, when our father died. I spent some time down in Florida with Ma while she was presiding over his last weeks in the ICU. Observing her careful consideration and poise during that rocky transition was an experience just as intense and precious as when the babies were little. Ma's better, twin-tending side seemed to really kick in if birth or death was afoot. I knew she was getting on in years and there was no family at all nearby in Florida. There was also the unfortunate discovery that Daddy had made no provision for Ma to cope alone in their Florida house; it was mortgaged to the hilt. On impulse, knowing that none of my siblings would consider tackling the job, I asked Ma to move home. Five minutes from my house.

And thus began *Operation Ma*.

I'm the self-appointed CEO/CFO of Op Ma: a series of maneuvers we siblings design as we go, to make our mother's years as a widow (left with suddenly limited resources and risky ideas) as comfortable and safe as possible. David is away on location many months out of the year, our three children are teenagers, and we have a temperamental old house, a dog, and two cats, one of whom, Marbles, has been with us since the earthquake and is now hanging on by a thread.

And I am pre-menopausal.

I voted against George Bush twice in a row. The second time, I campaigned vigorously for his opponent.

My mother told me she was voting for Ross Perot in 2000—she doesn't remember doing it now, and she doesn't remember why she might have. She began watching Fox News after 9/11.

—*The Muslims are taking over and he's the only one who sees how dangerous they are.*

—*Excuse me?*

—*They are evil, craven, and George Bush understands them.*

—*Sure he does. He did not have a passport when he was elected. He could not name the leaders of several countries, but somehow he understands Muslims.*

—*Susie, you don't realize how serious this is—*

—*Well, yes, actually, I do, Ma. That's why I'd like to have a president with half a brain.*

When Ma helped reinstall the president in 2004, something began to unravel in me. While she communed with Sean Hannity and Bill O'Reilly, I spent a solid two years compulsively glued to Jon Stewart and National Public Radio. Our consternation with each other increased, until things came to a head in 2006. I was in the middle of a rather tricky project, sending all three kids off on service trips to various third-world countries, and planning Eliza's twenty-stop college tour. I had asked Ma to try and avoid any urgent disasters for a few weeks until I got through that crunch. With her uncanny sense of timing, she managed to have her Toyota impounded for expired registration and close to a thousand dollars' worth of unpaid parking tickets.

Ma (dressed in Bergdorf's on credit, standing with me to pick up her car amid a sea of equally battered vehicles, taking in the long line of other dejected traffic offenders): *This is something I have in com-mon with Blacks.*

Ma was always a narcissistic driver, viewing things like Stop signs, speed limits, and No Parking zones as irritants installed and enforced with *no rhyme or reason by bureaucratic pencil pushers with nothing better to do.* Friends and family had hinted for years that it would be good to get her off the road. I'd passed these observations on to Ma, along with my own opinion, and definitely didn't let her drive anyone in our family around. But I didn't feel it was my place to apply too much pressure until the car's incarceration, when financial things were up to me. David makes a good living; he's well thought of enough to have steady work, but like most working actors, it's a living, not a Tom Cruise-like fortune. Plus, this was an opportunity to make the roads a little safer.

The deal I offered Ma for the impounded Camry was wily but appropriate. To her credit, Ma saw the sense in it. Operation Ma would bail the car out of jail as long as she would take a senior citizen's driving test to see if she was safe on the road. This seemed more than fair to her, mostly because Doctor Maxwell warned me on the phone that unfortunately most of his elderly patients managed to take this test and keep their credentials even though their families were sure they would not.

As far as I was concerned, Ma's driving was no worse than it had been when I was a child. This had nothing to do with her advanced age, but I figured at least if someone else judged her to be good to go, any resulting disaster would not be on my head.

The testing man, incoherent on the phone after Ma's exam:

—*I have never in my life*—*the other cars honking, I'm having these flashbacks, I tried to save us, but she kept calling me an ass.* Don't be an ASS, *she said.* What is WRONG *with her?? And I wanted to get my door open and JUMP for it, but she didn't STOP, she just*—*oh. I'm sorry, I'm going to tell her doctor the truth, I can't be unethical, I'm*—*oh, oh, I have to hang up, I'm not well* . . .

Doctor Maxwell, later that afternoon:

—*Susan Susan Susan.*

—*I know.*

—*Get rid of the car. And it might be a good idea to have your mother checked out for mental impairment.*

All this was going on in between trips to the Center for Infectious Diseases to get the kids' typhoid vaccines and malaria pills, and tense spats with our college-bound senior, Eliza, who wouldn't even look at schools in Ohio for some reason (what's wrong with Ohio?), let alone anywhere in an earthquake or hurricane zone. I was close to the breaking point.

For me, Ma's car trouble was simply an illustration of values she seemed to share with all those people cheering for George W. Bush. Pre-emptive war was necessary. Taxes, bank regulations, and parking tickets were not. And as soon as they turned eighteen, Ma's grandsons would need to lay down their lives defending her right to ignore them. Or something like that. It was a last straw type of thing, and I found I just couldn't deal.

It was the eve of the midterm elections in 2006. The Republicans were out of favor with most of the country, but there was that stubborn 30 percent still hanging on, and one of them was my newly indoctrinated neocon bible-thumping mother. What happened to Ma and me was classic. We saw it all around us: Our relationship, tenuous enough already, fractured along the red state/blue state divide. I told Ma that I would figure out what to do with the battered car, pay the bills, run the errands, and keep her safe, because I may be a bit of a brat but I was a Democrat brat and that's what good little Democrats do.

But I couldn't sit across the dinner table from Ma and smile just yet. Birthdays and all that pseudo-harmonious chitchat and folderol were not going to be happening this year.

Ring. Ring. Doctor Maxwell.

3.
The Answer To Everything

RING. RING.

—Hello?

—Hi, Ma.

—Oh, how are you?

—Okay, how are you?

—All right. There was a fire alarm in the middle of the night.

—Oh my gosh, did you have to go down the stairs?

—No. I called them, and they said *don't you worry about it, dear.*

Ma lives on the tenth floor of a nice, haphazardly managed building with a temperamental fire alarm system. It's what's known as a Nork, or Naturally Occurring Retirement Community because, with its twenty-four-hour doorman and easy handicapped access, it attracts a lot of senior citizens.

When the fire alarm goes off, sometimes the elevator shuts down. This unnerves older people on the top floors. Their general tactic is to ignore any alarms and cross their fingers. It's been hard since New Year's Eve several years back, when an especially ancient and addled resident left an electric heater unattended and burned her apartment to cinders. Ma was celebrating at our house so she missed all the excitement. Her friends down the hall, Dorothy (Lou Gehrig's disease) and

Bess (mysteriously accident-prone) described a harrowing trip down ten flights of stairs to join a milling throng of disoriented residents waiting for buses to drive them to temporary housing. You can't assume the alarms will always be false, and they happen a little too often for it to be fun.

—You didn't check the emergency channel on the TV?

—No I couldn't remember how to do that.

When they wired the building for cable, they gave everyone a special converter to connect with the camera in the front entrance. It doesn't make any emergency announcements; you just see what the front lobby looks like in real time. It's really to check out visitors before allowing them to come up. During fire alarms, you can try to read the attendant's body language: If he is running back and forth and his clothes are on fire, or if there are men trotting past with hoses and axes, it would be good to evacuate. Better than nothing, but the technique for getting the front desk on the screen is not senior-friendly. I find this counterproductive: How do they expect someone to start twiddling obscure buttons on their TV when a siren is blasting and they are rattled enough already?

—Oh, Ma.

—I know I know—Josie's on the other line let me tell her to get off—

Click.

I wish the phone company had never offered Ma call-waiting. She just can't let it go. If someone's trying to call she absolutely HAS to beep through; she can't bear letting her answer service pick up the call. Ma's friend Josie is actually my age; she has been beside herself about Ma's health all week—she lost her own mother when she was in high school and she and Ma have a special artist's bond.

Josie is one of a significant collection of people from my generation who, unlike my siblings and me, seem to truly appreciate my mother. Ma's more restrained, more able to resist the strong urge to correct and manage when she's dealing with friends as opposed to family. People like Josie seem to feel safe turning to her for advice. She must bother them, too, from time to time, but she doesn't hit their sore spots the way she can with her own offspring, still scarred from when we were tiny and vulnerable. Josie can laugh with Ma, make dates for tea, and confide. This has always confused me, but I do feel for her now and her urgent need to make sure Ma's getting the right medical help. If I were Josie, I'd be a little hurt to have Ma click in only to say she's got someone more important on the other line. . . .

Click.

—Well, I've been reading the book your sister sent me about how the intestine is the other brain and you know Tina had a bag and Whatsisname killed himself and I'm sure there's some emotional source for this.

—Yes, Ma, I've heard cancer can have an emotional source.

It's cancer.

We really didn't see that coming. We followed the ER's instructions and went to a colorectal specialist Josie recommended. He took me aside in the waiting room while Ma was still dressing after her exam, and told me he'd found a plum-size tumor on her rectum. There will be a colostomy bag in her future. For some reason, the doctor decided it's up to me to figure out when to tell Ma more specific details: They may have to remove an awful lot of her apparatus, and the bag may not be just for the recovery period. It may be permanent. This insider information weighs heavy on me.

We've been getting all the tests done. My favorite was the colonoscopy, scheduled as a priority rush on a morning that turned out to be icy. There's nothing like the challenge of driving on black ice somewhere you've never been before, dodging skidding cars and accident scenes, when your passenger is an elderly person in pain, on a massive laxative prep solution designed to empty her colon that hasn't quite finished its job yet. We're still collecting opinions, but it looks like it's going to be a long, hard slog, this cancer. Ma seems to be handling it with determination.

—Well, yes, and I think we all need this book now—it's so terribly important—you and David and Felix must all read it right now—

—Ma, stop it, this is what you always do, trying to force some new
idea you've got that can help *you* onto everyone else—remember YOU
are the patient at the moment.

There is a pattern. Ma's voracious intellectual curiosity and zest for
living has taken her down many interesting paths. When she finds something along the way, something she wants to pursue, her first impulse
(before she even knows what the details are) is to call up the family
and try to bully us all into it with her. This can be tricky, because quite
often the thing she's latched onto is actually something we all might
benefit from. But it's just too irritating to admit that.

My sister Colette lives in England. She has discovered she's good
at finding books Ma might be interested in. Now they have this handy
two-person book club on the phone, which fills the intervals between
shouting matches. I see where we're headed with this new one: If you
have rectal cancer, you need Colette's book. If you have trouble sleeping, you need Colette's book. If your teenager is moody, he needs
Colette's book. If your friend is going through divorce, she needs the
book. If you can't find your car keys, if you have a hangnail, the book,
the book, the book. It will get so incessant that I won't want to tell her
anything at all because she won't be satisfied until I have read the book
from cover to cover and applied it to every aspect of my life and gotten
Oprah to do a show about the frigging book.

I wonder if Josie's been given a copy of Colette's book yet?

And then, exhausted from dutifully adopting the complicated diets
and exercises and meditations the book recommends, having outfitted
my house with all the equipment that goes with it (the herbal remedies,
the special pillows) not necessarily because I want to but just to keep
her off my back, I'll find out Ma never read past the first chapter. She's
realized that actually Colette's book was written by a Freemason; it
may be subtly Satanic in nature and not a good idea at all.

When I was three, Daddy's drinking was hard to ignore. My parents
had married young, on the eve of World War II. It's difficult to say
exactly why *they* thought they should be together, but I think their

parents approved of the match because each had something the other's family found desirable: Ma was a genuine Old Philadelphia aristocrat, a gifted artist, and beautiful. Daddy had an exotic name, a promising career in the law, and family money.

They never really connected, though. When Felix was little, Ma decided having more children might fill in the vacuum between them, which was hard work because of all the miscarriages. By the time she finally had fleshed out their collection of offspring to four, she realized her plan had backfired, and they were stuck. She was understandably miserable, but too well disciplined in discretion to dare talk to anyone about personal problems. So she went and unburdened herself to the Carmelite nuns, because she found out they take a vow of silence and therefore can't divulge anyone's secrets. This led to a full-scale conversion, and we all had to leave the Episcopal Church and become Roman Catholics because the Catholics had The Answer To Everything.

In the late 1960s, when I was nine, The Answer To Everything became health food and vitamins. Ma doled out chewable vitamin C instead of candy on Halloween and filled our cupboards with things like soya rice cakes and those nasty little lozenges with the sesame seeds in them that bond permanently to your teeth. I eventually stopped inviting anyone for dinner, because it was painful to watch friends like Margaret, skinny as a twig and a seriously picky eater, not allowed to get up from the table until she had gagged down a plate of marinated salmon (that's raw marinated salmon, way before anyone knew about sushi), and okra sprinkled with brewer's yeast, with buckwheat groats on the side. Forget dessert. Colette's birthday cake one year was an uncooked squash with a candle stuck in it.

When I was ten, The Answer To Everything was the Power of Positive Thinking. There was a book. She'd recite affirmations like *whatever I eat, I get thinner and thinner; I get thinner and thinner whatever I eat.* And whenever we said anything negative, she would make us say *cancel-cancel!* which was like tossing verbal pinches of spilled salt over our shoulders.

Then there was Astrology and the Montessori Method, Transcendental Meditation and Silva Mind Control—that was a six-week course we all had to take, something about going to your subconscious level to make things all better. Occasionally, she'd fall in with people whose motives were a little suspect—she went through a period where if we knew what was good for us, we all had to sell our homes and move into Buckminster Fuller-style geodesic domes. She got so into those domes that she rented a conference center and had some guy come in and pitch the concept to all her friends. Whatever her new thing was, it was usually something that might have been useful in moderation, but Ma was so pushy and obsessive, and it had been crammed so far down our throats that we would come to loathe the subject and not want to have anything to do with it even if our lives depended on it. When you think you have The Answer To Everything, you should just keep it to yourself for God's sake.

Ma laughs.

—That's right. I'm the patient, so what about me?

—Did you call to get your thyroid medicine renewed at the pharmacy?

—Not yet because I just woke up because I was up all night with the fire alarm.

Today we'll get our second opinion from Scott Weissman. A friend in the colorectal field says Weissman is supposed to be the very very best, someone you would allow to operate on your own mother.

It should be noted that Ma's level of tolerance for doctors with suspiciously non-Christian names seems to have improved. She is staying calm and focused (focused for her), listening carefully to what everyone has to say, and letting me steer the ship. This is not the attitude I would have expected. When close friends or family have cancer, Ma scolds from the sidelines if they pick traditional treatment over holistic alternatives. When Daddy had an aneurysm and opted for emergency surgery toward the end of his life, she was against it, but didn't get there in time to stop them. She felt she was proven right when, to all our distress, he proceeded to spend his final three weeks in the ICU instead of bouncing back to life the way the surgeon had predicted.

I'll skip over magnets, full spectrum lights, Reiki, Blue Green Algae, and Twelve-Step programs, the last of which I'm truly grateful for—my father rejoined humanity with the help of AA. In the mid-1980s, The Answer To Everything turned out to be macrobiotics. Ma got herself a real Japanese mentor and proceeded to lose all her excess body weight, which was surprising because it seemed like all she did was cook and eat. Daddy began to get take-out a lot and used to call in desperation, asking how to prepare things like steak. When David and I came for a visit, we'd drop our bags and head for the grocery store first thing, because Ma's kitchen had become scary and witchlike; you'd sort of brace yourself before opening the fridge. Whatever was in there (thirty different varieties of seaweed, glass specimen jars with odd-looking sticks in them covered with bright orange fungus) would easily take away your appetite. Maybe she couldn't keep any weight on because the food was so slimy it wouldn't stick.

A lot of her friends at the club in Penllyn thought Ma had cancer in the 1980s because she looked so awful. Why else would you put yourself through such a restrictive diet? Ma didn't have cancer, but it's not inconceivable she might have been trying to set an example for friends and family who were foolishly trusting Western medicine to cure theirs. Either that or she had a full-blown eating disorder and thought it needed a legitimate focus.

She still claims she is macrobiotic, but she cheats. She doesn't eat meat, but she LOVES a good dessert. She has that compulsive tendency, if left alone with a platter of cookies, to eat until they're gone rather than till she is satisfied. I greatly enjoy pointing this out to her when she starts to lecture me about my own unhealthy eating habits.

Through it all to this day, Ma has maintained only middling respect for the medical profession (*doctors are ALL idiots!*). So it is impressive to see her obediently enduring test after test, not even batting an eyelash when they talk about chemo and radiation and surgery followed by bags. I appreciate her compliance, but I'm wary. Like her sudden willingness to let someone named Weissman poke around her nether regions, it's just not in character.

It seems that the latest and possible final Answer To Everything is Orthodox Christianity. She's been trying her darnedest to convert me, and I've told her I'm a little too old for this—I got off the train when we went back to the Episcopal Church in the late 1970s. The icons she's made me are beautiful, but I've got a whole trunk full of tracts and miraculous medals and paraphernalia she sent me when she joined a bunch of Catholics who liked to pray outside Planned Parenthood clinics and collect tin cans in the basement for the End Times. That really turned me off, and now I'm fine, thanks. Boy oh boy did that get her goat, she couldn't stand that I had finally had enough and wouldn't even give her the courtesy of listening, most especially because this time she really thought she finally HAD reached the last stop on the line, and all that other stuff was just a series of experiments.

I know Ma's been talking to her monks and priests, but I'm not clear where they fit into the decision-making process. A few years after she joined her first Orthodox church, which was Russian-oriented somehow, Ma had a difference of opinion with the priest (*he said I was a very difficult woman!*). Her friend Photini wasn't satisfied, either, and she eventually found the one they're with now: Saint Mark of Ephesus. It's Orthodox as well, but apparently without the corrupting KGB taint. Unfortunately, it's also two hours upstate, in a small town called Carlisle. Photini has actually moved up there, and Ma has trouble finding rides. When she had the Camry, she managed to visit several of the church's affiliated monasteries and convents around the country; now she mostly sustains herself through avid phone discourses with various members of the clergy she's met on her travels. I recently asked Ma to let me talk to one of them so I could get a feel for what's up on that front.

Ring. Ring.

—Hello?

—Susie?

It was Father Nicholas from the monastery in Seattle. He sounded cute as a button and told me all about his son who is an actor. Small world: my mother's monk's son is on TV, too.

Of course, it's all up to Ma, but if it were Father Nicholas, he said, he'd just give his Abbot Superior a copy of his living will, move up to the attic of the monastery, and let nature take its course. And there's always tonsure.

I keep hearing Ma mention tonsure as something that somehow factors into the equation, but she's vague about it. I know she and the holy guys have been contemplating this for her, and it is a big change of some sort. What I got from Father Nicholas is that tonsure is a ceremony where you become a monastic. Younger nuns and monks live in communities together, share the household duties, and pray. That's their job. In Ma's case, being female and elderly, she'd be a House Nun. Her job would be to stay in her home and pray there, which is pretty much what she does already.

Ma's favorite Orthodox prayer is familiar to me, but I'd always thought J. D. Salinger made it up. She has a slightly wordier version of this prayer Salinger's character Franny obsessively mutters while having a nervous breakdown in *Franny and Zooey*:

Lord Jesus Christ, have mercy on me.

I like Salinger. I'm pretty sure he was born half Jewish/half Catholic, and later practiced Buddhism and Hinduism as an adult. I feel it's best not to point this out to Ma.

According to Father Nicholas, there's a bonus with tonsure. The Church has noticed that when Orthodox people with dire illnesses receive it, Things have been known to Happen, and they've happened often enough to get everyone's attention. The tonsured person is sometimes miraculously cured, or else dies suddenly without any painful messy ordeals.

So that's what she's up to.

Weissman tells us he also wants to operate but, contrary to surgeon number one, he recommends the full course of chemo and radiation first. We realize we're going to need a third opinion, and things are getting complex. Ma's been sort of quiet, and after I walk her up to her apartment, I figure it's time to let her know where I stand. At the door, I tell her I'm with her no matter what she wants to do. Treatment, partial treatment, no treatment at all, I'll see if I can figure out a way to support her.

—Thank you, she says.

—I can imagine this is pretty scary, I say, and I don't want you to worry about me.

We look at each other.

—But, I say, I know what I would do. It's pretty clear that if you don't do something medical, and things progress, you might not like what you'll be going through.

—Yes, Ma says, I'm praying about it.

—And, I say, this might not be a good time to hold out for a miracle.

—I'm praying, she says.

—Right, I say. I really hope your priests and monks and things aren't getting your hopes up too much because—

—I'm aware of the situation, she says, and I haven't made up my mind yet. I'm gathering all the information and I know God will take care of me.

This, I think, is really hard. I don't want to beat her up about it, but this is really a big thing. It's one thing to say that with prayer someday your checkbook will balance itself or your illegally parked car won't get impounded. When those kinds of prayers aren't answered, you can still carry on somehow and Susie will get over it after she's had a minor conniption and recovered from cleaning up the mess. Now the stakes are raised.

—I hear you, I say. I'm with you if you decide to go the prayer route. I'm against it, but I'm with you. And if you do manage to be cured or even if you simply have a comfortable peaceful death without doing anything medical about this cancer, you just might convert me after all.

As soon as the words are out of my mouth, I am profoundly uneasy. There is an unmistakable gleam in Ma's eye, and her absolute composure both appalls me and rips my heart from its root. I burst into tears. The gauntlet is thrown.

4.

The Night of the Fork

WE ARE DOING THIS lying-on-the-foam thing today. The radiation department needs about two hours to get a mold of Ma, facedown in position. This mold will become her bed during treatment, to keep her perfectly still. They will also do a CT scan, and make tiny tattoos on her backside so they can point the beam as accurately as possible.

We have settled on an outfit called the Huntingdon Cancer Center. We like Huntingdon because it's not in Center City, and it has its own parking lot, which takes you right to the door. Also because Pete Johnson is a hotshot surgical oncologist there, and he used to be married to my cousin. When we sent Pete all the test results, he took charge in a very reassuring way, and we found ourselves saying yes to the full protocol: six weeks of chemo and radiation, followed by surgery.

At least, I think that's what we'll be doing. Ma has required a little coaxing, but she admits she has a thing or two to accomplish before she exits this world. So the plan is to try the treatment one day at a time with the option to quit immediately if she doesn't take to it.

The radiation subsection we're dealing with this morning is made up of a bunch of nurse types with shrill voices who are awfully wrapped up in the pleasures of their workday, hanging out in the halls and gossiping with one another. The patients seem to be expected to hop to it when they're told, and otherwise not to call too much attention to themselves.

This is sort of not really the way Ma likes to operate. I can tell they are pushing all her buttons; she's tired as it is. I wonder gloomily if we will be seeing a lot of these ladies over the next six weeks.

She emerges from the last segment of business, the CT scan, while I'm in the hall talking schedules with dreamy radiation resident Doctor Morris. She has two or three of the ladies in tow, and they're squawking cheery, patronizing last-minute salutations in high nasal voices.

Ma has a familiar demonic grin on her face, which calls to mind the famous Night of the Fork, around 1969 or so, when she decided she didn't like our dinner conversation.

—You're all done now!! says a nurse.

I wince. Ma hates it when people say they are *done* because technically it means they are dead. You are supposed to say *I have finished.*

—Oh, you're all DONE NOW!!!!! says Ma, mimicking the nurse in this really high voice with an exaggerated South Philly accent.

—You can get changed!! says the nurse.

Get changed is also bad grammar of some sort—I forget what. I brace myself.

—OH, GOODY!!!! You can get CHANGED, squeals Ma and she sniggers evilly at me and Doctor Morris, whose jaw has dropped. He looks to me for a cue.

When we were little, my siblings and I used to joke about the Men in the White Coats. These were the guys who had to come and cart you away from home if you were locked-up-type crazy. We thought it was a funny image, but under the surface was the possibility we didn't really talk about: that the White Coats might really have to come and collect our mother some day. Ma was mostly functional, but there were these outbursts when her frustrations got the better of her and she would lose it publicly in ways that were hard to overlook. Colette remembers a particularly turbulent summer when she was only nine or ten. More than a couple of people yanked her aside at the Penllyn Club to vent: Our mother *must* see a psychiatrist. This was the 1960s, when nobody said things like that unless the situation appeared to be desperate.

A few years before the Night of the Fork, when I was five, Daddy had his first heart attack. Quitting drinking was not discussed with the doctor, but apparently leaving his unsatisfying job as a corporate lawyer was. There was a modest income from a small family trust, and Daddy decided to look for a new country to live where the dollar could really be stretched. The criteria: golf for Daddy. There had to be Montessori, ponies, and dogs for us three girls, and Ma needed Catholics, a garden, and a decent social life. All of this boiled down to Ireland. There was added enticement: something about a baron Ma was related to, who was friends with racy people like the Guinnesses.

Felix had just graduated from college and was left behind to fend for himself. We girls spent a week on a Dutch ocean liner and landed in two worlds at once, the first being Old Fort: a farmhouse near the sea, named after the ruined sixteenth-century fortified castle that was crumbling picturesquely in the adjoining field, nestled in the lowland area of the magical, mystical Wicklow Hills. There were lambs frolicking, a few ponies and barn cats, a devoted yellow lab who produced baskets of puppies hand over fist, and new friends with names like Seamus and Grainne who had lyrical accents we quickly assumed as our own.

The second world was our parents' rapidly deteriorating marriage. Ma soon copped to the reality that her talented young Philadelphia lawyer had no intention of supporting the family in the conventional way, and instead had plunked her down in the middle of a dirty damp nowhere with three small children and untrained help. That's when she began to squawk. Plus she hadn't really thought out the whole social thing: We were serious Catholics then, and the Anglo-Irish crowd was allergic to Catholics—this was Ireland, duh.

Daddy could have made do indefinitely between the golf and the pubs and his weekly columns for newspapers back home and in Dublin (Mike O'Shisker amid the charming natives of the Emerald Isle— fables for our times). But Ma wasn't cooperating, and our household became a place where parents screamed at each other and slammed doors in the night.

As for us girls, we had to do a lot of coping on our own. We learned quickly not to make life more complicated by objecting when Things Happened. Like when Colette, the eldest, was ordered to put some excess newborn puppies in a burlap bag and drown them in a barrel because *that's what you did on a farm*, and I, at age seven, went into the ancient, cavernous kitchen for a snack and was fiddled with by the toothless old gardener.

There are some riveting memoirs out these days by people whose early years were incredibly intense. You keep checking the author's picture on the back cover for facial disfigurement and missing ears, or just to confirm the miracle that they survived. I enjoy these stories as much as the next person, but they kind of make it tough to justify my own need for therapy. My childhood, while it left a lot of scars, had subtler traumas that never really seemed to explain my personal level of angst. I keep thinking I must be a little boring:

—*Um, it was really really loud when they slammed the doors, and one time she threatened to leave, even. That really scared me.*

—*Of course, because she couldn't bear to see you all suffer. So she tried to drown you in the bathtub—*

—*No. She just put on her coat for a minute. But Colette had to drown—*

—*Okay, but she knocked you all unconscious that night and poured gasoline all over you and then—*

—*No.*

—*No? Are you sure you just don't remember? Do you have blackouts, multiple personalities?*

—*No, no blackouts. But—okay, the gardener groped me.*

—*How terrible! He violated you!*

—*No. He, you know, felt me up and sort of kissed me.*

—*You mean he repeatedly raped you over a period of years and told you not to tell anyone or he would kill your parents?*

—*Well, no. It was just the one time. But he didn't have any teeth . . .*

For me, it took a Meisner acting teacher to convince me to try therapy. She pointed out I was dodging conflict unnaturally in scenes and improvisations. My partner could be flipping out all over the place, yelling horrible things at me or whatever and instead of yelling right back, or at least admitting how I felt about what he was doing, I'd try to calm him down, or worse, I'd just giggle inanely. It's good not to get in an argument at the drop of a hat in real life, but my teacher wanted me to be able to go for it in the imaginary world, and I was clearly blocked. So I sucked it up and let myself unload on a series of therapists. I even took Ma's advice and tried Adult Children of Alcoholics.

It was exhilarating when the results started showing and I "came to life" in acting class. I could cry real tears and holler bloody murder all day long—in fact, I did, because expressing my true feelings felt so cathartic and pure, I couldn't bring myself to leave such liberating behavior behind in the classroom. If a bunch of construction workers tried to embarrass me with loud appreciative comments as I passed on the way home from class in Times Square, instead of ducking my head as usual and increasing my pace, I'd stop in the middle of an intersection and give them what for at the top of my lungs, complete with enough graphic hand gestures to make them all blush. I collared my landlord in a stairwell about our yearlong unresolved water temperature problem and informed him with gusto that he was a *flaming asshole*. My mother couldn't get away with *anything* anymore. I think David sort of regrets introducing me to the Meisner Technique.

What I had come to understand in therapy was that there were too many things we didn't talk about in our family. In the 1960s, people didn't realize that when a little girl tells her sister that the disgusting gardener defiled her one afternoon in the kitchen, it's not enough for her parents to fire the monster and pretend nothing happened. The little girl shouldn't have to wait till she's twenty-three years old to begin to face how utterly terrifying and life-changing that experience was.

Instead I was left to draw my own conclusions from the gardener episode and its aftermath. It's been a lifelong process. In Ireland, at the impressionable age of seven, I contemplated the elements that made up my small, dangerous world: the recent shocking introduction to horrors lurking in the kitchen, my basic lack of popularity with my older siblings (who had their own traumas to work through and weren't particularly thrilled by my *Special* status), my father's general emotional unavailability, and the strong possibility that my only ally was becoming more mentally unhinged by the day and might just leave if she didn't get what she needed. I figured I had to come up with my own strategy for coping.

It was pretty logical. If the world wasn't safe and Ma was the one person in the family who took a real interest in my welfare, and she was about to fall apart, then my personal survival depended completely on keeping her together so she'd stick around. Even though the role of the *Special* one was beginning to stink, I had to milk it for all it was worth. I had to take care of my scary, fragile mother any way I could think of. This solution would do nothing for my reputation with my siblings, but I saw no other choice at age seven. I became my mother's caretaker, because without her, I'd REALLY be left in the clutches of the next foul-smelling groundskeeper who blundered into our home in search of a place to stick his nasty old tongue.

Wicklow, 1966

So I became a habitual watchdog. When Ma ran to her room to cry, it was my job to follow her there and try to comfort her. And from that moment onward, I wasn't just reluctant to go out for a sleepover because I'd be homesick: I was afraid to leave her for too long in case she needed me to settle her down when she began to freak. This is partly why I switched schools so often—for a solid two-year period I pretended I was sick, so I could stay home all day and keep an eye on her.

Even Daddy came to regret the move to Ireland. He'd dreamed about Philadelphia every single night we were there. So it was not too hard for him when he finally faced facts and took Ma back to civilization.

By then, she was in the throes of a thyroid condition, complicated by undiagnosed perimenopause. It was too late. The marriage was still a disaster and no amount of country clubs, modern dishwashers, and wall-to-wall carpeting was going to help stop the battles that started when Daddy came home from the mishmash of jobs he'd cobbled together trying to make his life interesting. Still no lawyering and not enough money for Ma, which meant continued conflict.

We girls did our best to not be around for the fights, but we sure heard them down the hall at homework time. Nothing was ever said about their nightly hollering and stomping at dinner, when we all shifted seamlessly into Perfect Table mode. We had to set the table exactly right with *this kind of napkin placed exactly like this with the fork just like that beside, not on top of the napkin, and aligned on a diagonal with the glass—no, not that kind of glass, the one in the pantry on the third shelf and now we need the candles lit—no not just the little ones, the tall ones. Susie go get the tall candlesticks in the sideboard and then refold this napkin, its border needs to be showing in the upper left hand corner.* "Please pass the salt" wasn't quite right. It had to be *please pass the salt, Colette.* The topic of conversation had to be soothing, stimulating, and above all something Ma liked to talk about.

The Night of the Fork, everything was arranged just so and Daddy lurched in as usual to take his seat at the head of the table, wait for the blessing, and dig in.

Our father was as complex as Ma in his own way. It was really too bad he had such a problem with drinking, because when Daddy was in good form, he was absolutely delightful. He had a wonderful beaming smile and that special kind of manner that makes everyone feel appreciated. Going into the city with Daddy was a thrill because of all the different kinds of people who knew him and seemed so glad to see him—train conductors, waitresses, businessmen on the street. They all called him Mike, and he'd stop to talk to each of them. He was fantastic at names, so he'd make it seem as if it was his own particular pleasure to introduce us to everyone.

We loved Daddy a lot, but one of the things we'd all like to have changed was his appalling table manners. He was a huge, grunting, freckled redheaded ogre at the table, with chicken grease and melted artichoke butter all over himself.

So we were meant to keep eating despite the stomach-turning spectacle at Daddy's end, and help make *pleasant conversation* with Ma at her end, which was basically only anything Ma was interested in. We were, for the most part, unstimulated by Ma's topics, so the goal was always to try to engage Daddy, partly because he was more fun to talk to, but also just to get him to stop looking and sounding like a Neanderthal for a second.

That night was one of the good ones when one of us got his attention but, predictably, the subject matter did not pass muster with Ma. Daddy, perhaps too well lubricated to even register the degree of Ma's annoyance, wouldn't adapt to any change she tried. So she got up from the table and stalked out in the direction of the kitchen, where we heard her banging and crashing pots and pans around in a pointed, threatening sort of way.

When Ma's hysteria reached a certain feverish pitch, she often took it to the kitchen and expressed it by cleaning very very loudly. To this day, if David makes a certain kind of noise in our kitchen, my pulse quickens and I feel a reflexive urge to scurry to a safe corner of the cellar.

An ordinary family might have dispatched someone to soothe Ma, but by 1969 we had all given up the pretense of ordinariness. Even I, back in school full-time and successful with sleepovers by then, was beginning to think about easing my grip on the caretaker role and see what things were like on the other team. So I stayed at the table, and we all simply continued the offending conversation, which was probably about politics. Eventually we heard the kitchen door slam shut, and there was an ominous silence, different and confusing. Was she leaving us, and if so, was that a good thing or a bad thing?

Then ZAP, like in *Jaws* when the shark's bristling snappers fill the screen with a jolt: Ma appeared, teeth bared in a close-up just outside the darkened dining room window, rapping a loud staccato rhythm with a fork on the thin glass. It was more than *Jaws*, it was the Alien busting out of John Hurt's chest. It was Norman Bates, sweeping aside the shower curtain to the pulsing sound of screeching violins.

It was the *Here's Johnny!!!* moment in *The Shining* when the boy and his mother realize that the head of the household is not feeling quite as friendly as he was back when they decided to move into an obviously haunted hotel and get completely cut off with him in a blinding snowstorm for the entire winter with no help in sight, and the camera is close on Nicholson's wild-eyed face with his crazed, razzle-dazzle grin.

Here's Ma!!! Scwreech scwreech scwreeeeeeeeeech!

We all have mild PTSD flashbacks of the Night of the Fork. Even though we'd gotten out of Ireland in one piece and there was an ocean between me and that gardener, Ma was right outside the window and there was no telling what she might do next.

—*So she smashed through that glass with the fork, didn't she, and she leaped at your father like the Alien, and she gouged his eyes out right there in front of you, and strings of viscous eyeball gelatin splatted all over the melted artichoke butter while you screamed and screamed—*

—*Well, no, not exactly. But dinner was pretty much ruined. . . .*

This afternoon at the Huntingdon Cancer Center, she has no fork, but Ma's eyes are crossed, the grin is in place, and I think I see purple smoke coming out the top of her head.

It's been quite a while, though, since the Night of the Fork. The new improved Susie who had all that therapy just smiles at the doctor and the nurses, and looks at her and says "My, you seem very cranky!"

—Oh, not at ALLLL!!!! I'm so HAPPPYYYY!!!!! I'm DONE and I can get CHANGED!!!!! cackles Ma.

Several doors open in the hall, and people poke their heads out to see what the ruckus is.

I bat my eyes at Doctor Morris and tell them all we are very much looking forward to the beginning of radiation next week.

Sometimes I exaggerate. That gardener had at least two teeth.

Wicklow, 1965

5.
The Elephant in the Room

PICTURE AN ELDERLY WOMAN, three-thirty in the morning. She is standing in a pool of water outside her bathroom, barefoot, surrounded by broken glass. Her youngest daughter walks in and knows right away what to *not* do with the Elephant in the Room.

Twelve hours earlier:

We're sitting in a corner of the infusion room's waiting area. Ma is sound asleep, crumpled in a wheelchair. She's just had a chemo port installed under the skin of her chest, a procedure done under general anesthetic, so she's still pretty groggy. The next step is to get the poison hooked up and pumping into her veins.

We've been around Huntingdon enough to understand that it can take a lot out of you. Of course, you would expect a cancer hospital to take a lot out of you, a lot of *cancer*. But there's this collateral loss of time and energy that has to do with the sheer number of sick people. I had no idea. Our problem seems to radiate from this infusion area, which I've realized reminds me of airport lounges since 9/11 with the lines backed up and the planes overbooked. It's packed with people, mostly in pairs: one person usually wearing a kerchief, pallid in complexion, and a rosier-looking friend/spouse/sidekick who has a large shoulder bag full of reading material and knitting supplies.

What I find disappointing is that there is a notable contrast between our first meeting with the surgeon and the rest of the team, and what has gone on since we signed up. On the morning of our interview, we were greeted at the hospital entrance by a friendly grey-haired volunteer and whisked efficiently from one sign-in area to another. A handsome, official-looking blue ID card stamped with Ma's name was presented with a flourish. There was a brief pause in the doctors' waiting room, just long enough to appreciate its fireplace and picture windows looking out on beautiful landscaping. Then we had the full, focused attention of several very solicitous, intelligent experts who did their absolute best to make everything very clear to us before Ma committed to treatment.

The infusion room shares its waiting area with the lab. There are no fireplaces, no windows. We did bloodwork the last time we were here. I came unprepared, and as the wait dragged on, I yearned for my own shoulder bag like the ones around me. I'd have given anything for a garish orange-and-purple synthetic shawl to crochet. Most of all, I wanted to snatch the Nicholas Sparks novel from the woman next to me; it couldn't have been worse than sitting there with no distraction whatsoever. Instead I had to make do memorizing a pamphlet for a smoking cessation program. There are a lot of these lying around. I assume they are cleverly intended for the rosy sidekicks who don't yet know enough to bring their own entertainment and, left with nothing to do but take in the scene, become understandably terrified they will end up forced to wear bandannas themselves. Terrified enough to actually consider quitting smoking once and for all.

Today I've brought three recent *New Yorker*s to pass back and forth with Ma, but she's mostly been asleep since the tech handed her over after the port procedure. That was freaky, too. He just wheeled her out and shoved her at me, and there I was, alone with this unconscious person in a wheelchair, thinking *outpatient my ass*. It was quite a jolt to suddenly be the solitary custodian of Ma in such a helpless state. I first experienced the shock of having a vulnerable soul casually plopped into my utterly unskilled hands after our daughter Eliza's birth, when the nurse loaded the three of us into our car in the parking garage at Cedars-Sinai. The emotional contrast is not lost on me now, between the heady joy of a shiny new baby and the mixed emotional bag when a complicated octogenarian parent entrusts you with her life.

There was a little time before Ma's infusion "appointment" so I tried to get her some food, which was just silly. I could barely get her to wake up enough to find out what she would eat. The snack bar was packed; I had to elbow my way around people scrambling for something that didn't look too processed. You'd think they'd offer some reassuringly whole-grain steamed veggie miracle cure food, but the most natural options were pre-packaged salad (Ma can't chew it) or yogurt, which she doesn't think is healthy because of the sugar they put in the fruit. Perversely, she went for a piece of pound cake instead, and then fell asleep mid-bite.

Now I'm reading cartoons and "Shouts and Murmurs" and hoping nobody minds Ma's snoring. It's been three hours, and the door to the infusion room has opened maybe once this whole time. You could knit enough shawls for an army at this rate. The people behind the desk where you sign in are no help. They have these clipboards and headsets, and they announce things over a loudspeaker. They talk on the phone a lot and seem very hardworking, but they have a remarkable talent for not making eye contact when you are standing right smack in front of them, wanting to know what the holdup's all about. I would not want that job—it has to be wearing when people are irritated with you all day long.

Finally home, very late, both of us feeling drained. I'll be sleeping on the daybed in Ma's study next to her bedroom tonight because she is not safe alone after anesthesia. Which raises the Big Question, the rather large Elephant in the Room we've been tiptoeing around since the diagnosis: How much longer can she live alone? What are we going to do when she can't?

David's not going anywhere for a couple of days. Thank God, the kids have one parent in the house, or I don't know what I'd do. I make a brief call to my brother, Felix, hemmed in by the Vermont snow. He usually needs details and has been obsessing about Ma's beautiful white hair (*When does her hair fall out? I've got to get my driveway cleared so I can come down and see her hair!*). Colette is conveniently asleep in England, unreachable.

We're all adults now. I'm still *the spoiled one* to Felix. In my darkest moments, I imagine behind-the-scenes murmuring about the justice of Ma and her *Special* child partnered in this final lonely dance. There's a general vibe of sympathy and concern though, because we all know I never consciously asked to be groomed for the caretaker job. The siblings are trying to figure out ways to help, but still, what can they do? I'm the one who's here.

Colette may be right. She thinks I imprinted unnaturally on Ma at birth, like a foundling duck hatched accidentally in the nest of a needy, scatterbrained rattlesnake.

Ma has woken up enough for a little dinner. She now has a canister of chemo fluid strapped to her waist. It drips in via a thin tube attached to the port in her chest, and we're supposed to go have it refilled once a week in the dreaded infusion room. Tomorrow we begin radiation: five mornings a week. This will take six weeks, and then there's a rest period before they can remove whatever's left of the tumor. Ma has a reassuring 90 percent chance of recovery if she sticks to the program.

It's my first time sleeping in my mother's home since Daddy's last days in Florida. Funny to think of the journey from being afraid to sleep under a roof away from Ma, through the stage where I'd beg my friends to invite me for the night so I could get some peace, and now back at "home" again, even if it's just for a night or so. There's a scary teetering-on-the-precipice feeling to this—if I stay too long, I might get too comfortable, sort of fall metaphorically asleep and forget where I really live.

I'm older, more tired, and less patient now. The eccentricities get to me. There's a lot to do figuring out how to get Ma's clothes on and off around the canister, which nightclothes will work okay with this new obstacle and which will not, or where the right ones are for that matter. We lose her glasses several times. Ma has all these issues about her prayer ropes, her candles, and her special Holy Oil, and the phone keeps ringing. On top of that, there are the usual obsessive-compulsive rules: *Coats go in the coat closet, not draped over a chair!* She has a thing about bathroom doors (*they must always be kept shut!*). I keep having to go into the bathroom to look for things, and if I forget to close the door on my way out, I'm supposed to drop everything, rush back, and close it—and the trash cans (*Don't call them that. They're scrap baskets!*) are actually not meant for trash. If you put something in the one in the bedroom, like a small piece of scrap paper or Kleenex, you are supposed to empty it into the kitchen trash instantly because otherwise *it's too messy, living in an apartment is like being on a boat, everything in its place.*

When you're exhausted and you have a whole list of things ahead of you to do, that extra trip to shut the bathroom door can tip you right over the edge. But I hold my tongue and tell myself Ma's tired, too, she needs her order, it's just for the night. Looming over us is how we'll manage through the next six weeks. They say she'll be all right on her own till about the third or fourth week, then she'll start to feel ill and need help. There's that Elephant again.

I can't just move in here with Ma. I've got the kids. David will be back and forth doing an Anne Hathaway thriller followed by *John Adams*, so I have to assume he won't be around when I might need him. Nobody wants a strange caregiver to move into their home if they can avoid it, so that's a last resort. Besides, it's expensive and we have a lot of co-pays now. I'm not sure we could get the Long-Term Care Insurance to pay for live-in help or assisted living, when the affliction is curable cancer.

Do I dare even think this? Should Ma move in with us, even temporarily?

I have friends who have done it. Margaret (the picky eater) bought the house she grew up in from her parents, arranging the deal in such a way that the price was more affordable. In exchange, her parents get to stay there for the rest of their lives, in the master bedroom, for lord's sake. Margaret, her husband, George, and the two kids sleep up on the third floor. They all share the kitchen, and it is probably my imagination, but sometimes I think they seem a little overly pleased with themselves.

I have another friend whose mother is a prescription drug addict. The family tried a series of interventions, which accomplished nothing. They have disowned each other, and now she barely knows where her mother is. Having a friend whose mother is this much of a disappointment is a great solace to me.

It's really confusing. One month ago, I was hardly on speaking terms with Ma. Since I escaped to boarding school, I've had recurring nightmares about her that cause me to curse loudly in my sleep. David can do a great imitation of me, flailing spastically in the dark. (*Mfff. Mrrr, stop id you always mumff. Sprrgrm mad at yooghhh. Why do you spremf me I fffff . . . Prr stupid grr selfish. Oh, fff. Fffff. Ffff-ug.*)

It's only recently with this crisis that I've had it in me to spend more than an hour or two with Ma without blowing my stack, but as luck would have it for whatever reason, my relationship with her is the overall best of my siblings. And I have the biggest house, which means I'm the most logical candidate and we all know it.

It's not like it's the first time I've considered this. I knew the day would come eventually. Ma doesn't seem to want to move in with me any more than I want her to. The siblings have been funny. Felix's advice was to move somewhere like Boston and leave Ma to figure things out for herself. Colette is adamant, sort of:

—*I support you if you want to try, but I'm not asking you to do that.*

—*Good, Colette, because I don't think I can. I might turn into a lunatic and I don't think I can subject David and the kids—*

—*Good, Susie, because I think it would be a TERRIBLE idea.*

—*Right. Terrible.*

—*That doesn't mean I'm against it if you change your mind and decide to try it. I'll support you if you decide to try.*

—*Thanks.*

—But I'll support you if you don't, too. That would be completely understandable. Nobody should have to do that.

—I know.

—I'd do it for you if I could, but I don't think anyone should have to. She could literally suck the life out of you.

—I'm not going to do it unless she can't walk and she can't talk. Then I'll consider it.

—Good. But even then I will support you if you don't.

Colette is my confidante. She's a Libra, with the scales. I love Libras; I married one and then gave birth to two, deliberately. The boys were due on Halloween and when the doctor offered to give them a little shove three weeks early I leaped at the chance to dodge having twin male teenage Scorpios to cope with down the road. Libras are perfect for me, they're honest and loyal, they're tidy (not the boys, yet, but David and Colette sure are), but they can't make up their minds that easily. You should see David at the grocery store:

David picks up a jar of whatever. He looks at the label. He reads the ingredients for like ten minutes. He puts the jar in his cart. Then he takes it out and puts it back on the shelf. He wheels down the aisle and picks up some other item and reads that jar's label. Back on the shelf it goes. He goes back to the first product again, takes two jars, and puts them in the cart. He stares into space for a while. He puts one jar back and returns to the second product. He puts it in the cart next to the first one he chose. He starts to wheel away, then stops. He takes the two different jars out of the cart and sort of weighs them in his hands to see which one is lighter. He holds them up side by side and reads both labels at the same time.

When David goes to Whole Foods, he is gone for hours.

Ma's dishwasher's sort of almost full. I could have started it, but it's late and we'd hear it while we're trying to go to sleep. This daybed's not too bad. Ma spotted it at Ikea a few years ago and when she was out one day, I set it up for her as a surprise. I try not to fixate on the intermittent warning *beep* of the smoke detector that has needed a new battery for more than a year. Ma doesn't believe in smoke detectors and doesn't want to have it changed (she can't hear it anyway). I'd always figured it was her business, but now I wish I'd fixed it when I had the energy. I have earplugs for when David snores, but I forgot them. *I miss David and the kids.*

Our guest room is on the third floor, which wouldn't work for Ma: too many stairs. My office is on the second floor, and it has an attached bathroom outfitted for an old person with grab bars and things. *I could move my desk up to the guest room and put a bed in the office . . . we do get along remarkably well when Ma's sick for some reason. What a feeling of accomplishment, to do that for her. And think of all the bother I'd save myself if she were right there instead of at her place. I think we might possibly be able to do this. . . .*

By three a.m. I've managed to tune out the beeping smoke detector, so I'm finally dozing when a noise in the kitchen rouses me. The dishwasher is going, and it sounds like Ma's in there rearranging the cabinets or something. I listen for a while, not unaware of the behavioral contrast between my eighty-five-year-old mother in the kitchen tonight and the saucepan-rattling fifty-something Ma of my childhood. That Night of the Fork, you could tell she had a healthy head of steam building. Tonight, despite the odd hour, I sense no imminent eruption.

Swish.

Beep.

Rearrange.

Swish swish rearrange beep rearrange beep swish. . . .

I fight my way back to sleep, brooding on the month Ma stayed with us after she sold their house in Florida. She had a hard time adapting to someone else's house rules, like keeping the front door locked so burglars, rapists, and child snatchers won't get in, or not wandering outside to tell our lawn guys to cut David's cherished hedge down to the nubs (he'd been nurturing it for months to get it to just the right thickness and height), meanwhile forgetting she'd just left several pots of seaweed going on the stove at a very high heat and the entire downstairs was filling with smoke. Knowing her stay was temporary helped, but the kids were little then and sleep was precious and elusive. I found myself drawing the line one morning at five a.m. when Ma decided to make a phone call to Europe at the top of her lungs and woke us all up. In the wee hours, I tend to lose track of things like why it's important to be hospitable to old people in the midst of a tricky life transition.

Smash!

I leap out of bed. Ma's standing barefoot outside the bathroom. There is broken glass all around her on the floor. It seems she has decided she needs a special glass carafe of Holy Water by the bed. It simply can't wait till morning and, still unsteady from the anesthesia, she has dropped it.

I storm around finding slippers and dustpans, and when she's settled into bed, she doesn't dare ask me, Evil Susie, reveling in all my exasperated glory, to empty the shards of glass out of the *scrap basket,* and I don't stop after leaving the bathroom door open as wide as I can. I make a *special* trip to yank open the guest bathroom door, too, and another to take my coat out of the closet and slap it emphatically on the floor, just to make my point very, very clear.

The good news is it is now eight-thirty a.m. in England. Libras are also very accommodating about being dumped on when you need to express what you're *not* going to do about the Elephant.

Beep.

Beep.

Beep.

6.

Obstruction

HERE'S THE THING about Holy Oil and Holy Water: They are multipurpose and they never run out.

It's quite scientific. When Holy Oil starts to get low, you just add regular olive oil (*NOT Extra Virgin, only plain*), which magically makes the new oil Holy because it's been added to the already Holy Oil. The same goes for Holy Water. You get your original Holy Water from the priest and then just refill it from the tap when it's not quite all gone, and you've got a whole new batch.

Holy Water makes a very inexpensive hostess gift for a household lacking proper spiritual direction. All you need is an empty soy sauce bottle and a blank label. We have a few of these in the back of our cupboards:

Hello! My name is:
Holy Water

If you like, you can put Holy Water in one of those spray bottles for ironing or for misting plants, and spritz the air of a room that doesn't feel right or something. It's a good idea to spray your car, too. If you misplace your spray bottle, you can just drizzle some on your fingers and flick it at whatever is offending you, like your daughter when she starts getting uppity. This is supposed to calm your daughter down, but it mostly makes her laugh at you, which is better than nothing. I am sometimes a little damp after spending time with my mother.

Ma uses a combination of Holy Oil and Water to float beeswax votive candles in little red glass lanterns. She places these in front of the icons she has displayed in her apartment. The lanterns are supposed to be lit all the time, even when she's asleep or not at home. They can be only *100 percent beeswax*; anything else appears to be Of the Devil and definitely won't produce the right effect.

The family is beginning to descend.

Colette is my telephone lifeline and we talk almost every morning now, but she doesn't like to get in the way. This is too bad since she's really the most qualified person we have when it comes to colon trouble. Due to Crohn's disease, her husband, Badger, has had enough of his intestine removed to decorate a good-size Christmas tree, but Colette's been mum on details.

She's more focused on her job as Operation Ma's financial analyst. Colette's collecting my scraps of numbers to make up spreadsheets about the costs we're facing for things like the Long-Term Care's Elimination Period (they'll cover assisted living, but only after you've paid your own way for a hundred days or thirteen thousand dollars, *but what if they don't approve her at all? It can happen—Felix read about it in the* Times!). On top of everything, we'll have to keep the apartment till we know whether Ma will really be well enough to move back.

The alternative to assisted living is home health aides, also covered in part by Long-Term Care Insurance, which, thank God, I got years ago when I saw this coming (*IF they approve her! Remember the* Times!). The Long-Term Care has a limit. The odds are Ma will outlive it, and things will skyrocket after that. We'll need drivers to help get her to radiation when I can't, meals brought in if she stays home, and oh my gosh, the logistics (not to mention the costs) are insane and we're all doing our best not to panic.

Our brother, Felix, likes to depict the women in our family's behavior in crisis as a bunch of monkeys in a cage, running uselessly around screeching and bouncing off the bars after the winds shift and they catch the scent of the lions (who are obliviously napping, safe in their pens all the way on the other side of the zoo). We monkeys are not making any noise yet, but we're fidgety.

Felix arrived today, his Subaru Forester covered with mud collected on the messy drive down from Vermont. He used to drive a pickup loaded with chunks of tree trunk. He's always got pieces of trees handy for his sculpting, and they conveniently double as ballast on the highways. Felix favors Birkenstocks no matter the season, but layers them with wool socks for winter—he's a genuine, crusty, foul-mouthed weather-beaten prep-school-followed-by-Ivy-League renegade. The ladies tend to be drawn to him. He's been a bachelor for decades now, and his caregiving experience to date has been limited to a series of mostly self-sufficient cats, but he's willing to try anything as long as the instructions are clear.

David's gone to Richmond to be fitted with George Washington's nose for the *John Adams* miniseries, and I can't leave the kids for long, but I've postponed things like the boys' wisdom teeth extractions. We've lost track of how long it's been since Ma had a bowel movement, and it's not looking good. She unhooked the chemo canister before it could produce any results because it made her too sick. She's still not feeling well at all. We have to get her strong enough for radiation.

So we've spent a couple of days hovering and fussing around with hot water bottles, calling reports in to doctors' services (of course, it's the weekend), and to Colette, who mutters cryptic, ominous things like *what won't go down must eventually come up.* There was an interesting episode at the apartment waiting for the phone to ring. We figured out a soothing way to rub Holy Oil on Ma's lower back. When Ma instantly felt some relief, she swore she could smell roses. This was supposed to indicate a miraculous event.

Ma loves these sorts of mystical phenomena, and she's always on the lookout for them. I don't feel much need of visions and such to sustain my own faith, and can't always suppress the urge to scoff. But this will become yet another of those memories I secretly like to hold close, and ponder.

There's an experience Ma had at her father's deathbed. Grandsir was a flyer, a captain in the Army Air Service when Ma's mother left her first husband (a dull but acceptable banker type) and her four eldest children (my mother's half-siblings) to marry him. This was before there was an Air Force at all, when the use of planes in warfare was brand-new and very daring. He flew those little planes with the open cockpits, and he used to cause a sensation landing them on the polo field at the Penllyn Club—very Errol Flynn, with the goggles and the scarf and everything. Grandsir had a treasure trove of stories to explain his collection of physical defects: He was missing two fingers (shot them off in a hunting accident, age twelve) and he couldn't straighten one arm (got it sideswiped driving too close to another car on a narrow country road). When Ma and her younger sister, Bobs, were little, they lived with their parents on army bases in Long Island, Virginia and Honolulu. Ma had a patchy on-again off-again relationship with her father after he and her mother finally divorced, but she wanted to be there for his health crisis.

Ma felt it was important to acknowledge the obvious, and pointed out to Grandsir that he was dying. He responded indignantly that he was *not*. When he eventually did die, Ma was the only one in the hospital room with him. She swears that she saw a transparent thing of some sort float out of her father's body. She says it looked like the logo for Philadelphia's ice hockey team, the Flyers: an orb shape attached to a large wing, similar to the snitch in the Harry Potter books. She is positive she saw this thing waft upward and disappear into the ceiling above him. The point she makes now is that Grandsir had an instinctive, unschooled faith in the afterlife and, for some reason we may never know, Ma was there to see real evidence: her father's very soul on its way to the next destination.

I didn't see Grandsir float off to heaven myself, but it's interesting. This morning, I did think I sort of smelled the roses in the Holy Oil.

I know it started out as ordinary olive oil because Ma wouldn't allow it to be anything *but*. I'd bought the refills for her myself.

I arranged a visit from Michael (the reassuring administrator of the local Home Health Care service) for Ma to fill out her profile sheet and learn what they offer. Michael has an aide ready to come in anytime. The interview went like this:

Michael: I have a very nice, competent woman named Miriam who can come on Sunday morning.

Ma: Is she dark-skinned?

Michael: Um, yes she is. Why?

Ma: Is she light-fingered?

But the whole thing ends up with Ma moaning like an animal in labor, and me on the phone with the doctor on call at Huntingdon, trying to reach into the receiver and shake him (*she's not TALKING anymore, Doctor, she's just grunting on her hands and KNEES, rocking back and FORTH, so I don't think the milk of magnesia is really HELPING, Doctor*). They have no openings but want us to meet them in the ER—then *poof,* they call. A bed has been made available, which may or may not have something to do with the rose-scented Holy Oil, depending on who you talk to.

Ma insists all this makes perfect sense: The Holy Oil is why it is possible for her to even consider trying to take this trip without an ambulance. There's some confusion as to how to get her downstairs, highlighted by Felix and me debating the merits of using some bungee cords from the back of his mud-spattered Subaru to rig up one of the dining room chairs on a mover's dolly. Luckily, we scrounge a spare wheelchair in the Mills House. Ma is maneuvered into the Subaru, clutching her phone book with the priests' numbers and one of those bicycle water bottles with the pop-top I've filled with Holy Oil for the trip.

The doctor puts her on massive doses of laxatives, and Felix and I get to look at pictures of the tumor, which is behaving like an airtight cork and will continue to do so until they can get the treatment under way. We cancel Miriam. Ma's going to be in the hospital for a few days.

The winds appear to have shifted, and the musky lion scent has died down. I even get enough time to think of stopping at the liquor store to reward the monkeys with wine to go with our pizza dinner, before morning comes and Ma and I get the cage all to ourselves again.

I think it would be good to skip the details of how two or three weeks' accumulations of digested matter are safely and painlessly moved past a largish tumor when you are old and unable to get out of bed unassisted. Ma says the aides at Huntingdon are *saints*.

What strikes me right away is how much more there is to this place than I saw at first. There's the cozy area where they get you to sign up, and then there are the treatment areas: the dreaded infusion room with its rows of dentist chairs and individual TVs to watch while you get your chemo. There's the radiation area in the basement with its thick concrete walls. Now, we seem to have hopscotched over everything to the place with the beds, where the struggle is so much more immediate and real. In an ordinary hospital, our paranoia could be eased by happy sights: mothers being wheeled outside with newborns; flowers and bobbing balloons; orthopedic patients with casts on their legs. But this hospital is exclusively for cancer and now Ma has moved, hopefully temporarily, to the place you go when you might be dying. The hallways and rooms are very quiet and sacred, like a tomb, and they seem to go on for miles and miles and miles.

There's a very sick old woman in the next bed who is not up to socializing with her own revolving flow of visitors: saucer-eyed grandchildren and anxious adult offspring, optimistically approving procedures on her behalf. When they all step outside, the woman moans and protests to the aides that she has had enough. This has made Ma think serious thoughts, and she's asked Father Basil to come down from Carlisle. She wants me to meet him, so I work another quick trip to Huntingdon into my tight round of interviews at assisted-living places in anticipation of her release and the beginning of radiation.

I had been instructing myself all day to be on good behavior, and not to overreact if Father Basil turns out to be all pompous and patronizing.

Not just because I'm not Orthodox and who knows what Ma's been telling him about my heathen ways, but because I am a woman and I don't like what I hear about the role of women in this church.

My first contact with Orthodoxy was in L.A. I was filming *Deadly Intentions,* a TV miniseries based on the true story of a Sweet Young Greek Orthodox Girl (Madolyn Smith, the Other Woman in *Urban Cowboy*) who marries a Charming Young Doctor (Michael Biehn, from the first *Terminator*) with a Mysteriously Creepy Mother (Cloris Leachman—my favorite in *Young Frankenstein*). Things go downhill quickly when the Doctor turns out to be a Raving Lunatic trying to poison Madolyn and stuff, and she has to escape with the Baby in the nick of time.

I was playing the Spunky But Loyal Best Friend Who Suspects Before Anyone Else That Something Is Amiss. We filmed the wedding scene in a gorgeous Greek Orthodox church somewhere in the San Fernando Valley. When I got into my pink chiffon bridesmaid's gown a little too early for hair and makeup (Cloris's character wore white to her son's wedding, which should have been a tip-off), I slipped in to check out the church. The priest who would be performing the filmed ceremony offered a tour. This was long before Ma became Orthodox and I didn't know much of anything, but I was really impressed by the gold leaf all over the place, the wide Byzantine arches and the beautiful, vivid colors on the walls, with fantastically detailed old icons everywhere. What sort of turned me off, though, was when I asked if I could see behind the altar.

The priest said no. No women were allowed back there. I know from Ma that the women and men are separated during church services; they stand on opposite sides. Since I am most emphatically in accord with the team in the Episcopal Church that approves not just women but openly gay and lesbian priests and bishops, I've got a pretty healthy grudge going about Orthodoxy's apparent attitude toward women. I am not expecting to be disarmed by this Father Basil person. But as it turns out, that is exactly what happens from the moment he strides up to me in his sensible shoes, long black robe flapping, bushy grey beard halfway down his chest, and opens his arms to sweep me into a hearty bear hug, bumping me up against his rather substantial Santa Claus middle.

Father Basil gives off a jolly, unmistakably *past-life-as-a-motorcycle-dude* sort of vibe, which I take to immediately. I can tell right away that nobody's going to try to convert me or judge my lack of whatever. When Ma is taken out for a test, we go to the hospital library for a very enlightening session of Straight Talk that clears up a few mysteries for each of us.

Father Basil tells me he used to be a rock and roll musician. He comes from a complicated family and joined the Orthodox Church as an adult. His equally devout wife, who met him in high school and converted at the same time as he, is a nurse. (*Orthodox priests can be married? Hm!*) Because her father has rectal cancer, Father Basil's wife had already been helpful on the phone when we were learning about the disease. They have no intention of steering or influencing any of our decisions along the way. Father Basil makes it very clear that he really sees that Ma would be quite a handful. Not just now because of the cancer, but in general as well, especially for her children.

What's also fascinating is that my rather proper mother, who barely tolerated Colette's hippy teenage phase and has an extensive collection of well-thumbed *Social Registers*, genuinely *loves* this guy. What's more, he is truly fond of her. Father Basil and his wife put out an offer sometime recently to take Ma into their home and nurse her through the radiation. He says this offer still stands, but there is no pressure, only support of whatever she and her family decide to do. As we talk, it becomes more and more clear that Father Basil has something on his mind he's not quite saying. So I ask him what it is.

Turns out he got the wrong impression, probably because of the funeral plans. A few years ago when she converted, Ma announced to the family that she would not be able to be buried as planned at the Church of the Redeemer. This is a lovely old Episcopal church on the Main Line where a lot of Ma's maternal ancestors were installed, going back to the 1800s. There is a family plot kept in perpetuity. While my parents were both Roman Catholic at the time of my father's death, we knew he didn't care much what Ma did with him as long as she was happy. So after the military honors Daddy wanted in Florida, she had him cremated.

—*Margaret thinks Roman Catholics can't be cremated, Ma.*

—*I know, but there isn't enough room for any more full-length graves. Just two little spots are left, near Mummy.*

—*How about a nice urn?*

—*He'll be fine with the box from the funeral home. You know Daddy; he was a rebellious dresser and wouldn't want a big fuss.*

—*At the Redeemer, with all those huge monuments, surrounded by the crème de la crème of Philadelphia's old guard? You're going to just stick him into the ground with his mother-in-law in a* cardboard BOX??

After some reflection, it made a tiny bit of sense. Granny and Daddy did get along well (they shared a fondness for cigarettes, crossword puzzles, and whiskey), and Ma would eventually join them.

Or so we thought, until our mother became Orthodox and a whole new, more elaborate set of rules kicked in. Orthodox Christians are even more allergic to cremation than traditional Roman Catholics and Ma seemed to have no intention of taking chances with her own remains. They also can't be embalmed, and they have to be buried in an Orthodox plot.

Ma's even got her own personal Orthodox shroud. It's a special white baptismal robe she was given to wear when they dunked her in the River Jordan. She brought it to a family picnic at the Penllyn Club after she got back from the Holy Land because she wanted all the grandchildren and great-grandchildren to see what she'd be buried in. She made them pose for a picture: All of them lined up next to her on the grass in their dripping swimsuits and water wings, holding her death shroud spread out between them like they've been shaking sand off a big white beach blanket. Ma is beaming. Everyone else looks sort of spooked.

So our family had to adjust to the idea that Daddy would spend eternity with his mother-in-law and a bunch of highbrow strangers. I'm thinking Felix should take Ma's empty slot if he doesn't get around to marrying anyone else so there will be at least one blood relative to keep Daddy company. We decided that while Ma's funeral was going to be tricky, it was manageable, but that was before she and Photini switched from the local Orthodox church to Saint Mark of Ephesus, two hours upstate in Carlisle. That's when I suggested it might be helpful if she gave me some clear instructions.

—*What sort of instructions?*

—*Well, if you can't be embalmed and you can't be cremated, and the church is out in the middle of nowhere—*

—*So sorry to be such a burden to you.*

—*No, it's okay.*

—*I want all my descendants to go to my funeral together. That's the most important thing.*

—*Right, Ma, that shouldn't be a problem. As long as they're not having an ice storm in Vermont. And Colette will just have to somehow zap herself here from England before you start to sm—*

—*If that happens, just go ahead with it anyway. You can have a big party after everyone gets here. I'm sure you'll all have a wonderful time.*

—*That's nice; your own children won't be at your funeral because it's more important you obey a bunch of wacked-out religious—*

—*Susie.*

—*I'm sorry. I know this is important to you. I really do want to get it right for you.*

—*It's very important, Susie, and you should be thinking about it, too.*

—*Yeah, well, David and I are going to be scattered on Mount Desert Island.*

—*Oh* (dripping with an unvoiced opinion) . . .

—*I don't want to hear it, Ma.*

—*Well, I'm sure you'll be very happy there, and your children will never know how to find you.*

—*What do Orthodox people do if they die on vacation over-seas? God forbid, I screw it up so badly that you end up in the wrong heaven. . . .*

Ma did all the research and came up with a detailed contract from a funeral home near her new church that knew how to make Orthodox preparations. I paid for the burial plot and filed the particulars. But I balked at emergency evacuation insurance for the remains of vacation-ing Orthodox types when Ma admitted the priest said rules could be bent a little for extenuating circumstances. I also refused to put down a nonrefundable deposit with the funeral home, on the basis that she had a solid track record of switching religions. Who was to know whether Ma wouldn't have something else in mind when the moment was upon us?

My lack of faith in her faith made Ma quite indignant despite my assurance that I would definitely adapt to her wishes according to whatever the religion du jour was when she took her last breath. I was presented with several long handwritten pages of rambling explana-tion about why this church was indeed the Final Definitive Answer To Everything, which I think I filed somewhere, too. But I didn't budge on the down payment, and apparently she shared her version of our stand-off with Father Basil. He drew his own conclusions about my fears based on his past experience with concerned family members, and sees this as his chance to finally reassure me.

—Oh, that, I say. No, we definitely don't think you're running a cult. My mother's an idiot, but she's not completely stupid.

—It's good you feel that way, he says dubiously.

—No, it's just that she switches around so much. No offense. If she wants to be buried in Carlisle, that's fine; none of us will have a problem. But she's like a dog with a bone with each religion, and we've been through too many different bones. It makes her really mad when we don't just sign right up.

—Oh, he says. I'm always advising my wife to go easy on our kids about that, too.

My mother may be a little nuts, I think to myself, as Father Basil and I bound back down the hall like two old buddies to see how the test went. But at least she's not a Moonie. And she does know how to pick her priests. Father Basil has class.

7.
The Walk

THERE'S THIS THING I hate hate hate having to even think about, and now it's time to do it.

Colette and I have talked it to death over the years:

—I won't be able to do it, Coco. Kissing her good-bye and walking out of the room and down the hall. That's the killer: the part where I walk down the hall and home to my family.

—Well, maybe one of us will be there with you.

—Oh gosh. That would be SO helpful.

But nobody's here.

The whole idea of this assisted-living place I've found is that Ma can stay here for a month or so while she's having her radiation treatment. She won't have to fix her own meals, and if she needs a shower or something, they will help her. Then when she's back on her feet, she can go home. That's the idea.

That's not so bad, right?

So, the new place. Grammy and Grampy's Happy Hide-Away (or whatever the hell it's called). It's a good one, we hear. The other inmates seem comfortable. They're all trundling cheerfully around with their oxygen caddies, and the dining room has linen napkins and a pretty view of the woods. There are friendly notices on the bulletin board about Saint Paddy's parties and visiting day from the elementary school; pictures of happy, smiling old ladies making cute little crafts.

There are even people here that we know: Mrs. Martinelli—her husband was Daddy's doctor once and I used to play with her daughter. When I came for the tour, there was Mrs. Martinelli. She looked so fit, I figured she must be visiting somebody, but then it seemed to take her a minute or two to figure out who I was.

The occupational therapist at the hospital gave Ma her first walker. It works really well. It's red, with four wheels and a padded seat, so if you get tired you can stop and sit. The seat opens up with a hinge to a basket underneath into which you can fit a lot of other things like a purse or a bunch of bibles.

I began to believe that Happy Hide-Away was necessary when I stopped at the post office box on the way home from the hospital yesterday, the day before Ma's release. There among the heaps of mail I hadn't gotten around to collecting, was a notice from the school about Sam. He's all messed up and behind in his schoolwork, and I didn't even know.

The kids are smart enough and they work hard, but David's been away so much and I've barely been able to focus on them. According to Sam, his latest research paper stumped him; it just froze him right up. He says he sat staring at the computer in a trance for three nights in a row, and it was like dominoes. All the other work got neglected, and now he's in a real jam. I get the feeling if I, his actual mother, had been there checking in now and then, he might have snapped himself out of it.

It's ninth grade and the GPA counts. Sam's in the generation of kids where college acceptance is at its most cutthroat. I simply won't let this crisis mess up his chances. So Sam is moved to the top of my list for now.

I've got to check in with his teachers, which is difficult because they're busy, too, and during the day, I really need to work on Operation Ma, picking up what she needs at her apartment and organizing rides to radiation when I can't do it and stuff. I have this new compulsive relationship with my cell phone. It rings all the time now, and I can't resist answering it even when I'm driving, which is unsafe. There's no time to shop for a Bluetooth gadget, but we have an old headset that connects with a wire, and I wear it all day, clipped to my waistband. That way, when I'm in the sporting goods store looking for the spandex bicycle shorts Ma's physical therapist thinks will help support her back, I don't have to stop what I'm doing when Sam's advisor finally calls.

This is why I don't have a job. This *is* my job. I know there are people who manage it, single working mothers with aging parents. I just don't know how. How do they take care of the kids, the parents, and *then* go to an office or wherever and accomplish anything anyone would actually pay them to do? Honestly, it's beyond me to even understand, much less be capable of it.

And this place, this place, this place, it's not working out very well. I don't understand why everyone else here looks okay, because Ma's just not. Maybe we're not assisted-living material. When we arrived this morning, they didn't have sheets on the bed and people kept coming in with paperwork, saying *where are the sheets?* And we'd say *yes, where are they?* and they'd say *it's not my job.* So fine, Ma sat on her padded seat in the middle of the room until finally somebody whose job it *wasn't* took pity on us and found some sheets.

This got me thinking. Ma's using her first walker ever, and it's hard to get out of bed quickly. She just came off massive laxatives. Bed linens are hard to come by in this place for some reason. Put that all together, and it seems like I'd better make sure they know it would be a good idea, for the first night or two, to have some extra sheets handy for heaven's sake and maybe a person available whose job it is to get them if something were to happen in the middle of the night. So I ask the head nurse if she is prepared. She says *of course, not a problem* and puts it in the notes for the night nurse to see when she comes on tonight.

It's hard to figure out who to talk to about things. There are lots of women walking around in scrubs, laughing in the hallway, but when I ask them things like *who do I talk to about my mother having breakfast in her room on a tray,* they say *I'm private duty,* and that seems to mean they don't really work here. What's that all about?

I'm determined to get all this settled in time to be home for dinner and homework.

We have a geriatric psychologist who said *make sure your mother has familiar comfort things like family pictures,* so I've brought some of those and a couple of her icons. And because I can't just keep it simple, I grabbed our little portable DVD player and a handful of movies like *My Big Fat Greek Wedding,* which I hear is a huge hit with the little old ladies, especially future Orthodox nuns.

I've made several thousand trips back and forth from the car. It's funny because everywhere I go, I see Mrs. Martinelli.

I get in the elevator to go downstairs from Ma's room and it stops at the second floor and Mrs. Martinelli gets in. I say *hello, it's Susie von Moschzisker,* which seems to ring more of a bell for her, so that's who I'll have to be. *Oh, hello, Susie, how are you?* (We already established how I am this morning, but anyway.)

We travel down to the lobby together. I go out to the car to collect the next load of stuff: a quilt and the DVD player. Everything is getting a little tangled up with the wire from the phone headset, which gets somehow shut in the car door. And when I try to walk away, my ear-piece is ripped off my head and the phone yanks off my waistband and lands on the pavement and the battery clatters out, but it still seems to work, thank God, and I hook everything back up again and I go back in and push the elevator button and after a while the door opens and out pops Mrs. Martinelli.

—Hello again, Mrs. Martinelli, it's Susie von Moschzisker.

—Oh, hi, Susie, how are you?

I wonder which of Mrs. Martinelli's kids has my job. Maybe we can have coffee sometime and talk each other out of killing ourselves.

When I get back to the third floor, Ma announces that Father Nectarios will be here any second to give her communion, and isn't that nice because I will get to meet him finally.

—*So* nice, I say.

Nice for her but *help*. I don't have time to wait around for that to get done, it's almost time for dinner and I'm going to have to pick up some takeout as it is. The kids really need a calm meal before homework. I show Ma the DVDs. She's being uncharacteristically decent about everything, which sort of makes it hard for me to feel inclined to take any of my monkey-in-a-cageness out on her, which is a good thing.

I'm trying to figure out how to get the DVD player to work. This gadget belongs to the boys, and they know how to work it, but I have not got a clue. I've got the directions, but half of it is in Spanish and the other half is an obvious translation from some other language altogether, using one of those word-for-word programs on the Internet:

Making to Play: Please be setting the proper input button on your DVD device. Wires installed correctly will to avoid hazard instead.

So I've laid all the different wires and batteries and things on the floor, and I'm slowly making some sense of them all when Father Nectarios and his wife, Matushka, arrive. This business about Matushka took some concentration. Father Basil and Father Nectarios are at the same church. They both have wives named Matushka, because apparently that is what your name is when you are married to an Orthodox priest. (You get your own special Orthodox name when you're baptized. Photini used to be something much simpler. They call Ma Anna now instead of Marjorie, which could be hard for Mrs. Martinelli to get the hang of if it ever comes up.)

Anyway, Father Nectarios and Matushka are here, and I'm still figuring out how to be setting the correct AV cable to acquire proper according to the output frequency of this component or something, but I drop everything and shake everyone's hands and ask if they would rather I come back tomorrow.

But Ma wants to see *My Big Fat Greek Wedding* in bed tonight. So we decide I'll just keep on sorting the DVD player out while Father Nectarios and Matushka do whatever it is they do. This turns out to involve a lot of walking around with candles and decanters of wine and special cloths on Ma's head and some very long and drawn-out chanting. I have to discreetly climb around them with all my wires while they do all this stuff.

I get the thing working, and I sort of hover till they come to some kind of break in all the chanting and walking around, and it feels rude, but I ask:

—I'm sorry, is it okay if I just go over this with Ma I mean Anna for a second before I go home?

Not a problem, so I show her how to turn on the power and put in the disc and what to push for play and pause, and I kiss Ma and I shake everyone's hands and thank them, and thank God I got that taken care of so Mrs. Martinelli and I can grab a minute to catch up on things in the elevator on the way down to the lobby.

What's amazing is that there is so much going on, I don't even pause for a second to register the fact:

That walk down the hall I was dreading?

I just did it.

I kissed Ma good-bye and walked out the door. And surprise surprise, she wasn't alone like I had always imagined. She had Father Nectarios and Matushka, and Holy Communion, and she was kind of happy.

And yes, I *did* that walk down the hall by myself, but in my recurring horror fantasy I never pictured Mrs. Martinelli waiting for me in the elevator, a reminder that this kind of thing happens to lots of people whose children are not selfish jerks any more than I am. Maybe we're all going to manage.

So we have an excellent stew from the take-out place, and Sam and I get to talk about his situation. I sort of pace around all evening trying to think about what else could go wrong and how to stop it. David calls and gets an earful and he wants to speak to Sam, and then he starts to wonder if he should pass on this Broadway play he was thinking of doing, which is really a bummer but maybe that's the thing to do.

—Maybe not, I say. Don't pass yet. I think it may be under control.

I call Ma first thing in the morning to see how the night went, and yikes.

—I have to go home now.

—What happened?

—There is something very very wrong with this place.

—What? What happened?

—Well, a person came into my room in the middle of the night and woke me up and started yammering.

—Oh my *gosh*, was it Mrs. Martinelli?

—Who?

—Never mind, who was it?

—I have *no idea.* A nurse.

—What did she want?

—She was shrieking *what's all this about having to change the sheets all the time. I'm not set up for this!*

—What?! Wait, you needed the sheets changed?

—No, I didn't need the sheets changed, I was asleep. I didn't need anything.

—Are you sure you hadn't been bothering them?

—No, I hadn't been bothering anyone. I didn't have anything to bother anyone about. It's completely unnecessary for me to be here.

—Well, what *did* she want?

—She had a chart and she was waving it at me and howling. I was quite frightened, but I didn't want to wake you.

—So what did you do?

—Well, she finally went away and I couldn't sleep. So I watched your *Big Fat* movie over and over for the rest of the night, and it was awfully good. Susie, they were all Orthodox in it and how did you find that movie, it was perfect.

—Well, that's good.

—Yes, but Susie, this really won't do.

The thing is she's going to radiation at ten today, and I don't know how we'll manage if she moves back to her apartment, and we know what we can't do with the Elephant, and it feels like a trap is closing in on me. I'm so worried for her and Sam and David's job and all of us, so I say *please, I'll talk to them and try to sort this out.* I get the kids fed and drive them to school and then I go home to call the admissions person at the facility, who sounds very apologetic and says they'll work things out with the night nurse, who must have felt unnecessarily overwhelmed about the note in the chart about the sheets.

Ma's friend Diana is going to drive her to radiation today. Just when it's time for her to be picked up, Ma calls:

—Why didn't I get any breakfast?

I *told* them about her breakfast, so what the heck's *that* about? I drive over there to talk to someone, and I end up in this little office with the head of something or other and the admissions person and they're all very sorry about this. I ask them:

—What is going on here? I thought Assisted Living meant you got Assisted with your Living. You don't have anyone to put the sheets on the bed, nothing is anybody's job it seems like, and now what? Do they need me to buy Nurse Ratched an extra supply of sheets? Should I drive over here every morning and make sure my mother gets some breakfast?

They are really very very sorry and it's just a series of miscommunications. The aide didn't file the right instructions about breakfast in the room; *your mother hasn't had a chance to fill out her menu choices yet. Here, you can talk to the Director of Nutrition and fill out her meal choices, and it won't ever happen again.*

So the Director of Nutrition is wheeled in: a surprisingly corporate man in a pressed polo shirt. He gives me a stack of forms with choices for things like prunes or fruit cocktail, eggs boiled or scrambled and what kind of toast. I'm looking at it and I am trying hard to think, I'm really trying to focus: *What would Ma want?*

And now I know exactly how Sam must have felt, staring and staring at the computer, frozen stiff, blocked. I put the menus on the desk.

—I'm sorry, I think maybe I need medication. *I can't do this.*

And they look at me with great compassion but no idea what to say. They must have seen this a million times.

So I get up and I walk like a zombie out past Mrs. Martinelli, who stops as I go by, trying to figure out where she's seen me before.

I go home and lie down for a while and call Colette for the millionth time, and we decide the thing to do is to call that Michael guy with the hopefully not light-fingered people who help you at home because that's what Ma wants: to make a polite departure from this lovely facility, and be in her own home while she's going through all this. And David says, of course, you don't need medication, this is just like when the twins were born, you will be all right, you're figuring out how to make this work, it's just that this all matters so much and you care so much. *I know you can do this;* I'm coming home soon.

Okay.

We got through *that.* And now we'll try *this.*

Yes. I can do this. Yes.

8.
Subject: Items

On March 12, 2007 <susanmorse@myemailaddress.com> wrote:

Dear Siblings,

Don't mind me, I just need to get something out of my system.

Till now, Ma's actually been pretty decent about asking me to pick things up for her. She usually gives me some warning and says not to worry, just get it when I have time. Now that we're in the third week of radiation, she's becoming desperate and lunging at anything she can think of to ease the discomfort. We have reached this frantic stage where she's not able to be considerate, and it seems like there is no way to win.

- Item: *Calming Pills*

She called her acupuncturist, Bella, to ask for more homeopathic Calming Pills to help her sleep. Bella told her she would order them and would call when they came in, hopefully Friday. Ma calls me on Friday without checking with Bella, and tells me *Bella has the pills and can you pick them up.* I go to Bella's. No pills. No Bella. I leave Bella a message and she calls me later to tell me she told

Ma she wasn't sure about Friday and she will call when they come in. I hear nothing more about the pills, including from Ma who doesn't appear to mind that she doesn't have them because she never mentions them again.

- Item: *Triple X Ointment*

A home health aide told her it would help with the burning. Radiation burns the skin, as we know, and we're all very glad the radiation nurses talked Ma out of using Holy Oil to heal the burns because now she has stopped basting herself like a turkey before getting roasted. It's time to try Triple X Ointment, and at the drugstore there was a small package and a large one. I got the small and told Ma if she liked it I would get the large. We went through this whole big thing about trying it and she decided it was *marvelous* so I later got her the big box. Marvelous marvelous.

- Item: *Bras*

Ma said her bras were wearing out. This should have been easy because I knew what bra she had -- I introduced it to her. I said do you want the same size and what is it because I am going to the mall tomorrow. We checked her bra and noted the size. The mall doesn't have this bra anymore, I discovered, but this was okay because I could order it online. So I ordered it. The bra arrived a week later and I dropped it off ASAP.

Ma calls me and announces that in the last week she has noticed that she is *one cup size smaller*. I say why didn't you tell me before I ordered the bra. She says she didn't know I would get it right away.

- Item: *Night frigging shirts*

Ma has had to simplify her wardrobe because of all the discomfort. She wears nothing but these nightshirts so she can lie on the sofa with her legs in the air no matter who is coming over, like she used to do when she sunbathed by our pool. (Colette: This habit of exhibition-ism is something I know you accuse me of inheriting from Ma, and you're probably right. When the twins were born and David's teenage niece Caeli was visiting, I used to parade around wearing nothing on top but a back brace and a nursing bra with the flaps open. So I don't really have a right to criticize, but the Triple X Ointment Ma uses for the burning and itching gets all over the nightshirts, and she walks around with stains on the back.)

When I pointed this out to her, Ma was really unhappy about it. She said it was hard to clean the only two she *has* often enough, and I offered to buy a couple more. This meant ordering from Vermont Country Store online. I called her while online and asked what size she wears because I can order them right now. She checked and said *large*. I said are you sure it's not medium since you've lost the weight during treatment, and remember the bra. *No, it's large*. I order the nightshirts. Ma calls the next day and says she thinks she should get *medium*. I say why didn't you say that when I was ordering them. *Oh,* she says.

• Item: *Cancer tea*

This is some stuff Photini's husband recommended, an herbal cleansing tea he uses for his lymphatic cancer or something. They want to give him chemo, but he's been tak-ing this nasty swill for years and seems to be hanging in there. This is the one holistic cure elixir Ma's asked for. I've indulged her, even though I had to run around buying all this stainless steel paraphernalia to brew it and strain it. I have to store it in *dark glass bottles only*, which believe me are nowhere to be found except in a liquor store. I went and bought three bottles of some expensive god-awful vodka because it comes in dark blue, and poured ALL OF IT down the sink so I could use them. I sterilize all this crap every couple of weeks when I make a new batch, and then we have a huge witch's cauldron-type pot bubbling all day on the stove and nobody wants to linger in the kitchen. I really hope it helps, but still . . .

- Item: *Regular olive oil*

She uses regular olive oil to make Holy and rub on anything that hurts that's not in the radiation zone, and to put in her religious lamps. If I get Extra Virgin, I have to go back and get the right kind. We have been through this. She literally goes through a gallon or two a week. She has just recently asked me for another of the large cans, and I'd better take care of it right away.

- Item: *Kleenex*

She likes the small boxes because they are pretty, *but not if the box is decorated with bright colors. Neutral, please.* She uses Kleenex when she is out of toilet paper. I ransacked the store for neutral boxes the other day and delivered a ton of them in beige stripes.

- Item: *Toilet paper*

Ma goes through reams of toilet paper, and I have tried about three different brands; each one hurts. She wants the kind from Superfresh. While I was gearing up to find out what that brand is, she called to say *Josie just came and dropped some off.* Yippee! Four days later, Ma says she has *no toilet paper.* By then, I know what I'm looking for. So I am going to Superfresh, on a special trip, because Ma sounds pretty desperate. It is a *toilet paper emergency* right this second.

- Item: *Bubble ice packs*

This is the best description I can get from Ma:

—*You get them at CVS and dip them in hot water and they become ice packs.*

She also wants some of my ice cubes from home because she has run out and she needs to put them directly on her *tail,* because it turns out she is allergic to the Triple X

Ointment after all. And she is allergic to the Kleenex in the neutral boxes because the Kleenex inside the boxes is beige and she is *allergic to beige*. She has welts all over herself and she describes them to me in minute detail:

    —There are enormous bumps in the creases that turn into bubbles and --

    —Stop, Ma. Call the doctor.

If she weren't so sure she was allergic to Benadryl, I would recommend that. I pray to God that she doesn't ask me to pick up Allergy Pills at Bella's. After the wild goose chase for Calming Pills, I would like to skip Bella's for a few days.

    •   Item: *Moist Wipes*

I got her four boxes last week.

Today is my day to pay bills. It takes about five hours and I can usually run one little errand, but I prefer just to focus on the bills or I will make a horrible mistake. But Ma is having a toilet paper emergency and an ice cube emergency. So. Also there is no rush, but the olive oil I dropped off yesterday *is perfect for the lamps but not for cooking,* can she have *a small bottle of Extra Virgin, as well?*

I print up info about colostomy for her to study in preparation for the meeting with Surgeon Pete in two weeks. Maybe she will be so busy reading pages and pages that she will fall asleep or be too tired to call and ask me to pick things up for her.

I look through the bills before going out on this quick errand. A bill has arrived from Bella for the Calming Pills. I call Ma to find out if she got them somehow. *No,* she says. I call Bella, who says she dropped them off with the doorman more than a week ago. I wondered all this time why Ma was not complaining about wanting Calming Pills anymore. It appears that Ma has simply not noticed that they were dropped off, and neglected to process the evidence in front of her nose: She had plenty of Calming Pills all along, despite the fact that she asked me to pick them up ages ago and I didn't.

I put the ice cubes in a cooler in the back of the car so they will last while I am at Superfresh getting the emergency toilet paper, the olive oil, and some garlic. I arrive at Superfresh after failing to get the bubble ice packs at CVS. I have asked two pharmacists and called Ma, but CVS does not know what we are talking about. I call and get Ma's machine and tell it I am giving up on the bubble ice packs.

I go to Superfresh. In the parking lot, David calls to tell me that Ma has called to say *stop looking for the bubble ice packs*. I do not need this direction, but okay, I will continue to not look for the bubble ice packs. I get everything else, and pause by the Moist Wipes. But I think *nah*, she just got four boxes last week and she knows I'm at the store, she can't have run out.

When I arrive with the garlic and olive oil, fifty rolls of toilet paper, money to pay the housekeeper, the pages and pages of colostomy info, a bag of ice, and a big blue bottle of her cancer tea, I go in the closet to unload the toilet paper. There is a full, unopened package in there already. Not only that but it looks a teensy bit different than the kind I brought. (America's Choice Plush versus America's Choice Super Plush or something, *oh, darn,* I literally bought tons of the stuff, *oh, scheitzenheimer.*)

I put the ice in the freezer and I'm kind of pissed, so I pick this moment to not very nicely tell Ma we have to work on our system here because it feels like I am getting nowhere.

—*I can't help it; I don't need to hear this I am in great distress* (she is; it's a fact).

I say I am sorry she is in distress, but getting me

to run around buying her useless things is not going to change that, and I have to go pay bills. I make my move for the door.

—*Don't talk to me like that*, she says. *Do you want to see?*

And she lifts up her nightshirt and waves her backside at me. It looks truly awful, but all this makes me think about is the millions of times that Ma gleefully paraded her backside at us over the years (in the dressing room at the Penllyn Club, standing in front of her fireplace with her skirt hitched up to her hipbones. Prudish teen-age friends used to tease me about it) and I am sick of her flashing, I have no sympathy. In fact, I am beginning to suspect she may have asked for this problem somehow, because this whole thing seems to have a huge psychological component. Maybe Ma deliberately got this cancer so she could *legitimately* wave her backside around at me and a whole lot of other people -- why on earth this gets her off, I don't know. But I think I understand now how our niece must have felt, even though she never said anything about my open nursing flaps, and I sincerely hope I never do anything like that to anyone ever again.

As I am making my exit at top speed (unfortunately for-getting to give her the cash for the housekeeper, and also forgetting to point out that the ice is in the freezer), Ma shakes an empty Moist Wipes box at me and says *what do I do with this?* I say how about throw it away. *Oh*, she says, *have I run out?* I say, I don't know, HAVE YOU?

Yes, indeed she has.

Okay now I feel a little better, I'm going to start pay-ing the bills. I wonder if she'll check the freezer. If any of you call her, will you tell her the ice is in there? I'm off duty for the day.

XXSusie

9.
Capitation Tap Dance

EVER GET THE FEELING you might have been adopted?

Ma and I now spend so much of our time together that our incompatibility is showing. We drive around to doctors and talk on the phone several times a day. We've been getting along surprisingly well, for us. But it's as if we're partners in an odd business enterprise, thrown together by circumstances.

Those women in the movies whose mothers are their best friends—I know some in real life, too. They go on spa vacations, shopping sprees, lunch dates. They share confidences. How do they do that?

There's a therapy exercise where you make a list of what you do and don't have in common: Let's see, Ma and I both got married young and postponed the development of our artistic talents to raise a family. And we both like asparagus.

That's all I can think of. Here's what I really like: tap dancing.

When I was eight, I loved to watch Fred Astaire movies on Channel 29's *Saturday Matinee*. I begged and begged for tap lessons, but I got ballet instead. That was all the dancing there was in our area.

Ballet was okay, but it felt restricting. I found that my toy building blocks fit inside the soles of my knee socks and I could sort of tap around a little that way. Colette used to laugh when I soft-shoed vigorously through the kitchen instead of helping her with the dishes. Daddy was nice about this. He had been through dancing class as a child, like most boys and girls in his circle. Sometimes he would put on the record player, let me stand on his feet, and fox-trot around the living room. Other than that, it never seemed like anyone in our family shared my interest.

I didn't follow through with ballet for long, but I tried modern dance at college to get out of the sports requirement. This led to a little bit of performing. I don't think I was particularly good, but it seemed to partially satisfy a hunger.

There was a small commotion my sophomore year when a new freshman named Lacey turned up. She was a bona fide Rockette from New York's Radio City Music Hall. Williams College was dominated by nerds and jocks, so Lacey was exotic; an anomaly like the Marine who roomed in my boyfriend's suite and told dramatic stories about his service in Vietnam.

We had a special January break between semesters where you only took one class. Students could teach little mini-courses as well, if they had anything to offer. When I saw that Lacey was giving a beginning tap workshop, I pounced, and for the four short weeks of classes, I felt like a hound dog let off the leash in the woods.

In New York, I dabbled in some wonderful classes: You could put down ten dollars and walk right in with the real Broadway hoofers. I took a one-day workshop in African dance with Eartha Kitt that almost crippled me. She was really tough. There was this bongo drummer accompanying, and Eartha was screaming at us in that trademark raspy Catwoman voice. I felt like an ignorant klutzy white woman, but still I was thoroughly transported. Eartha was a force; I couldn't help doing everything she said even when I wanted to collapse on the floor. I couldn't manage the stairs of my apartment for almost a week.

I also skulked around at Alvin Ailey for a while and eventually managed to flounder in the back of a class taught by the great Judith Jamison. I never really clicked with it the way the pros did, but dancing was in my blood somewhere, it had to be. Who *were* my real parents?

For some reason, I didn't try tap again, although having another go did cross my mind from time to time. In California, it turned out Fred Astaire was a member of our Beverly Hills church. He kept a low profile, but one Sunday morning I had to leave early and when I stepped outside, I froze: There he was, his silhouette unmistakable from the back with those wonderful loose dress pants. Balanced slightly more on one leg than the other, as if poised for a take-off down the church steps. It was like spotting a rare kind of woodland animal. I didn't even want to breathe.

David had to learn ballroom dancing for a TV movie he did during a hiatus from *St. Elsewhere*, and we bought a series of lessons. Tango, cha-cha, swing, mambo. We weren't bad. The best was when we went to the final party at the end of the show's last season—I wore a fire engine red dress with a short skirt that flared out when he spun me around.

We eventually forgot most of our moves, but we can still pull off a few at the odd wedding. David's a good sport about helping me find chances to satisfy these urges I get, but I think it's a little tough on him—he's shy and thinks he's a dork on the dance floor, though he's not. We don't go to clubs because we get self-conscious about people looking to see what *that actor* dances like. We mostly stick to private parties and weddings, and there aren't really enough of those for my needs. If David isn't there, I get lucky sometimes and find a kindred spirit. I struck gold once when I spotted a cousin of the bride who used to dance with the Joffrey. That guy really knew how to jitterbug.

And then there was Uncle Tommy.

David's nephew was getting married in Maine. David was in the middle of a six-episode gig on *House*, so I flew the kids up to represent his branch of the family, and see his sister Diane's son Nathan tie the knot with Tiffany at a picturesque inn on the coast.

Diane was in rapture—this was her first time as the mother of the groom. She'd been broadly hinting about grandchildren since the first time Nathan showed up with Tiffany, who is not only sweet, but drop-dead gorgeous. The whole family was there—David's mother, his three sisters, the husbands, most of their grown kids, and lots of cousins we didn't know.

The kids and I were delighted to see Uncle Tommy. He's not related to David by blood; he's actually Diane's brother-in-law from her second marriage. You can tell right away that our backgrounds don't quite overlap, but the first time we met a year or so before, we clicked. Uncle Tommy is the kind of guy who can click with anyone. He's a cheerful little fellow, kind of runty and he walks funny—he wears a back brace and collects disability, but he's got a great attitude and rather nattily groomed facial hair, like Al Pacino on a good day.

Oh, and there's this thing nobody told me: Before the whole disability business, Uncle Tommy had a brief career as a male stripper.

It was great to see him again, and we sort of hung out together during lunch. When the music started, I was on the edge of the dance floor with the kids. I wasn't aware of Uncle Tommy at my elbow—he's not very tall. But then he began to shimmy, and I grabbed him.

Of course, I had no clue about Tommy's dance background, but he seemed surprisingly loose for a guy in a back brace and it was clear he had some moves. In ballroom dance, you are trained to assess your partner's style and adapt. Tommy seemed to be having a very good time, so I pretty much went with it.

Actually, my mother did teach me some useful rules of etiquette: *Bring a hostess gift when you come to visit. Send a thank-you note.* There are a few she forgot to mention, like *no dirty dancing at an in-law's carefully planned New England wedding.*

Nathan and Tiffany's nuptials were memorable for the whole group of in-laws and friends. Not just for the pleasure of seeing this picture-perfect couple joined in holy matrimony against a magnificent ocean backdrop, but because it was the exact moment that the mid-life crisis David's wife was apparently having finally found its peak.

I don't have much recollection, but I hear Tommy and I pretty much cleared the dance floor. I think we kept most of our clothes on, but they say we were at it for hours. Cell phones came out; videos were messaged instantly to David. His mother seemed politely impressed. Our children were mortified.

When we'd just moved to Philadelphia, I found a Saturday morning tap class for our kids. On the first day, I sat in the waiting room with another mother listening to the music and the beat, and again I felt that hound-dog urgency. I kept tapping my feet on the floor in front of the bench where we sat and saying to this other mother (who had never met me before in her life), *isn't this great? Don't you want to join them?*

By the end of the class, my new friend was as jazzed as I was. When the teacher came out with the kids, I told her how we wished we could tap, too, it sounded like so much fun, and the teacher said *why don't you?* And I looked at my new friend and said, *I will if you will, oh, please . . .*

So for about three weeks, this lady and I joined a class of kids who came up to our waists. We were going to be in the recital and everything. I tapped all the time, disappearing for hours to practice on the concrete floor of our unfinished basement. The kids refused to participate; I think they were sort of upset. I was so disappointed when they staged a minor rebellion: One day I just couldn't get them to go, and that was the end of my tap career.

It was devastating. I still wonder if that lucky woman actually got to be in the recital without me. . . .

Lately, I've had to be satisfied with Dance Dance Revolution in the arcade when I chaperone the twins and their friends at Dave and Buster's. I'm terrible at it. Ben says I drew a crowd once, but I think they were probably the type of people who like to make fun of early rejects on *American Idol.*

I'll get back to tap some day, but right now Ma needs some tests.

I found one other thing Ma and I have in common: We both think there's something fishy going on at Stone Mills Hospital.

I'm pretty much okay with the whole HMO-referral thing now that

I know what we're supposed to do. I get that the insurance companies don't want to pay for unnecessary treatment. Ma inherited Daddy's health insurance: Medicare with a supplemental policy for former employees of the state of Pennsylvania. When the supplemental's premiums began to go way up several years ago, Ma opted for a cheaper HMO. One big difference between traditional Medicare and an HMO is the HMO has a list of approved primary doctors, one of whom she had to sign up with. All medical decisions start with that doctor. This is supposed to keep Ma from running around willy-nilly wasting insurance money having expensive unnecessary things done to her.

Getting the hang of the system was intimidating at first. I was so afraid Ma would go to a specialist she needed without remembering to get approval from her primary doctor, and then we'd have to pay for it in full. But from what I can tell so far, doctors won't let this happen to you. Even if you are sitting in their waiting room, if they don't have the referral from your primary, they will make sure you know it, and tell you what to do to fix this before they'll let you in. I guess they know you'll be reluctant to pay the bill if the HMO balks.

We know what to do now anyway. If Ma wants a cardiologist, say, she calls some friends and gets a few names of doctors they like. Then I call one and ask the office if they subscribe to her HMO. If they do, I make an appointment and ask for their subscriber number. I then call Maxwell, her primary, and give his office the name of the doctor, the subscriber number, and the time of the appointment. Maxwell's office is supposed to know us well enough to decide whether or not she needs this appointment, so there may be a little chatting about her symptoms first. When we get to the specialist, they generally have received Maxwell's referral through the computer. If they haven't, things tend to work themselves out.

What gets Ma and me apoplectic is when we have to deal with outpatient tests at the dreaded Stone Mills Hospital.

Maxwell's practice is a valiant little one-man outfit right in the neighborhood. His HMO patients are therefore *capitated* to Stone Mills Hospital. Capitation is apparently a word invented in 1983 especially for HMOs, and it is just beginning to make sense to me. I understand now that it means certain tests may only be done at the primary doctor's nearest hospital.

For a while I had to play mind games with myself to keep from forgetting the word, and I would say to doctors' offices *she had her CT done at Stone Mills Hospital because she has that thing that sounds like decapitation but it isn't.*

The Huntingdon Cancer Center, of course, has all the CT machines you could wish for. If Ma was allowed to do the tests there, then Pete, her surgeon who is *right down the hall*, could have the results in a twinkling. But no, these monthly tests to monitor the cancer must be ordered not by Pete, the guy at Huntingdon who actually wants them, but by Maxwell in Stone Mills, who is not really in the loop enough to know exactly why they need to be done.

And not only that: Instead of having the order, tests, *and* results all in one hospital system from start to finish, the patient (or her daughter) must trudge back and pick up the results at Stone Mills the day after they are given, so she can hand-deliver them to Pete's office *all the way across town.* This is supposed to be in the interest of curing a sick person who needs every chance she has to rest. Does it make sense to anyone at all?

The procedure is this: Pete Johnson at Huntingdon tells Ma to get a CT scan and a chest x-ray before her next checkup when he'll see if the tumor has grown. I call Maxwell's office and tell them to take my word for it: Ma needs these expensive tests. They take my word for this and call the scan and x-ray in to Stone Mills Hospital via their computer network, and I call Stone Mills Hospital to schedule the tests.

And Stone Mills is where the whole thing gets bollixed up.

Ma's been dealing with an unfortunate affliction, which may or may not be a side effect, depending on who you're talking to. On certain random days when I call her, it's:

—*I'd better stay home today; I'm having the fiery tail again.*

Radiation's been over for a couple of weeks, but the side effects linger. It's still pretty hot down in places we won't mention, and the sensation can be very hard to ignore. We've tried all kinds of remedies from ice packs to a strategically directed portable fan; nothing provides much relief for long. They say this will pass, but for now, outings have to be timed between Ma's unpredictable attacks, and must be kept pretty short. Fiery tail is not at all compatible with Stone Mills Hospital's current system for processing prescribed, pre-approved outpatient tests.

Today, we have no discomfort so far. This is good, but it takes time just to get Ma there, so who knows how things will turn out. We find a parking spot close to the outpatient testing entrance, which I take as a good omen. We plod inside, sign in at the desk, and wait. It doesn't take too long before someone in a cubicle calls us in. She (usually, it's a she—today it is Ayesha) takes the insurance card and looks Ma up in the computer. I tell Ayesha we need a CT and an x-ray, and I have the prescriptions right here.

Usually from there, we totter around the corner and down the hall to the x-ray waiting room, turn over our paperwork, and settle in for another wait. No good, Ayesha tells us today. We're all set for the CT, but we can't have the x-ray because the thingy isn't in the computer, which means the doctor hasn't called it in. The thingy could be pre-approval or pre-certification or pre-authorization, I forget which—they all mean something different believe it or not, and it doesn't really matter because whatever it is, we don't have it and we won't get the test until we do.

I sense a monkey fit coming on. I sprint outside and call Maxwell's office to see what's gone wrong and ask if he can send this thingy over pronto.

Ring. Ring.

—Hello, this is the office of Doctor Andrew Maxwell. We know it is a Friday afternoon, but we have decided to take an unexplained vacation just to inconvenience you. We will be out of the office until Tuesday. If this matter cannot wait until then, Doctor Suchandsuch is on call at . . .

I call Suchandsuch's office and, of course, they will have to *see*

Ma before they can prescribe an x-ray. We might be psycho-deviants hoping to get see-through pictures taken of our chests to share on the Internet with a global ring of perverted x-ray fiends.

I call Pete, the surgeon at Huntingdon, and get his assistant—can they help us?

—Why doesn't the hospital just do the test and get the authorization later when your primary's in the office?

—Good question!

She says she'll try to pull some strings and get back to me, but we wait and wait and the strings don't work.

What it boils down to is we can't have the x-ray today no matter how hard we try. So Ma does the CT scan and we have no choice, we have to give up on the x-ray and hope another nonfiery tail day turns up soon.

Now, here's the part that makes me mad:

I call Maxwell's office when they all (all three of them) waltz in from their long weekend (mental note to revisit the group practice idea, we love Maxwell, but honestly since when does an entire office get to go on vacation at the same time?) and they tell me they actually did send the x-ray thingy in, at exactly the same time as the thingy for the CT. So it was the hospital that lost it. If I had just insisted last week, we might have that stupid x-ray behind us. Now we have to go back.

I've run out of old *New Yorkers* to read while we wait, and lately I've found solace in Sudoku. It's actually a bit of a problem. Addiction runs in our family. Instead of losing myself in a bottle or pills, I tend to get overinvolved in things like Spider Solitaire on the computer. I once had to see a chiropractor because I got too compulsive with a little hand-held game of Tetris.

I have a nice pocket version of Sudoku, not too easy and not too hard, and I remember to bring it with me the next time we go over for the x-ray. We park near the entrance, lumber in, sign the clipboard, and wait for our turn in the cubicle, with Irene this time. Today is unfortunately a fiery tail day for Ma, but Pete needs this x-ray now, so she waits standing up. I sit with the Sudoku. We tell Irene in today's cubicle what we're there for, and:

Still no thingy in the computer.

This is not good because Ma can't put up with this too much longer. We don't have the patience to call all the doctors and wait for them to resend the thingy. Anyway I know it's there; I just have to get the hospital to admit it. So I ask Irene to look again. While she looks and Ma hovers, I fill in a few numbers: *a 2 and an 8.*

—She's not in here, says Irene.

—That's impossible, I say. Why does this happen every time we come here? It's like your computer system's a black hole. Does this happen to everyone? How do you get anything done?

—No, says Irene. This never happens. Your doctor must have messed up.

We've all heard that before. I know Maxwell sent in that darn thing. This is crap.

—How about try under M instead of V—her last name is two words. (*I fill in a 6.*)

—Not there under M.

Ma is beginning to pace up and down the hallway outside the cubicle.

—Look, I say, and I'm barely even looking up from the Sudoku.

I was one of those decent students who did their homework in front of the TV. It's best to multitask because I bore very easily. It's a little rude, but I've been through this so many times. The process is fairly mindless, and I spend so much time at it between my mother's appointments, orthopedic people for my athletic children, orthodontists, pediatricians, vets for the pets, and on and on. For my own sanity, stimulation is essential if there's a wait. This woman has her screwed-up computer to keep her entertained, so I get to play with my Sudoku. It's part of my battle plan. With Sudoku to keep me occupied, I figure they can't bore me out the door, and we will get the x-ray even if it takes all day. But each second that ticks by may bring us that much closer to a fiery tail attack, and there's no way of knowing how long Ma can hold up. Well, we've been through this. Maxwell's office assured me the authorization is in there this time. We are not leaving until Ma gets her x-ray.

—Look, my mother is in real discomfort and can't be kept waiting again. You are obviously trying hard, but this seems to be beyond your scope. Who can I talk to get this done? (*A 3 and a 3 again.*)

Irene seems completely stumped.

So often we assume the people behind the desks know their jobs better than we do. It can be liberating when you realize it's time to make a stand.

—Okay, forget it, I say, raising my voice a few notches.

Step. Slide. Heel-ball-change.

People in the waiting room can hear us and are looking.

—Maybe we should just go home, stop monitoring the cancer and DIE. Let's go, Ma.

—No, no, Irene says, I'll take you to the manager.

So we box-step around and around, past stacks of file cartons and other mess that's not for public viewing, to this tiny office with one extra chair. There's a lady sitting behind a desk who looks somewhat startled to see us. I plunk myself down in her one chair since Ma can't possibly sit still and she's shifting her weight from one foot to another and sort of squirming. I still have the Sudoku book in hand as I speak to the woman:

—My mother has a rectal tumor, which is being monitored monthly. We were here last week for a CT and an x-ray, which were prescribed, pre-ordered, pre-authorized, pre-approved, pre-certified, and called for by her primary doctor. Ayesha couldn't find the thingy. We went home because we believed the hospital. Now we know the thingy has been here all along. My mother is very uncomfortable and needs to get this test done and go home as soon as possible, and Irene has tried very hard and she can't find the authorization any more than Ayesha could last week. But this time, we aren't leaving until she is x-rayed because she has to bring the results of these two tests to her surgeon's the day after tomorrow. Can YOU find my mother's thingy?

Ma is pacing again, and she is beginning to slap her hips. I take a moment to fill in *a 9, a 4, and a 2.*

The manager gets it, thank God. She scoops us up and leads us through to the x-ray department where there are about six people ahead of us. We all promenade around them into the work area, where the manager collars an x-ray tech holding a clipboard. He looks like he is in the middle of something.

—Your mother can go with him, she tells me. You can go back to Irene in her office and get her paperwork.

And the manager disappears.

—I have to find a bathroom NOW, says Ma. She is jumping up and down, and it looks like she is getting ready to hitch up her skirt and do something unseemly.

—Where is the bathroom? I ask the tech.

He blinks at us and looks distractedly down at his clipboard.

—I can't do an x-ray without paperwork, he says.

—SHIT, says Ma.

A few years ago, my mother announced she had a confession to make. I had no inkling of the guilt she'd apparently been wrestling with for quite some time.

It seems there were plenty of tap classes to be had near our home when I was a kid. She knew her little girl would have died and gone to heaven for a tap class; everything down to my toes needed to *tap, tap, tap*! But Ma had her own ideas, and sent me to ballet class instead.

Tap dancing was not for *our kind of people.* Tap dancing was *vulgar.* Ballet would be *much more appropriate.*

—SHIT, says Ma. She wiggles her hips and hops.

The x-ray tech can't begin to appreciate the profundity of this moment. My well-bred mother has unexpectedly been transformed into a potty mouth and appears to be fixing to shuffle off to Buffalo, and there's nobody but me and this stranger to admire the significance of her amazing breakthrough.

Guess I'm not adopted after all.

He points to a bathroom door and Ma makes a dash for it. I had no idea she could move like that. She leaps in and slams the door.

The tech is trying to sidle around the corner.

—Oh, no you DON'T! I call out.

He backs away further and I charge around to block his escape, brandishing my Sudoku book. I point my pen menacingly at his chest.

—Where are YOU going? She doesn't know where to go when she comes out. I'll get the goddam paperwork, but *you* have to *stay* with her till she gets this x-ray done!

In the car going home, x-ray in the bag, so to speak, we are warriors galloping back to camp with scalps and prisoners flung across our horses' necks. We holler like the winning team on the bus back to school. If Ma knew how to high-five or bump my chest, and what it meant, she would do it right now. If I had a bottle of champagne, I would pour it over her head.

For a long time afterward, Ma keeps telling friends and family about how I blasted those buggers without skipping a beat in Sudoku. I myself will never get over Ma's climactic jig in the hallway, and especially the S-bomb.

Weeks ago, I gave the hospital's archive room a copy of the Power of Attorney to put in the computer so I can pick up test results without Ma's signature on the release. The archive people seem to lose everything, too, but I have made a friend there, Iris, who recognizes me now. She knows very well that she will have to look in three or four places to find that POA. She never tells me I'm wrong—we both know it's in there somewhere. I'm just now putting this together with the recent thingy problem, and a pattern is emerging. Next day, I go to the counter to pick up the CD and reports of the tests, and I'm glad to see Iris is on duty.

—What is it with your computers here? Nobody seems to be able to find anything and they all act as if it's this big mystery and it only happens to us.

—Don't you let them tell you that, says Iris. They took away the good computers to save money when we went private. Now nobody can't find *nothing* around here.

I wonder how long they'll keep someone like Iris around. She's a little too smart for her own good.

10.
Proof of Life

GRAFFITI ON A DESKTOP in the Anthropology 101 classroom freshman year:

> *God is dead.*
> —Nietzsche
> *Nietzsche is dead.*
> —God

Lately, I've been fretting about transportation.

When they canceled Ma's driver's license after the car impoundment debacle last summer, I committed to help her figure out how to get wherever she needs to go. Her friends and I do most of her transportation, and there are a couple of useful local people who can be hired. Still there have been times when we've found ourselves in a bind.

There's a city service you can sign up for called CCT Connect. They have small vans that transport senior citizens door-to-door for a pittance. They can even take you if you're in a wheelchair. All you do is fill out a short application and send it in with a copy of your driver's license, birth certificate, or passport.

—Don't take the passport. I might need it.

(I'm at Ma's apartment getting ready to root around for one of the things on CCT's list of options.)

—Why? Are you going somewhere? You still haven't had your surgery.

Ma's been stalling about the surgery. She says she'll make up her mind by the end of the summer. I don't think she has a trip set up, but I'm always a little suspicious. Colette and I wring our hands a lot over Ma's travel bug, so she has learned to keep her plans to herself—she finds our remonstrations about travelers' insurance and her lack of overseas health coverage to be just so much *negative thinking*. Whenever she can get her hands on some money of her own, she's off, usually somewhere religiously oriented. She's been to Yugoslavia (the site of some apparitions of the Virgin Mary), Russia (to see their icons when she joined that first local Orthodox church), and the Holy Land (baptized in the Jordan). Her present spiritually themed dream destination is Greece, because that seems to be where her current crop of priests and monks are more closely aligned. She thinks I don't know this, but it's obvious—she's trying to learn Greek, and she has a new, gigantic *National Geographic* atlas of the Greek islands displayed prominently in the living room.

—Of course I'm not going anywhere now. I keep the passport in my purse for identification because they took away my license.

—Right, well, it looks like it has expired, so good luck with that. Where do you keep your birth certificate? Is there a file?

Most people know how to find their vital documents when they need them. I have my own special file in my office where I stash any number of things: marriage certificate, baptism records, proof of immunizations, passports. There's even a card with Eliza's tiny three-year-old fingerprints, made by a group that visited her pre-school to simplify identification in case something unspeakable happened.

Ma has beautiful files, at first glance. She hired someone to come in and organize her life several years ago. Everything is alphabetical, and not hand-labeled like mine. Whoever did the work had a gadget that typed the headings on the little cards. They even slipped them in the slots on the files in a perfect descending pattern, like music scales. It's impressive, until you go looking for something and find yourself in a netherworld of complete and utter chaos.

There are nine drawers. Each one holds items that are meant to be compatible. In the accounts drawer, there are three different places she can file her bank statements: under CHECKING or BANK or NATIONAL PENN (depending on her mood I guess, because there is certainly no system I can identify). INSURANCE has a couple of obsolete car insurance policies (not the most recent one) as well as some Explanations of Benefits from her HMO. The rest of the HMO stuff is filed under HEALTH PLAN, but it takes up a lot of space because mixed in with it is a five-page history of the state of Pennsylvania.

Daddy was very organized; I'm sure he could have told me where their birth certificates and things were at all times. He used to spend hours in his study, sitting behind the desk he inherited from his father, the Chief Justice, working his way through a vodka bottle in the bottom right-hand drawer and poring meticulously over figures. Daddy also had a sense of humor: For years, he kept a paperweight on the bureau, with a giant clip holding a check carefully filled out by Ma:

> Date: *$106.40*
> Amount: *Marjorie von Moschzisker*
> Pay to the Order of: *March 5, 1969*
> Signed: *The Mills Hardware Company*

After he died and we kids formed Operation Ma, I didn't inherit the desk, but I did get the job. The way Ma kept her accounts made me tear my hair out. My picky-eater friend Margaret would speak up for Ma when she could. Her husband, George, is an artist, too, and according to Margaret, their brains don't *do* orderly financial management. And that's quite an understatement.

If Ma's organizational talents equaled her artistic gifts, she would be like a top-of-the-line Macintosh with all the latest software updates. She had a lot of solid training abroad and in Philadelphia before she raised us. (Painting, drawing, and sculpting—it's funny to think of a young debutante doing all those nudes. Come to think of it, maybe that's why she's so immodest.) As far as I'm concerned, Ma is the real deal. She was always working on something or other while we were growing up. My earliest childhood memory is downright Proustian: sneaking into her mysterious studio upstairs at age two to smell the turpentine, stretching up on tiptoe to peer over the edge of the table at a stained palette's shiny blobs of rich colors, and finally, unable to resist, popping the lid of a paint tube into my mouth. I can still taste the grit. Ma and I practically lived at the Philadelphia Museum of Art on weekends, and I vowed never to do that to our kids. As a result, they haven't learned much about art from me.

Ma's creative pace picked up a lot when the house was finally empty, during The Separation. Daddy had Ma on a strict allowance and, needing to supplement, she managed to launch a significant career as a portrait painter. People would wait their turn for years. Some of the last ones she did were of our children:

Eliza, Ben, Sam

There's been some rumbling among my siblings about the extensive collection of Ma's artwork in our house, but I say tough luck. She needed the money badly after Daddy died, and we were willing to pay for the stuff. It's lucky that David really does like her work. I try not to insist on displaying everything. We've got a bunch of gifted friends and family whose work we really love, but Ma's art is pretty much all over the place. David says it's not just the quality; it's the scope, the journey of her work that he admires. He's only uneasy when my dealings with Ma are particularly fraught. He says it's hard for him to see me worn down while surrounded by all these potent reminders of my mother, no matter how wonderful they are.

But for me, it doesn't seem to matter how upset I am with Ma, my feelings never transfer to her art. I can be screening her calls except to occasionally scream at her and hang up, waking from nightmares about her almost every night, but my relationship with Ma's pictures and sculptures is on a separate plane. I'm in awe, and I love living among them.

There's probably something in psychology textbooks about this, but, whatever. It doesn't feel unhealthy to me. I even admit to a degree of gloating over certain particular treasures, like these two little bronzes I have:

That's Colette, age two, strangling Pussle, the cat. (Pussle really had nine lives—she survived swallowing a needle and thread when she was a kitten, and being dropped repeatedly from the second floor balcony by eight-year-old Felix. She was found once, after an unusually long absence, under a sewage grate in the street. We had to get the fire department to extract her.) The bull is special because Ma's favorite childhood home was in the country. She's so subtle with these gems; they're like sketches almost but you can tell how much she delights in the subjects. I've always felt miffed that Ma stopped sculpting before she could do one of me, but at least I have these two beauties.

Ma keeps trying to give us a portrait she did of me during college, but it's enormous and I don't really like it—I don't think it's her best work and besides, she did nothing to hide the fact that I was bored out of my mind. She has it in her bedroom:

If this piece had a title, it would be *Young Woman on Stairs with Cats, Holding in Her Stomach and Wishing She Had a Cigarette*. Ma let me read that book near my elbow when I got desperate, but mostly I passed the time trying to make her laugh, mimicking her concentrated expression while she painted: head tilted back, eyes squinting, mouth hanging open. She would snort when she turned from the canvas back to me.

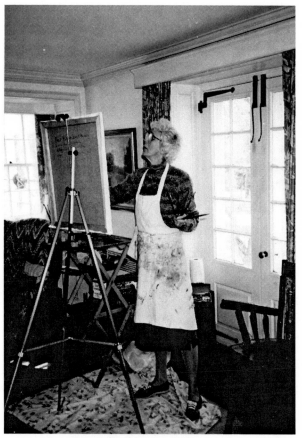

Ma at work, 1980s

I wish she could have put me in this oil below—a Christmas present. She based it on a photograph I took of David and the kids at our club in Penllyn. I had no idea Ma was working on it, and it may be my favorite. That's Sam with his back to us in the too-long swim trunks he insisted on wearing that summer. His bony shoulder blades are poking through his towel, which depicts a Central American village scene, a gift from a babysitter from El Salvador who helped us through the aftermath of the earthquake. Ben looks almost manly. Eliza's there with her elegant neck and her bag of chips, smiling for the camera, and David is David, keeping a quiet eye on the brood. That's the polo field in the background, with all its history from my own childhood, of egg-and-spoon races on the Fourth of July, Sunday afternoon teas on the lawn, and riding ponies along the far tree line with Colette. This is my world, and Ma's, too—she saw her father land his plane on that field. Sometimes he would take her there at four a.m. to look for mushrooms in the dew. She watched from the roof of her grandmother's house when the club's barn burned down one night and the era of polo came to an end.

I have my own personal relationship with that leafy branch in the foreground; in fact, every single stroke of this simple but remarkably accurate sketch is part of my DNA. It's my special people enjoying my special place, and it was made specifically for me by the one person who clearly knows how important that is.

I can't remember if it's Colette or Felix who once said *when you really feel at the end of your rope with Ma, remember the art.*

Here's one we have that I'm in. It's a *Where's Waldo.* This is the backyard of the first house David and I bought in Los Angeles, just up the hill from Universal Studios. If you look carefully, you'll spot me (actually only my legs) working on a wannabee starlet suntan by the pool. David designed that wall and the gate, and I tended the roses. The house came with a pre-installed mean old white cat with a crooked tail named Missy, who shunned us. She lived mostly in that rose garden (when David wasn't chasing her around the house in a rage, bleeding from their turf battles). Missy's buried there now. We still wish we'd kept this house . . . and it's so typical of Ma to bravely let that blue striped umbrella take up a quarter of the canvas. I imagine a therapist might have questions about that—what exactly are we hiding and whom are we hiding it from?

Ma gave me a fascinating pencil sketch of Daddy. She dashed it off on the day after they were married, during a train ride on the way to report for his height-finder school at the beginning of World War II. Neither one of them had any idea what they were doing; they were not emotionally equipped for marriage and hardly even knew each other. They hadn't really had a honeymoon at all, but look at how she did his lips in this picture:

So we've got something from just about every one of Ma's different phases. We drew the line at the abstracts she tried in the late 1960s to early 1970s: paintings of stripes done in masking tape, caged in primary colors. Ma has recently realized that her cages were a subliminal way of expressing how she felt back then: trapped. She would be the first to agree the stuff was not worth keeping, but I think she should get credit for experimenting.

Looking at the portraits, it really is fascinating how someone can be such a nuisance and also have this superb gift for expressing the soul without words. Maybe it's because they're of our children, but those three portraits can bring me to tears. Ma identifies with Mary Cassatt, who often painted her own family. She believes portraits are most effective when the subjects are linked to the artist by blood. She's also figured out that all the faces she worked on over the years were actually getting her ready for her great passion: Byzantine icons.

Since Ma began to make icons, it's been hard to get her to paint anything else. (Icons are *made*, not painted. The artist never signs an icon. It's something about humility. Ma flatly refuses to sell them to non-Orthodox people. It would be blasphemy or something.) Icons are always of the saints, the angels, and the holy family. She says the whole point is to help the viewer to feel close to those unseen heavenly beings, like having a comforting photograph of a loved one that is far away. Here's a *Mother and Child* she gave me:

What I found intriguing when she started is that there's a whole series of prayers and meditations to do during each of the stages of making an icon. It's very hard to get it right, and therefore most people, Ma included, can't just paint alone at home. They have to go to a master iconographer for workshops, which are seven-day exhausting marathons. At first, if she didn't get the prayers right, Ma found that the layers of clay, gesso, egg tempera, etc. wouldn't set: The gold leaf would peel off the board or something, even if her materials were perfectly prepared. Maybe there's some more concrete explanation, but it sure is interesting if it's the kind of spiritual phenomenon she implies. There's something so profound about the eyes in Ma's icons. I don't dare tell her that or she'll assume I'm ripe for conversion.

As with many things, Ma doesn't really know when enough is enough. Icons must be shared with the Whole World, and she has decided that this colossal task is completely up to her. For about fifteen years, she has been determined to make a video about icons that will once and for all convert everyone on this earth and save our souls, amen. (I have a sneaking feeling that besides the trip to Greece, the world's need for this video is what is motivating her to go through with the cancer treatment instead of just moving into Father Nicholas's attic to let nature take its course. I'll take it, if that's what it is. Far be it from me to quibble about what Ma wants to live for.)

So, of course, in Ma's study there are a lot of compartments just for icon stuff: file after file of bizarre unpronounceable Russian and Greek names (*Deesis. Hesychia. Kazanskaya. Vladislav Andrejev*). I'll bet Ma hasn't even a clue what's in there.

I skip the icon cabinet and try one last drawer that looks promising. There's a file for each of us children, one for Daddy, and an intriguing section devoted exclusively to MANNERS, which contains some of the lists of dos and don'ts she has inflicted on me and the kids when she's feeling a particular urge to boss us around: *Do not brush your hair at the table. Do not put your knife in your mouth.* But I see no sign of a file for BIRTH CERTIFICATES or anything remotely like it, and while the SOCIAL SECURITY file gets my hopes up for a second, there is actually nothing in it at all.

So the options for identification are as follows:

> Driver's License: *Confiscated.*
> Passport: *Expired.*
> Birth Certificate: *Misplaced.*
> Social Security card? *Nope.*
> Medicare card?!? *Sorry.*

—Ma, you don't seem to exist.

—I don't seem to *what*?

—*Exist.* We have no proof of your existence.

—*Really*, Susie. You're being very negative.

Okay, here's the bright side: Without that passport, she won't be skipping off to Greece for a while.

11.
Preparation

SEPTEMBER 10, 2007

IT'S TONSURE TIME.

I'm peering down Ma's hall, past her gallery dominated by all the inscrutable patrician ancestors, watching her closed confessional bedroom door.

I wait.

Suddenly, the door opens and out bursts Ma with the Bishop. She's smiling.

The Bishop is based in Carlisle, but he travels constantly to perform jobs like this. I've actually been curious to get a look at him because I've heard he cuts a dashing figure. He's a lot younger than I expected, thirty-five at the most: tall and lean and very serious. His long beard is black, and he has a thin, equally black braid hanging down his back that reaches all the way past his waist. On the table by the icons and beeswax votive candles, he places a black hat that has some folded pieces of paper in it.

—Those are all the names, says Ma.

She and the Bishop have agreed on an assortment of saints' names that might be appropriate for Ma's new nun title. At the end of the ceremony (and I am not making this up), he's going to pick a name out of this hat, because apparently it's up to the Holy Spirit to decide.

There are also some scissors on the table. The tonsure ceremony is basically a haircut. You abandon your everyday life and are reborn to one of prayer and service. At the climax of the ceremony, the Bishop will cut off a lock or two of Ma's hair—something about symbolically shearing away all her worldly passions. From then on, she'll eschew haircuts for good, just like Father Basil and the rest of the clergy.

Oh my gosh, hair scissors. Names out of a hat. Why aren't my siblings here. National Geographic *should cover this. Where is my camera?*

My mother's friend Photini says it's okay to take pictures, and it feels a little awkward, but that's what I definitely have to do. The Bishop, the priest, and the mousy guy in blue jeans Photini introduced me to earlier do all the standard chanting and walking around Ma's living room with the crucifix I'd seen at Happy Hide-Away. Photini helps with the responses. No attempt is made to get the rest of us to participate. It's not clear why this is but I'm hoping Ma's friends Ellie, Olivia, and Babbie are as okay with their infidel status as I am, and can just appreciate what I am beginning to realize is something singularly momentous under way, right under our noses.

I take pictures. The chosen ones chant and chant. Ma seems so small and fragile in her loose cotton nightshirt, and so humble and totally sincere that she catches me off-guard, and by the time they get to the hair business, I'm beginning to blubber all over my camera. It doesn't matter how big the chip on my shoulder is about the succession of dogmas she's tried to force on me. It's almost irrelevant because *this* is; I don't know what *this* is, but it sure is *something*.

It's like the spectacle of David beginning his vows at our wedding twenty-five years ago. Determined, intent, face drenched in sweat and tears, David was so focused and serious and overcome that I began to giggle inappropriately. This spread from me to Ma and back again, gaining momentum. We pretty much howled raucously through the rest of the service. People who were there still ask what the joke was. Watching Ma now, I have an image of David's wedding face, and all my years of loving Ma while she was driving me out of my mind, and all the times I've been unutterably furious at her, and the love she's capable of, and I can barely keep the camera steady.

Photini holds a white linen cloth to catch Ma's hair when it's cut. They hang a black square thing covered in red embroidery around Ma's neck. A larger black cloth is draped over her head. She is given a long, thin candle to hold and a hand-carved crucifix, and I'm almost hyperventilating. Maybe it's the hormones, but it is so overwhelming to see this woman who has been in many ways such a problem for me, decisively leaving herself and all her faults, and being literally reborn. Who knows if she'll succeed, but that's almost beside the point. In this suspended moment, she's not my mother. The big, imposing, Bergdorf-clad fork-wielding creature I've been shielding myself from has morphed into someone opposite; gentle, peaceful, ego-less. She's so old. She's come such a long way. I am moved beyond words.

Oh my gosh, maybe she's really done it: Ma's actually found The Real Answer To Everything.

Ma's favorite prayer, the Jesus Prayer, is also called the Prayer of the Heart. The version J. D. Salinger gives us in *Franny and Zooey* is *Lord Jesus Christ, have mercy on me.* The longer version Ma uses is *Lord Jesus Christ, Son of God, have mercy on me, a sinner.* The point being that when your ego is in charge, you can't help sinning. They say if you repeat the prayer without ceasing, rhythmically timed with your breath, if you really get it right, it becomes one with your heartbeat. Your ego is trampled and God will hear the prayer. I'm no expert, but if that's what Ma's supposed to be doing right now, I'd say she's mastered it.

I've been so busy with my catharsis all over the camera that I missed the whole *Harry Potter* Sorting Hat segment of the service. The next thing I know, *presto change-o,* Ma has a new name.

Introducing: Mother Brigid.

When you become an Orthodox nun, you wear no jewelry except a cross around your neck. You can wear black if you like, and you have to put on a special habit when in the presence of bishops, priests, and other monastics.

I thought black clothes would be out of the question for Ma, who's always been exactingly creative about her wardrobe and accessories. But she has assured me that simple black is all she wants, and she's embracing it. In the back of my mind has been a rather catty thought: If this is what it takes to slow down her spending, far be it from me to object.

So . . . Brigid.

I'm pretty sure this was one of the Bishop's ideas, and not Ma's. Before the ceremony, she rattled off a slew of impossibly long Greek names she was hoping for, that rivaled the standard set by von Moschzisker in their impossible-to-spell-or-pronounceability. So when the new name is announced, there's the slightest glimmer of a pause as Ma considers this first joyful step on the road to spiritual obedience and humility. *Black clothes, okay. Give away my jewelry, fine. Try to be an angel living on the earth, devoted to a life of prayer instead of terrorizing my children—I'll do my best. But* Brigid? *Isn't that an* Irish *name?*

Sorry, says the Holy Spirit. *I know you wanted to be Theotockos Nephpactos Hierotheos of Whatchamacallit Boopty-opolis, but you're going to make a much better Mother Brigid of Carlisle. Get used to it.*

Ma smiles. Believers and infidels alike gather together around Mother Brigid and the Bishop for a picture.

Oh, and one more thing, Mother Brigid, says the Holy Spirit.

Yes? says Mother Brigid.

You have a colostomy coming up in a couple of weeks.

Ma, Philadelphia, 2007

12.
The Wizard

IT'S FOUR P.M. on a Friday. We've been sitting here in the waiting room for an hour and we are both fit to be tied.

—Let's go home.

—Ma . . .

We borrowed a wheelchair today at the door of Franklin Hospital. Ma's back is bothering her, so luckily she can't storm out on her own steam. This appointment was almost impossible to get, and we need it. The new surgeon has agreed to perform his specialty, TATA, and I don't think he and Ma have spoken candidly enough about what they're getting her into. TATA will give Ma a reconstructed rectum sans tumor, with no dreaded colostomy bag. This would be fantastic except that the new rectum won't be as clever at communicating its plans in advance as Ma's original model. If you're old and prone to bouts of mobility impairment, there is a real lifestyle concern. If things go as planned, Ma will have to stay within close range of a bathroom at all times.

Ma thinks Doctor Lawson is a genius, because he's very sympathetic to her aversion to permanent colostomy. He quickly slotted her as one of those patients who'd rather die than have a bag, and he's right. This is why she moved on from Pete, who was recommending a simpler procedure, the one I still think she should have. Ma kept looking around for more opinions—she would not have agreed to do anything at all if this Lawson fellow hadn't promised a new (albeit temperamental) rectum, and she thinks it's very *negative* of me to assume the worst about this plan. I just want her to be able to have a life: overnight trips to the church in Carlisle, lunch dates with friends.

Ma's been too discreet to get into the details with Doctor Lawson. When we scheduled the operation, I was overjoyed she had finally agreed to do something, and I figured we'd sort out the specifics later. But at this point, I can't decide whether I want to hug Lawson or kick him. The man's office is like Fort Knox. He won't correspond with me by email the way Pete did, and he hasn't responded to my phone calls and messages. Surgery is on Monday, and if it weren't for today's appointment, I'd be plotting to throw myself across his operating table, demanding an audience.

The more we sit here, the crankier we get. There's a flat screen in the corner of the waiting room. It plays nothing but irritating ads on a loop: soft gauzy lighting showing how happy everyone is frolicking through the leafy meadows, all hopped up on their breakthrough medicines. Around the corner near the door leading to the exam rooms, there is a small, hopeful cluster of professionals dressed for success with their briefcases full of drug samples: pharmaceutical salespeople, waiting to pounce on any doctors that appear.

We haven't had time to shop for black nun clothes yet. Ma's been determinedly wearing the darkest nightshirt she has every day since the tonsure, along with that cloth thing with the red embroidered Greek lettering. She is harrumphing through the one piece of reading material in the room, a pamphlet with dull hospital news. I'm playing Spider Solitaire on my phone and beginning to worry about the battery reserve.

A noise is coming from the lower rib-cage area of a woman sitting at my other side. There is a crackly, ventriloquistic tone to it, like she's hidden a walkie-talkie up her shirt and someone on the other end is passing gas into it. The woman pokes herself and it stops. I have been hearing about issues with gas in colostomy bags. The sound does seem more disturbing than your average run-of-the-mill fart: *unnatural,* as Ma would say. It's a good thing Ma's hearing aid doesn't work well, or she'd really want to make a dash for it. It has now been an hour and a half since we got here.

Ma shifts in her wheelchair.

—This is ridiculous.

—What?

—There's no point.

—What are you talking about, Ma, this appointment or the surgery?

—Both. I feel fine. Let's go home.

Aargh. I go up to nice little Cindy behind the desk, the one who took all my messages, the messages Lawson never answered.

—Excuse me, my mother is so tired of waiting that she has decided to go home now and not have her surgery after all.

—Just a minute, says Cindy, as if this happens nine or ten times a day. She calls back to see if we are next. We are, and it should only be a few more minutes.

Twenty minutes later, I'm down to one bar on my phone, and Ma says *get me out of here, this is ridiculous, why can't I go home.* I get ready to say what I have said a thousand times before because she keeps forgetting that *shrunken rectal tumors grow back and cause bowel obstructions, which lead to everything backing up. What can't go down must come up, remember, and you'll be begging anyone available to remove that tumor. What's more, by then it will have spread to your lungs, liver, and bones. Lungs are okay because it's like drowning, which is manageable with morphine. Cancer in your liver is bearable, but bones, forget it. Cancer in your bones feels like rats chewing on you, and they say the painkillers can't do a thing. Four out of five doctors have told you that it's all very well to say avoiding surgery is a reasonable course to take when you're old and frail. It's not when you have a rectal tumor.*

But this lady with the walkie-talkie rib cage is right next to us, and because of the bad hearing aid, I'd have to shout. So I go back to the desk and tell little Cindy that I have to wheel my mother out of range and talk her off a ledge again.

We find a quiet corner and start with *what can't go down* and so forth.

—It's all right, Ma says. That's what happened to Grandsir and he was fine, he just went ahead and died.

(It has been bothering me, this business about my grandfather's mysterious but horrible death and its similarity to what we're dealing with. Mental note: Schedule my own colonoscopy when the surgery crisis is over.)

We switch to *chewing rats.*

—Nonsense, I have a very high pain threshold, and besides, my cancer tea may be working. Let's go home.

Sigh.

—Ms. von Munch-spritzer?

It's Doctor Lawson's assistant Gina, not a moment too soon. She leads us past the hovering salespeople toward the inner sanctum. Ma tries to ditch the wheelchair on the way, probably so she can hide her current feeble state, which might cause Lawson to reconsider his new rectum offer and suggest the permanent bag instead.

We pass several office staff members in the hall, and it may be my imagination, but they all seem to be trying to keep very busy and not notice us. These people are most likely victims of my recent increasingly tetchy phone and email assault. Ignoring us is not an easy feat, what with the wheelchair and the two gigantic Memory Foam seat cushions that we keep forgetting about and leaving all over the place, Ma's weird nun thing around her neck, my huge red file folder not to mention our mutual state of seething agitation. We are like an enormous pulsating Rose Bowl float trying to maneuver around the corners jammed tight with workstations that seem to have mushroomed haphazardly in tiny pockets here and there outside the exam rooms. The rectal reconstruction business must be positively booming.

Lawson's personal office is surprisingly homey. Here we wait again, this time on comfy leather chairs. Ma has abandoned the wheelchair after all because there's no room for it here, but I've managed to park it conspicuously outside the door. There are many personal touches surrounding Lawson's enormous desk and his computer with emails on the screen (wish I could get close enough to make a note of his direct address).

—Look at the drawings by his children, aren't they lovely? says Ma. He obviously has his values in order, Susie, don't you think?

Ma knows I'm still hung up on the last surgeon Pete's superior communication skills, and she's trying to bring me around. Lawson's children appear to somehow sense their father's patients' need for reassurance while they wait, because the wall by his computer is lined with their drawings and notes:

MY DADDY IS THE BEST.
HE IS VERY TALL.
AND MOSTLY NICE TO EVERYONE.

Mostly nice?

Back on the wall in a corner by me, where Ma can't see it, there is something that looks like a stone tablet carved with unreadable words. Hebrew? I'm interested to know if Lawson is Jewish and if so, how this will figure with Ma. I can't decide whether it will help or hurt to call her attention to it.

Ma is cooing over the children's drawings. There's a handout on the desk describing the procedure. Instead of wasting more battery life on Spider Solitaire, I decide to check this out.

TATA (pronounced the way it looks, like ta-ta!) was a big breakthrough back in the day. Also known as *transanal abdominal transanal radical prosigmoidectomy with descending coloanal anastamosis*, the surgery involves two stages. First you get your cancer removed, a new rectum is built using a healthy piece of your colon, and you receive a temporary colostomy to give it all a chance to heal. Second stage, some months later, they take away the temporary bag, reconnect your plumbing, and teach you how to work your new rectum. Pretty wonderful in theory but I'm convinced it's not for Ma.

The wait drags on, and I check Colette's list of questions: *"How many eighty-five-year-old people have you done this to who didn't end up incontinent?"* I'm beginning to work myself up with some pretty mean thoughts like, *Who does he think he is? He's younger than me. Okay, he's got a nice office and he's all busy and everything, but this could easily be a smokescreen. I'm not about to let some whippersnapper use my mother as a guinea pig.*

I look around the room again, and that's when I see it. How could I have missed this before: a rather large wooden sign, displayed prominently on a bookshelf—a gift from a former patient? It takes up quite a bit of space, so Lawson must really like it:

Nobody gets in to see the wizard!
Not nobody!
Not nohow!

All of a sudden, everything becomes extremely clear.

I was Glinda the Good Witch in *The Wizard of Oz* in high school. I've watched it thousands of times with the kids. I could jump out of my chair and perform the exact choreography of the Lollipop Guild dance for you right this second if you needed me to.

The Wizard of Oz lives in the Emerald City. Dorothy and her friends go there for help. The Gatekeeper is played by the same actor who plays the Wizard—the point being that the Wizard turns out to be a big fake, or Humbug, who can't actually help them at all. Glinda has to come to the rescue in the end. But we find that out later.

Here's what happens at the gate:

They ring the bell. The Gatekeeper opens a little door and sticks his head out, perturbed.

Gatekeeper: Who rang that bell?

Dorothy, Scarecrow, Tin Man, Cowardly Lion: We did!

Gatekeeper: Can't you read?

Scarecrow: Read what?

Gatekeeper: The notice!

Dorothy and Scarecrow: What notice?

Gatekeeper: It's on the door—as plain as the nose on my face! It— Oh . . .

He hangs the notice and goes back inside.

Dorothy, Scarecrow, Tin Man, Cowardly Lion (*reading notice*): Bell out of order, please knock.

Dorothy knocks. The Gatekeeper sticks his head out again.

Gatekeeper: Well, that's more like it! Now, state your business.

When they explain that they want to see the Wizard, because the Scarecrow wants a brain, the Tin Man wants a heart, and so forth—I probably don't have to make this any clearer.

Gatekeeper: **Nobody gets in to see the Wizard! Not nobody! Not nohow!**

And boy is that ever right. I've been trying to get Ma this final consultation for the past month. It is only by some miracle that we have slipped in under Gina's and Cindy's fierce radar. My mother has no ruby slippers (they are not a part of the nun uniform), but she does definitely want to go home *and* she wants a new rectum. Unfortunately, I am not Glinda the Good Witch, I just played her in high school. Suddenly, it's cataclysmically clear that we're not the first people to have to claw our way in for an audience with the Great and Powerful Wizard of Franklin Hospital.

In fact, other patients have been here in Lawson's incongruously welcoming private chamber before us, many in crisis themselves. And at least one of them *must* have come out the other end okay at some point (possibly in diapers or making farty-crackly noises, but alive) and with enough free time on their hands and sufficient sense of humor, good will, and gratitude toward the Great and Powerful Doctor Lawson to want to *give* him this sign commemorating their ordeal with him.

Not only that, but Lawson himself comes more into focus. He has decided to *display* this sign, which means he must at least recognize the difficulty we've had getting in here as a common affliction among the visitors to his office. Either he thinks it's funny, which is a little annoying, or maybe he just enjoys the power in a warped sort of way, which if true would be very annoying. But one thing about him that I like (besides the nice chairs) is that he has some self-awareness, which is always good. Especially when you're the guy who's about to take my mother apart and put her back together again.

I see light at the end of our tunnel. Maybe someday we, too, will not be so mad at Doctor Lawson, and grateful enough to crackly-fart our way up here to present him with some funny, insightful memento of our own time with him, so other poor souls can sit their tender, cancerous fannies in his comfy leather chairs (for two hours) and contemplate the meaning of *our* gift after fantasizing about various ways of getting him offed.

It may be hard to spot, but there's a recurring theme here I don't feel like admitting to, but I guess I should. I may have this leetle bitty slight tendency to mistrust doctors, and it may be the teensiest bit unfair sometimes. Just sometimes. Because most of the time all doctors are either stupid or out to get you.

I think it should be out in the open that I am aware of this tendency. It's possible that I have acquired it from someone close to me.

That's all I feel comfortable saying for now.

Finally, Lawson comes in looking as ready for a squabble as we are. He looks at me, then Ma. He stops to take in her thing around her neck with all the red Greek embroidery.

Ma (*imperiously*): That's my schema. I am Mother Brigid of Carlisle.

Pause pause pause.

(I just keep my head down. It's all good! It couldn't be more clear to him that she might not be making a rational, informed decision about her surgery than if Ma had smiled up at him and said *by the way, before we start, you should know that I am Nuts.*)

When we get into things a little, it becomes clear that Lawson has read my emails, and he won't give an inch about how poorly we have been communicated with. He seems to think this meeting, which I have fought like a tiger to get, was all his idea. He claims he has explained clearly the pros and cons of TATA. (He *has* explained them but not clearly enough for Ma—he doesn't know her like I do. She will forget whatever she doesn't want to know and besides that she is deaf deaf deaf deaf—it's very handy to have her kind of memory and hearing issues. You have to hit her over the head with the facts she needs for her own good, hit her with them over and over again at the top of your lungs till she is *whimpering.*)

So I say to him *my mother doesn't tell you this, but she has trouble getting to the bathroom on time. She tries to downplay it, and she is so weak right now with her bad back that we needed a wheelchair to get up here. So tell me, Doctor: For someone in her age and condition, is TATA, with its potential resulting incontinence, really the optimal choice for my mother?*

Pause pause pause.

Lawson: No it isn't.

Me (*in Ma's good ear*): DID YOU HEAR THAT, MA????????

Pause pause.

Me (*loudly*): What would you say IS the most optimal surgery for her?

Lawson: A permanent colostomy.

Me (*in Ma's ear*): A PERMANENT colostomy?

(Thank you.)

Lawson: But!

(Oh my gosh.)

Lawson: But! You can always wait to make up your mind about the second procedure after you have the first. If you want to stop after that, keep the temporary bag indefinitely and even skip the reconstruction surgery altogether, you can.

Ma: You CAN???????

Me: You CAN??????? Do you like that idea, Ma?

Ma: Yes, I do.

Me: Okay, so that's settled, you'll have the colostomy and decide later if you want it to be temporary or permanent, right?

Ma: Yes.

Pause. We look at Lawson, who takes this in.

Lawson (*pulls out a handy printout of the colon and makes illustrative marks on it*): Or, I can remove the tumor and leave the muscle intact, not rebuild the rectum, put the colostomy here instead of here. Then later, if you want me to, we have two more surgeries—

Me: Did you hear that Ma? Two more—

Ma: TWO more? Why—

Me: TWO MORE?????

Lawson: Okay, wait a minute.

Pause pause pause. I can see his gears turning. He crumples up his colon printout.

The Wizard, remember, is a Humbug. There's a little man behind the curtain pulling levers. He has no spare body parts stowed away anywhere, and he ultimately fails miserably at getting Dorothy back to Kansas. That turns out to be Glinda's job. (I believe I mentioned who played Glinda in high school.)

There's no way to be sure how much investment Doctor Lawson has in that sign he's got so prominently displayed behind his shoulder. But he is, after all, the only doctor out of five who has been able to get Mother Brigid of Carlisle this close to an operating room. It's beginning to dawn on me that a significant portion of a surgeon's skill has to be the ability to simply convince certain patients to agree to be helped in the first place.

Pause pause pause.

Lawson: What if I just decide what to do when I get in there?

And he *winks* at me.

Ma: That would be fine.

Me (*totally irritated by the wink, but if it means that at the very least my two cents' worth can no longer be overlooked, then*): Okay!

Ma: Can we *please* go home now?

Yes, Ma: There's No Place Like Home.

13.
Family Tree

—WHAT'S THE DIFFERENCE between Gaga and *Auntie* Gaga?

(Every so often, I gather my wits and attempt to get this straight. It's extremely confusing. Just try to breathe through it.)

—Gaga was my mother's mother. Auntie Gaga was Gaga's sister.

—Which one of them was Muzzy?

—Auntie Gaga was Muzzy, but that's only what her children called her. Her real name was Gertrude. *We* called her Auntie Gaga because of Gaga being her sister.

—Wait, Ma. *Two* sisters?

—No, *five* sisters. My great-grandmother had three boys and five girls. Actually, she had six girls, but the first one, named Susan, died right after she was born.

—Wait. Wait. Okay. No. Okay, so, Ma: Let's just stick with this Gaga thing for a second. Your grandmother, your *mother's mother*, was Gaga. Oh. That's funny!

—Why's it funny?

—Because Gaga, you know, *gaga*. Your grandmother was *gaga*.

—No, she wasn't; she was very rational.

—Whatever. Then why did they start calling her Gaga?

—It was instead of Granny, because we already had a lot of grannies. The name *Gaga* helped keep track of who's who.

—Well, that doesn't explain why her sister was called Auntie Gaga. How is *that* keeping track?

—It is, Susie, because Gaga was our grandmother and so her *sister*, who was our great aunt, was called *Auntie* Gaga.

—And one of Auntie Gaga's, *your great aunt's,* one of her children was Cousin Buckety, right?

—Yes, because Buckety's sister couldn't pronounce Buttercup.

—Her real name was Buttercup?

—No, it was Gertrude.

—Ma. Wait a minute. Auntie Gaga was Gertrude *and* Cousin Buckety was Gertrude, too?

—Yes.

—*And* she was Buttercup.

—Right.

(I have a life-size white plaster bust Ma did of Buckety's son Johnnie in our downstairs loo. It was probably a practice casting for the final bronze, which is now with Buckety's family. My copy has no base, so it looks like Johnnie's body is stuffed in the bathroom cupboard with his head sort of popping out of a hole in the countertop next to the sink. When you sit on the pot, Johnnie's looking at you, right at eye level.

This kind of intimacy bothers the men in our house. Sometimes I'll go in there and discover that Johnnie has been turned around to face the corner. I think somebody was too rough with him recently because he has a newish chip on his temple, and now he has to wear hats. I like to dress him up on Halloween—he looks best in an electric blue Cleopatra wig. He gets a Santa hat at Christmas.)

—So, Ma, who was it that married Max von Pappenheim?

—That was Nee. Gaga's and Auntie Gaga's sister.

—And what was his deal?

—He was a German count they met while they were wintering in Rome. He impressed Granny Wheeler, till they found out he had gambled away all his money. So before Nee married him, there was almost a duel with her brother. But instead, they tied up Nee's money so Max couldn't get it. That made him go away after he married her and found out. It was because of Max von Pappenheim we ended up related to the baron in Ireland. Granny Wheeler liked all that—

—Granny Wheeler, was she the one with the bonnets?

—No, that was *Little* Granny, Granny Wheeler's mother. Little Granny was a nineteenth-century Quaker. She always wore bonnets. Granny *Wheeler* was Episcopalian. Her name was Susan, too—you were named after her, and she was your great-great-grandmother. She had the five daughters. Four of them looked sort of the same, very blonde because of the Swedish ancestry . . .

(The Wheelers were Swedes who came to the new world to trade with the natives for beaver pelts in 1638, which was just before William Penn was born. That makes for a *whole* lot of grannies before this bunch even. They later made their fortune in ironwork—they forged the huge chains that George Washington strung across the Hudson and Delaware Rivers to block enemy ships during the Revolutionary War.)

— . . . But Gaga was different, darker, and particularly beautiful. That's why they called the five sisters Four Wheelers and a Hansom.

—And she married a count because she was so beautiful.

—No, her sister Nee married the count, but it didn't really last.

—Okay, Ma, let me see if I've got this: Little Granny was your great-great-grandmother, the Quaker with the bonnets.

—Right.

—And Granny Wheeler, who you named me after, Susan, was her daughter and therefore your great-grandmother.

—Yes. And Gaga was—

—*Hold on with the Gagas*, Ma—I'm not there yet. Little Granny wore bonnets and gave birth to Granny Wheeler and some other unidentified people. THEN, Granny Wheeler gave birth to the five girls (not counting the first one who died and the three brothers). One of them was Gaga, your grandmother, who was both beautiful and a Hansom, and one was Countess Nee Pappenheim, and one was Auntie Gaga, whose children called her Muzzy.

—Exactly.

—And Gaga, your grandmother, had your mother and some other children I'm not able to process right now. And your mother, Gaga's daughter, is the one I called Granny.

—Right.

—Ma.

—Yes.

—My grandchildren are going to call me Hot Mama.

—*What?*

—It's decided, Ma. David and I agreed the first year we were married. I'll be Hot Mama and he'll be Gramps and there's nothing you can do about it.

Ma humphs.

—So, Ma. Did you call Gaga Gaga, too?

—Yes. And then Auntie Gaga was her sister so it was logical.

—Right. Logical. Except that she was also Muzzy.

There were a lot more women than men in my mother's family, and it's the women who fascinate me. Most of them had multiple daughters and only one or two sons. Sons tended to either die in the wars or just take generally background-ish positions in the family. Same for all the women's husbands, who often expired or fell out of focus somehow. Throughout the generations, it seems like strong women were often at the center of things, calling all the shots. And the one who intrigues me most right now is Muzzy, my great-great-aunt, known to me as Auntie Gaga.

There's a family photograph in Ma's gallery of Auntie Gaga with her parents and seven siblings. It's one of those pictures where everyone had to not move for a long time, so they're all sort of glassy-eyed. The youngest ones look like they may have had to be tranquilized to keep them still for the camera. I'm guessing it was taken in around 1888, because Auntie Gaga looks about thirteen. She wasn't the youngest, or the oldest, or even the most beautiful (the prettiest was definitely her sister, the Hansom: my great-grandmother Gaga), but she has superb posture, pale blue eyes, and this wonderful unmanageable lion's mane of wavy flaxen hair tumbling down to her graceful waist.

I've just finished reading a biography her son Charlie Thayer wrote, called *Muzzy.* Charlie was in the Foreign Service in places like Russia, and he wrote a lot of books, including this fun one about his mother. Auntie Gaga was the center of the matrilineal line for a lot of years. She lived on the Main Line (they all started out there), and her house, Kyneton, was where everyone gathered for tea every day and also on Christmas Eve, which was a real tradition.

She died when I was five, but I vaguely remember going in my velvet party dress for what may have been her last Christmas Eve, down a long driveway to a hill in the dark. The tradition was that everyone came and it seemed a little like visiting the queen. I remember she was really really old, and she sat in a big chair by the fire in the drawing room. You had to go up and kiss her, which was scary. Someone came out dressed as Santa with a big sack of presents, and every single person who came got something. In *Muzzy,* it says Auntie Gaga even gave presents to all the servants and the servants' children, too. I think mine was some chocolates.

Ma's portrait of Auntie Gaga, 1960

Today is Ma's follow-up visit with Doctor Lawson. Surgery was successful; she's coping relatively well with the bag. Her appointment finished sooner than we expected, and Ma's happy to be out in the world for a while. I thought she'd like to have lunch somewhere, but she says she's not hungry. So I ask, since we're sort of in the neighborhood, if she'd like to see if we can find Auntie Gaga's old house, Kyneton.

Auntie Gaga had six children of her own, including Buckety, George, and Charlie. When they all reached school age, she built a schoolhouse on her land and hired a teacher for them and some of the neighbors' children. The Kyneton School had a hundred students at its peak. She also had something to do with introducing field hockey to the United States, and her husband was football captain at Penn.

—We had Sunday touch football games on the lawn at Kyneton, and it was very intimidating. They were all so competitive and I was hopeless at it, says Ma.

—Why did you always go to Auntie Gaga's house instead of your own grandmother's?

—Because my grandmother was never there. She had taken care of Granny Wheeler till she died. By then, she was a widow with a lot of friends all over the world, and she liked to go to stay with them.

I snort.

—You mean she was always off on the Isle of Wight trying to rub up to the royals.

—Well, I don't know where she was, but we didn't see her much. Auntie Gaga was always there, with all the children and the grandchildren. It was very nice, except for the football.

From the book, it did seem as if life for Auntie Gaga's children and guests was one long athletic event after another. Ma loved the country atmosphere at Kyneton, but what meant most to her was the strong sense of a large family going back in time. Since Ma never felt much stability in her own immediate family growing up, she was terribly glad to find it through Auntie Gaga.

Ma's own mother, who Ma called Mummy and we called Granny (there really were an awful lot of grannies running around), was what some call a bolter. The bolter phenomenon began in England around World War I, when an engaged or married woman of significant social standing and means gave it all up to run off with some dashing but inappropriate chap for love and excitement. Ma's mother was the first in her family to dare bolting, and it was quite a shock to everyone. Ma believes her mother didn't technically bolt. She thinks what happened was more forgivable, but you can't get around the fact that Ma's mother actually did divorce two husbands, and there were two sets of children involved who didn't end up with her.

Ma's mother's first husband, Sidney Brock, was wealthy and socially acceptable. He came approved, even recommended, by her mother, Gaga. Ma's mother had four children with Mr. Brock, and when he went off to war, she became entangled with Grandsir (my grandfather, the accident-prone flyer). Grandsir, born Harry Drayton, was descended from an old Charleston family, but their money had run out. This seemed to be happening more and more by the twenties: Old establishment families must have made life so easy on their children that the ones coming up didn't necessarily have the juice to step forward if things got tight.

Gaga consulted with her well-heeled son-in-law, Sidney Brock. They both thought it best for everyone if Ma's mother (Gaga's own daughter, mind you) didn't bring her four children when she bolted with her impoverished aviator (her second husband, my Grandsir).

Ma's mother was deemed an unfit parent, by *her own mother.*

Ma's parents, Granny and Grandsir, went where the army took him: first to Virginia, where Ma was born, and then to Long Island, where her little sister, Bobs (short for Barbara), was born. Grandsir was eventually transferred to Honolulu, Hawaii. This must have been pretty exotic—imagine what Hawaii would have been like in the Roaring Twenties, all Zelda and F. Scott Fitzgerald under the coconut palms. There's a fascinating picture of a fancy dress party with a crowd of partied-out grown-ups, probably from the army base: Grandsir's a pirate, Granny's a gypsy or something, and there are one or two people in blackface, which is awful, but there it is.

When I was little, I had a favorite story I'd get Ma to tell me over and over at bedtime, partly because it seemed to soothe her nerves, but also for my own pleasure:

—*Tell about the goat.*

—*Well, Bobs and I were both in bed with the mumps.*

—*And you were soooo bored.*

—*Yes, we didn't have anything to do for weeks and weeks.*

—*And there was a nanny goat who died.*

—*Yes, Grandsir went hunting with his sergeant and the sergeant shot a nanny goat by accident. The nanny goat had a little kid and it had to be fed, so Grandsir brought it home for us.*

—*And you and Aunt Bobs were in your beds and—*

—*And we heard something outside the door:* meh-eh-eh!

—*And it was a little baby goat!*

—*Yes, and it was so lovely because we weren't bored anymore— we had the little kid. We could feed it and it got on the beds with us and everything.*

For years, I thought Honolulu must have been the absolute best thing ever, but it turns out that like Ireland was for us, there were more layers to Honolulu than you realized, and things got tough. The people on the army base weren't interesting enough for Ma's mother, and there wasn't much money for servants. Neither of Ma's parents knew how to cope (i.e., cook, clean, get children to school) which is pathetic, but that's the way it was. They drank and fought a lot, and Ma's mother would go back to Auntie Gaga's in Philadelphia for long stretches of time, to "get her teeth fixed."

Eventually, Ma's mother bolted a second time, to her final true love: Jack Henderson (known to us as Granjack), who was also not particularly well-off. This culminated in a standoff in San Francisco when Ma was about eight years old. Ma's father's term in Honolulu was over, and he had just brought the little girls back to the mainland. Ma's mother showed up with her new husband and told Ma and Bobs that she would take them with her to their place in Wayne, Pennsylvania, or wherever it was. Ma must have had a precocious backbone, because at age eight she took it upon herself to speak up. *No,* she said to her mother. She and Bobs would be living in stability, in Penllyn with their father, Grandsir, and his mother, Grandma Drayton—

—Ma. Time out.

—What?

—Who's Grandma *Drayton* and where did *she* come from?

—She was my *other* grandmother.

—I can't deal with Grandma Drayton right now.

—Don't say that! Grandma Drayton was very important, and I loved her! She was my father's mother, your great-grandmother.

—*Grandma Drayton. Grandma Drayton.* You left your mother, who I called Granny and you called Mummy, and went to live with your father (my Grandsir) and his mother, Grandma Drayton.

—Your Granny, by the way, was *not* a bolter, Susie. Sidney Brock kicked her out, and then she and Grandsir fought so terribly much that she had to leave. She couldn't take her children because she had no money. And she just loved Granjack. He was an old friend she'd known all her life. He was descended from Washington Irving and related to Elizabeth Barrett Browning, he played the piano beautifully, and I was very fond of him.

Whatever.

I have a few memories of my mother's mother (aka Granny aka Mummy, aka the bolter) mostly to do with croquet and dogs. Like Auntie Gaga, my Granny played a vicious game of croquet. When I knew her, Granjack had died and she was living within range of Manhattan in Seabright, New Jersey, in a moldering 1930s-era bungalow she named *Malgré Tout,* which means "In Spite of Everything." She had card tables set up in almost every room for her ongoing jigsaw puzzles. There was a stash of empty bottles by the bed, and enough lawn for both croquet and a sizable pack of carelessly trained poodles, who generally preferred the masses of newspapers lining the floors inside the house. She wore wigs and had long cigarette holders, and made sure our visits were relatively bearable by keeping up her membership at a wonderful Victorian beach club we all adored.

Almost every picture of Granny includes a small dog—that was her thing, dogs. In fact, Ma and Daddy met when *his* mother went to buy a poodle puppy from *her* mother. My guess is the dogs filled the void left by the two successive households of children she didn't manage to keep, or else they always had priority to begin with. Just a guess.

So little Ma and Bobs went with Grandsir, which is where his mother, Grandma Drayton, comes in.

Ma and Bobs had the best years of their childhood to date with Grandma Drayton, who gave them more stability than they had ever known. They even managed to connect with their older half-siblings and spend time over at Auntie Gaga's trying to play touch football. It's possible that they would have gone with Grandsir to his next army posting down south, but this got canceled when he had his elbow side-swiped in the car and instead needed to spend five years having a series of operations at Walter Reed Army Medical Center. They were able to keep in touch with their mother and Auntie Gaga, while living with Grandma Drayton in the country, in her house named Warley.

And Grandma Drayton was such a relief. She gave them a predictable routine, and religion—grace at meals and prayers and things. She loved her garden and believed in fresh air, so they took long walks every day with a "companion" hired especially for them. Everything Grandma Drayton did was carefully thought out—she was a widow and wore only black all winter and nothing but white in the summer. Ma and Bobs became pre-teenagers, and did happy teenager things like secretly painting their toenails up on the third floor and smoking hand-rolled cornsilk cigarettes behind the barn.

—She was so thoughtful to us, and so civilized. I listened to the symphony on the radio with her on Saturday afternoons, and the coverage of the Lindbergh baby's kidnapping and the stock market crash. The crash worried her—you knew always when Grandma Drayton was worried because she used to fiddle with her wedding ring.

When Ma and Bobs's father was discharged, he got a job in insurance and settled with them in Philadelphia. His drinking escalated. Grandma Drayton was determinedly oblivious, but Ma was not, especially one morning when Grandsir was going to drive her to the eye doctor. Her father was obviously drunk already, Ma says. She tried to get out of it; she went to the servants, who clearly didn't have the authority to protect her. Grandsir and Ma eventually set off. They were headed straight for a pine tree along the side of Warley's driveway when Ma decided to open the door and make a leap for it, out of the moving car.

Ma, age thirteen, dusted herself off and marched back into the house. Grandma Drayton was in the front hall looking out the window as her son's tailpipe as it disappeared around the bend. She had on her winter black, and was silently twisting her wedding ring around and around.

—*He's DRUNK,* said thirteen-year-old Ma.

—*He's NOT,* said Grandma Drayton.

So Ma took a deep breath, and then took her thirteen-year-old self upstairs to the phone and called her mother (who lived with Granjack on the other side of town). Ma told her mother that she and Bobs couldn't stay there, it was *too much.*

Her mother told her to sit tight and eventually called back. She asked if Ma would be willing to stand up in court to explain why she and Bobs needed to get out of their father's care.

This was the law in that area at the time: If children wanted to have their custodial circumstances changed, they could only get it legally done by testifying in open court.

So that's what Ma did. She went to court. It must have been horrible because her father was there that day, of course, and Grandma Drayton, too, who loved them like a mother should, loved them to pieces and must have felt terribly betrayed. Ma told the story of the near-accident on the way to the eye doctor and lord knows what other stories, but whatever she said did the trick. The judge gave custody to the bolter.

Grandma Drayton got very ill some months after Ma and Bobs left. They wanted to visit her, but since their mother and Granjack didn't exactly feel welcome at Warley, there was endless debate about how to handle the delicate trick of taking Ma and Bobs all the way out to the country to see their father's mother. By the time Ma and Bobs were delivered, everyone seemed busy and preoccupied. Someone was in with Grandma Drayton, and nobody invited the girls to go in and see her. They waited in the hall outside the bedroom, listening to their favorite grandmother's moans of pain, until finally someone (Grandsir?) came out looking distracted, to say it was not a very good day for a visit.

Grandma Drayton died soon after. So the last time Ma saw the only truly dependable adult in her childhood was on the terrible day when she had to tell all those grown-ups in open court the truth nobody wanted to face. That kind of wound never goes away.

Ma's and her little sister's bumpy childhood must have been a sharp contrast to the other world Auntie Gaga ruled over at Kyneton on the Main Line. They were lucky for their foothold in it through their mother: this vibrant, jolly club where people mostly stayed married to each other, met their responsibilities to their children, and there were enough means for staff, afternoon teas, and what have you.

Supposedly, the house still stands, although the land surrounding it has long since been subdivided and developed. We've tried one road that Ma thinks was their long elegant driveway. This used to go through the fields to the main house, but now it dead-ends at a much smaller building that looks like a little converted barn.

—The schoolhouse! says Ma.

Holy mackerel, this is Muzzy's schoolhouse! People actually living in it, with a mailbox and their cars parked out front and everything. We back around and go out to the main road again. Not far down the way we find another road that Ma says hadn't existed. It's called Kyneton Road, which sounds promising, so we try it.

One McMansion after another line both sides of the street.

—This doesn't look right at *all*, says Ma.

—Let's just go to the end and see what happens.

The road ends in a cul-de-sac, and we pause self-consciously. We are the only people on the sleepy suburban lane besides a crew of gardeners swarming with mini tractors and leaf-blowers all over a garden to our left.

—None of this looks right, says Ma.

—What's up that hill?

There's a longish uphill driveway disappearing somewhere above the gardeners.

—We need to go see what's up there, Ma.

A woman in an SUV comes down the driveway, waves at the lawn crew and heads off to the main road.

—Darn, we could have asked her. Let's go up.

—Susie, this is trespassing!

—Ma, we're having an adventure. We've come all this way, why don't we drive up there and see? Just act like you know what you're doing.

So up we go past the gardeners, who don't look like they're going to report us. At the top of the hill, we round a corner.

—Oh my, says Ma.

—Is this it?

—Yes, this is it!

I've had a huge estate house in my mind, with tennis courts and outbuildings, a ballroom, but Kyneton is actually sort of normal looking. It clearly has a lot of bedrooms, but it's not really anything to jump up and down about. Still it's fun—somewhere below here among the newer houses was the tennis court and the actual touch football field. This is where Auntie Gaga lived and died, drove one of the first Model Ts, and much much later, age eighty-two, woke herself up at four in the morning to see the first Soviet *Sputnik* overhead.

—That oak tree has always been there. *Always*, says Ma.

I remember a grand old oak mentioned in *Muzzy*. Auntie Gaga and her husband, George, bought their twenty-five acres of land around the time they married in 1902. The only tree on the hill where they built the house was a single massive oak. It was supposedly still standing when *Muzzy* was written in 1966, so this must be the one. The gardeners are working their way up the driveway, too, but I get Ma out because who knows when we'll ever come back here? I give her my arm, and we teeter across the driveway to take a picture by the ancient tree.

It's gnarled and lumpy and a lot of its older branches have had to be lopped off. It must be really ancient now, but it's here.

Ma leans on me as we go up over the grass to stand at its base. I have to back myself up to get as much of the huge tree in the frame as I can. Ma looks so small, but she's standing on her own, and behind her the trunk of the old oak spirals majestically up, up, up, with sunlight coming through the leaves near the top.

The remaining good branches are sturdy and long. If you look at the picture closely, you might be able to see Auntie Gaga up there on one of the limbs—she still climbed trees in her seventies. And maybe you'll see beautiful Gaga, and Cousin Buckety, Granny with her poodles arranged along a branch beside her, and the countess, and Aunt Tiny who wasn't really tiny. This tree is so old, maybe even older than truly tiny Little Granny with her Quaker bonnets, and older than all the other grannies we know about, and Grandsir and Bobs, and Grandma Drayton in her summer whites. But still, the old oak is here.

And so am I. And so is Ma.

Ma, Villanova, 2007

14.
The Fall

PAPERWORK MAKES ME GRUMPY, and it's worse than ever this year. Bills all over the place. Elaborate forms to fill out for Ma's Long-Term Care claims. Phone calls to places like Eliza's new college, trying to make sense of their supposedly efficient, indecipherable online paperless tuition payment system. They won't let Eliza look at her grades till I sort it all out, and it's a labyrinth of passwords and login numbers and user IDs with unexplained charges popping out of nowhere.

Ring. Ring.

—Hello?

—Susie, did you hear about the Baumards' rapprochement?

—Yes. . . .

—Isn't it amazing? It's just astounding. . . .

(*I can sense it coming, here it comes I just know it's religious and I'm going to get cranky. I should get off the phone quick before I say something mean—*)

—Don't *you* think it's astonishing, Susie? Their father wants to see them after all these years!

Ma's deceased sister, Bobs, married a Frenchman named Baumard, and they had a lot of children, my cousins, who are now scattered all over Europe. Following the divorce many years ago, the children's relations with their father have been strained. Ma feels very maternal about Bobs's children.

—Well, I don't really know them as well as you so . . .

—It's the Holy Spirit! The Bishop *said* this kind of thing might start happening in the family when I became a nun and—

(*Too late.*)

—So, Ma. You think this reconciliation between the French cousins and their father is our family's first legitimate miracle? What about *your* rapprochement with Daddy thirty years ago when you two were separated and he joined AA and started going to church with you at Saint Mark's? An Episcopalian miracle!

—What does that have to do with anything?

—You're saying anything good that happens in our family from now on will be because you became an Orthodox nun. All those other good things that happened before were hoaxes because they were the wrong religions.

—But it *is* the Holy Spirit. I'm going to light a candle for the Baumards when I get to Carlisle.

—You do that. Look, I'm being a pill. I should go; it's the bills; they're making me nuts. Sorry.

Mother Brigid is going on a trip. She's making her first official church appearance to celebrate Orthodox Christmas at her home church in Carlisle tomorrow. It's a very big deal. She has been spending much of her time this month figuring out how to assemble the nun habit.

Her friend down the hall, Bess, is good with computers and things, so Ma finally enlisted her when she couldn't make sense of the elaborate handwritten diagrams sent from one of the convents. There are all these pieces of black cloth you have to wrap around yourself and layer over one another and tie together in hard-to-reach places. It takes forever and is exhausting. At the end of their first try, Bess needed a glass of wine and Ma looked like she had joined the Taliban. I have a grim record of the result of their ordeal: a snapshot of Ma, haggard, glaring out from under masses and masses of black fabric, like an exceedingly irritated, swaddled old bird. I've posted it on our bulletin board, next to a reproduction of Picasso's *Jester on Horseback* and my favorite George W. Bushism:

> *I know how hard it is to put food on your family.*

But she's really in the groove—cancer-free as far as anyone can tell, and her Wizard surgeon is very pleased. In fact, Ma's had a pretty smooth recuperation in her apartment throughout most of the autumn, attended by cheerful home health aides thanks to the Long-Term Care policy. She's now ready to risk ruining everything by going on a Christmas adventure.

The siblings were full of helpful advice for how to handle this:

Colette: That's not safe; it's a terrible idea. Tell her she can't afford it.

Felix: Tie her up and lock her in a closet.

Home care had taken some figuring out at first. When the acute care rehab clinic released Ma about a month after surgery, their social worker (a rather limp, portly man named Fred who seemed to have pressing business elsewhere) told us she needed twenty-four-hour supervision for the first few weeks.

Me: Who pays for that?

Fred: Well, the family usually provides it.

Me: I can't provide it. I have kids and my husband's away and there's nobody else in the family who can do it.

Fred (offering me a printout): Here is a list of home health care agencies. . . .

Me: Long-Term Care Insurance only pays for about eleven hours a day of that. Who pays for the other thirteen hours a day?

Fred seemed at a loss. He gave me a number to call for city services to the elderly: our tax dollars at work. This was really just an experiment. I knew we could finance aides on twenty-four-hour care for a short time, but I was curious about the not-so-distant-future when needs like this might be more permanent, so I decided to get the ball rolling and see where it went.

First we got a visit from another social worker: Vicky, a short, roundish bustling Mrs. Tiggy-Winkle sort of person who started with some questions about general fitness. I like to be there to translate for these interviews because Ma pretty much speaks a language unknown to the average person.

Vicky: Do you use a commode at night?

Ma: Yes.

Me: No, you don't; you go into the bathroom with the walker.

Ma: Yes, I use the walker, but then the commode.

Me: Not exactly. She goes into the bathroom.

Ma: Yes, I go into the bathroom and then I use the commode.

Me: Ma. A commode is a portable toilet by the bed.

Ma: I know that.

Vicky: So you go into the bathroom and then you go back out and use the commode?

Me: Oh, I know what you mean, Ma. The toilet is down too low, so we took the commode apart and put the seat bit on the—

Ma: Yes. The commode is on the po-po.

Next was the mini-mental. This is basically an oral memory test, very quick and easy to pass for someone as together as Ma, but somewhat nerve-wracking due to strong convictions and her need to share them when opportunities arise.

Vicky: What country are we in?

Ma (pityingly): The United States.

Vicky: Who is our president?

Ma (smiling smugly at me): Well, we're very lucky it isn't Hillary.

Me: Ma, just answer the questions.

Ma: It's George W. Bush, thank God.

Vicky: What holiday is coming up next week?

Ma: Halloween, but that's not a real Christian holiday. It's a made-up excuse to sell candy and confuse the children.

Vicky put in a request for home aides and told us not to expect the HMO to agree to more than two hours a week of help. This seemed pretty useless, but you never know. A week later, Ma called me:

—*Susie, who was that person?*

—*What person?*

—*She was crazy. She didn't introduce herself when she called, she just said, "Would you like me to come over and give you a bath?" I said, "No, I wouldn't. I don't even know you."*

—*What was her name?*

—*I never found out. An hour later, she called again and asked for directions. I thought you must have sent her so I told her where I was. But all morning, she kept calling over and over, lost. She'd say things like "I'm at Talbot's. How far are you from Talbot's?" and I'd say, "Who ARE you?"*

—*Who on earth was she, Ma?*

—*Susie, you don't know, either? Finally, she called from the street outside and said, "Where should I park?" Then she called from the fifth floor and said, "Where are you, I can't find you," and I said, "I'm right here on the tenth floor, where are you?" Then, Susie, when she finally got here she was DETERMINED to give me a bath.*

—*This is really crazy. Maybe it was—*

—*Yes, it was crazy. I didn't want a bath at all. I'd already had one, but she wouldn't listen.*

—*Well, I didn't schedule anyone other than the usual people you've already got, so it must have been from Vicky—*

—*Who's Vicky?*

—*You know, Ma; the one who came to talk about George Bush and Hillary and the po-po.*

—*Oh yes.*

—*So what did you do?*

—*Well, I told her I wasn't interested. Then she took out an apron and started filling the bath, and I told her to GO AWAY.*

And this is our tax dollars at work.

So we're using Michael's ladies, paid by Long-Term Care Insurance, and as predicted, Ma is slowly becoming more self-sufficient. Now the walker's in my basement, and she is down to a few hours of help in the mornings and evenings. We have her two favorite aides on a schedule, and things are pretty smooth.

We also managed to get Ma over to our house for Christmas, which was *not a real holiday, just another made-up excuse to sell things and confuse children.* The Orthodox Nativity of Christ is on January 7, and the main thing to do is church, for like six hours or something. Ma is psyched. The rest of us are braced.

Ma's church, Saint Mark of Ephesus in Carlisle, is a two-hour drive along the Pennsylvania Turnpike in the farmlands. Nothing was going to stop her—she found a cheap but well-referenced driver to take her there, recommended by her friend Babbie. The idea was that he would drop her at the church and leave right away. Ma's friends there had a place for her to stay, and someone to drive her home the next day.

The night before the trip, I stop in to say good-bye and drop off a paycheck for the aide who'll be coming early next morning to get Ma ready. The lights in Ma's apartment are dim and the candles lit. She's in the bedroom, all settled under the covers with a cozy pink cashmere shawl around her shoulders. When I lean down to kiss her good-bye, I'm more aware than usual of this role reversal we live with: I've been the mother of my mother ever since that turning point in Ireland with the gardener. In therapy, I've identified this seemingly unavoidable habit of mine as something I should watch closely. I have to remember to protect myself because of the intense frustration it causes. Tonight Ma seems so happy, like my children when they were small, wriggling with anticipation and delight, Santa's cookies and milk set out at the foot of the bed. I'm surprised by a flood of real maternal passion, an urge to capture this precious moment and take a picture. Like Ma's real mother could have felt, but most likely did not.

I spend January 7 tying up yesterday's paperwork mess and taking down our tree, thinking about how excited Ma must be, and wondering if she managed to get into that nun habit on time this morning.

Sometime late in the afternoon, the phone rings.

—Susie.

—Father Basil?

—It's—yes. How's your mother?

—What? I thought she was with you.

—No, I had to stay at the church. I'll try to get over to the hospital tonight.

—The *hospital*?

—Didn't Seraphima talk to you?

—*Who*?

It takes a while to piece this together from different eyewitness accounts, which include Father Basil, Ma, and a soft-spoken young church member named Seraphima. Seraphima's been leaving me a series of updates on the cell, which I won't pick up till the next day because my phone is turned off in my purse:

Ten-fifteen a.m.: *Susie? This is Seraphima. Mother's had an accident but she's all right. My number is 267-555 . . .*

Twelve noon: *Susie? Mother Brigid's hip seems to be broken, but her arm may not need surgery and the doctor is talking to her now. Can you call me? God bless you. . . .*

Two p.m.: *Susie? I'm with Mother at the hospital, can you please call us? Christ is born, it's Seraphima, and my number is . . .*

It seems Mother Brigid (in full costume) was delivered safely and efficiently by Babbie's driver, a retired gentleman named Hopper who was missing a leg (really: *Hopper*, with one leg, on crutches).

Saint Mark of Ephesus has a big open worship space with no pews. You're supposed to stand. How they put up with this for hours at a time, I'm not really sure, but apparently it's not unusual for worshipers to come and go and generally mill around. They do have seats on the perimeter for the elderly, and that's where Father Basil immediately put Mother Brigid when Hopper went crutching back to his car. Ma was a lot earlier than expected, and Father Basil didn't want her to get into any trouble, so he instructed her to sit still and not go anywhere.

—But you know your mother, Susie. She does what she wants no matter what you tell her.

The fall occurred ten minutes into the Nativity service when Mother Brigid of Carlisle defied orders, got up, and started bumbling around fixing and lighting some candles near the front of the church (*of course, the Baumards' rapprochement!*). Apparently, she tripped on the hem of her voluminous nun habit, and splat.

Ma is now in the emergency room at Carlisle Hospital, two hours from home. She is in no shape to be brought back here for the surgery. A hip *and* a shoulder are broken. Some doctor I've never laid eyes on, Winkleman, wants my permission to operate first thing tomorrow morning. So Ma is looking at an extended stay.

On the phone, Ma is giddy from painkillers:

—I did *not* trip on my habit. I just wasn't steady on my feet. Somebody's candle had fallen on the floor; it was still lit and nobody noticed it. I could have told someone, but instead I got up to fix it myself.

—Oh, Ma . . .

—And then I decided to light my own candle, and when I turned I stumbled and landed on the anbvon—

—What's an *anbvon*?

—It's the platform in front, where the priest stands during the service. I was right by Father Nectarios when it happened because that's where the candles are as well. I was so thrilled to be there, I must not have been thinking straight. It was very stupid of me. Impulsive. You can't be impulsive like that. And Susie, Hopper may be missing one leg, but it's only the *left* leg, so his driving is perfect.

—So what did Father Nectarios do?

—Well, the service had already started, and he was *so marvelous,* he didn't miss a beat of liturgy at all. Susie, it was amazing, he was saying all the prayers and I lay there on the floor next to him and said *OUCH!* and *DON'T MOVE ME!*

—They tried to get you *up*?!!

—No. They called the ambulance. We waited till the paramedics came to put me on the stretcher and *that hurt.* I'm afraid I made a lot of noise then, saying *OUCH, OUCH, OUCH,* but that Father Nectarios, he is *amazing*. He just chanted louder and *then* before they wheeled me out, he asked me if I wanted communion because it was time for communion.

—That was thoughtful of him.

—Yes, it was. He gave me communion right there on the stretcher by the altar and the candles. And Seraphima put a little prayer rope in my hand, and off I went. It was a lovely service from what I could tell; I wish you could have seen it. But Seraphima's here and Matushka and I'll be all right, don't feel you have to come right away.

—Of course, I'm coming. I don't know how long I'll be able to stay, but I'll get on the road the minute the boys go to school tomorrow.

I look up Doctor Winkleman on the Internet while he's with me on the phone. I have never heard of the schools he attended. His group is called the Susquehanna Clinic, which doesn't exactly have a reassuring urban ring to it, more of an ominous *Deliverance/Dueling Banjos* twang that makes me think of creepy mutant people in the wilderness with Burt Reynolds's broken leg bone poking out of his skin. Winkleman does appear to have two eyes, two ears, a nose, and a mouth in his picture, though, which are all essential for any good surgeon, and he explains the situation very clearly and patiently.

I call Felix, who quickly gets an old buddy from Yale in orthopedics to bestow his blessing on the proposed procedure. So I give surgery the go-ahead, cancel the aides, update David, arrange a ride home from school and dinner for the boys tomorrow, email the siblings, post the bills, drag the tree out to the curb, and pray. For another Orthodox miracle.

15.

Run Susan Run

THERE'S THIS GERMAN MOVIE David and I love: *Run Lola Run*.

Franka Potente (in a wife-beater undershirt and light green pants, sporting a big tattoo around her belly button and an awesome chin-length neon-red hair mop) is a young woman named Lola. In the opening scene, Lola gets a phone call from her boyfriend, Manni. He's frantic because he has lost a satchel containing 100,000 Deutschmarks that belongs to his crime-lord boss. She has twenty minutes to get the money and save his life.

Ready, set, go! Lola races to borrow the money from her banker father, dodging obstacles in the streets of Berlin along the way (an ambulance, a barking dog, workers carrying a huge pane of glass across the street). When her father refuses to help, she rushes back to Manni just in time to help him rob a store. They flee the police, and Lola is fatally shot in the chase. Just as she is about to lose consciousness, Lola says, *Stop!* Then the film starts all over again at the beginning with the same desperate phone call from Manni.

This time, Lola runs in the same direction but handles each obstacle a little differently, thereby altering the outcome of a series of background stories. Things go even worse with her father, and this time Manni gets fatally injured, run over by the same ambulance Lola passed before. When Manni dies, they're back at the beginning. It's like a video game, with Lola and Manni using up their lives: Super Mario or Lara Croft trying to beat the level.

I'm thinking Lola's neon-red hair is doable for me. Something to add fun and flair to the rat race I've found myself in.

After the hospital released her, my mother ended up in a rehab center not far from the church. I've made the mad dash to Carlisle four times in the last three weeks. I drop the boys at school and then I drive home, do the dishes, check my lists, and load up with assorted provisions (things Ma needs from her apartment, and especially food: the menu at the rehab place, Cloverfield, is limiting for a nonmeat eater). I gas up the car, drive two hours on the highway, get off the highway, bolt a quick bowl of soup at Panera, order some hot and fattening takeout for Ma, and drive through the farmlands to Cloverfield: *Run Susan run*.

I allow three hours at Cloverfield tops. I unload the stuff into my arms, stagger with it down the hall to the skilled nursing wing, and dump it in Ma's room. I then scurry back and forth between Ma and whoever I have to meet with there: therapists, nurses, social workers, business office people, whatever it takes to make sure Ma has what she needs to get better. Then it's time to rush home: through the farms, onto the highway, *run Susan run*, to pick up the boys in time for dinner and homework.

This extended stay in Carlisle has pluses and minuses. The distance is rough on me. But Ma is happy to be close to the church and all her friends, and it's mutual. They've been very gracious to me, too. Father Nectarios is a nurse in real life, so he really knows the ropes. He steered Ma to the right surgeon at the hospital, and helped me narrow down the list of options for rehab facilities. Father Basil and his Matushka even offered to put me up if I was sleeping over, and everyone seems to hope that Mother Brigid will stay permanently. I'm not sure how I feel about that and neither is Ma, but we're keeping our minds open. It's the bright side of a tough situation: She doesn't get to see these people much as a rule, and she's seeing plenty of them now. I get the impression the church members have been thronging in for audiences, which is a great comfort. Photini says they treasure Mother Brigid here, because she's literally the only monastic in Pennsylvania. Their convents and monasteries are in other states, and if Ma had been younger and more active, she would have gone to live in one. Apparently, the people here in Carlisle feel blessed to have unlimited quality time with my little old mother. It's sort of interesting to find I'm connected to a celebrity besides my husband.

Today there's a Care Management meeting at Cloverfield, and I'm invited. Ma's not totally happy with the therapy, and I've got questions about health insurance. So *ready, set, go!*

I get there by twelve and do the stagger thing past the front desk with my mountain of stuff. There's a tiny woman by the nurse's station peering into a huge birdcage with several parakeets. Her eyes are sort of rolling around in her head, and she and the birds are all screeching rapturously at one another. Ma's nearby, in her wheelchair, determinedly reading the paper. There is an untouched bowl of pasta on a tray at her side.

The physical differences between that Ma the night before Christmas, in bed with her pink shawl, and this Ma at Cloverfield are becoming a bit of a worry for me. She's starting to look more and more like a molting, disheveled *Whistler's Mother*. Her hair is growing; it's at that awkward in-between stage. Along with getting used to Ma's weight loss (more pronounced each time we see each other), I track the progress of this wispy pure white nun hair that will grow and grow till I don't know what—it's trailing off behind her. Soon we'll have to figure out a way to put it up.

On the way to therapy, we meet a favored aide I've been hearing about, whose name tag reads *Fran*.

—This is *Frohn*ces, says Ma. (Ma has an aversion to certain nicknames.)

—Oh, lah-dee-dah, I'm *Frrrohn*-ces! says Fran, flattered. I can tell she likes Ma (she calls her Mother Brigid, of course).

We discuss the laundry situation, which seems to baffle not just us but everyone in the facility—nurses, aides, residents, and even a furtive guy in the hall who eventually, when cornered, did admit to Felix last week that he was the laundryman.

Washing clothes is tricky. Mother Brigid must wear soft, black, non-itchy cashmere, which means Dry Clean Only. This makes *Frohn*ces snort, but we settle on her using the delicate cycle in the laundry machine and hanging dry instead of sending the woolens out to be destroyed by the furtive laundry guy. This is a huge favor she'll be doing for Ma and not one of the included services.

(Felix, it should be noted, came up trumps. He threw a small fit, at first, about the disruption to his annual post-New Year's diet and exercise regimen. He likes to cut out his wine and spend up to three hours a day on the rowing machine, working his way through all the art house movies on his Netflix queue. To his credit, he got over himself pretty quick and voluntarily drove down through the snow right after Ma settled in. He spent three days in the Sleep Inn down the road from Cloverfield, figuring out ways to make Ma comfortable and giving me updates on his cell phone.

—*Suse, this place is decent but it's fuckin' weird. They have a mangy old long-haired dirty white cat that sits on the couch in this room called the Activity Room, and it never moves. I thought it was stuffed! I tiptoed in to check out the computer, and there was a guy up at the front giving a lecture to about ten or fifteen old farts just sitting there in a semicircle in their wheelchairs, all snoring their heads off.*)

Ma's therapist is a strapping woman who appears to be trying to telegraph some level of frustration to me. I sense a comradely history of dysfunctional, unresolved conflict. This can't be good. Ma's been here less than two weeks and already the staff are rolling their eyes at her the way I do. . . .

There is a sort of floppy woman slumped on a low padded table in the corner of the room. She's being gently manipulated by two very solicitous therapists, who are trying to get her to sit up straight. She has amazing inner poise, but keeps listing back and to the side like she has no concept of up or down. This makes the therapists laugh, and they pull up a full-length mirror so she can see what she's doing wrong.

—Do you see yourself?

—Unfortunately, yes, she says, with a beautiful German accent.

There's also a tiny woman over in another corner, facing a wall. Her back is so crumpled that it might as well be only about three inches long. She's using a machine where her arms have to pedal like a bicycle. She continues to pedal away extremely slowly the whole afternoon. None of the therapists seem to realize she is there.

Ma shares her therapist with an elderly gentleman who can barely speak—*stroke,* I think. When they're parked opposite each other during a lull, he leans toward Ma gamely and makes a quavering attempt at small talk, as if they've been seated together at a formal dinner party:

—Do you know what day it is?

—What? says Ma.

She progresses from tedious ankle weight reps to the big stuff—walking between the rails. For this, I pull out my cell phone to get some videos for siblings. We have been hearing the rumblings about Ma not liking the way exercises are being doled out. We want to know what's up.

The exercise routine is hard, complicated by something wrong with Ma's disposable briefs—they seem to be poking her somewhere and it hurts to move her leg. She stops, shifts her skirt around, and fiddles with her undergarments, while the stroke gentleman politely averts his eyes. There is no real privacy in nursing homes.

It's time for the big Care Management meeting in the conference room, so I leave Ma and hurry down the hall. *Run Susan run.*

In the conference room, I meet what I guess is the "team" of supervisors—therapy, nursing, social work, nutrition, at least six ladies and me. I think they must be bound by law to invite me to this meeting. They don't look all that excited to see me.

I take out my list of questions. I'm working on switching Ma from her HMO back into Medicare with an American Association of Retired People's supplemental, hoping to get out of the seventy-five-dollar daily co-pay for skilled nursing. I want to know if the HMO will remain in control till this particular incarceration period is complete. It's becoming more and more clear this HMO is for the birds.

But what Carol (head of therapy) wants to talk about is that Ma is not cooperating. Carol says she has to send weekly reports to Ma's HMO. (You only have to send them monthly to Medicare, which is another good reason to switch.) If they sniff a lack of progress, they will cut Ma off from rehab exercises just like that. And in a split second, she will become another old lady in a wheelchair forever and ever, amen.

This is bad, so it's *stop Susan stop.* The meeting shifts to why Ma is not getting with the program and what to do about that. I thought I was just checking on how they are treating her, but it seems I have turned up at a major pivotal moment in Ma's recovery.

I explain that she is definitely motivated to get better and has always worked hard on her exercises for past injuries. But I do have the feeling that Ma is not getting along with this particular person she has been assigned. Carol takes this well. She offers to give her another therapist and see if that helps.

Meantime I get the full explanation of how if Ma doesn't knuckle under *now,* her HMO will pull the rug out. Also Ma will lose the tiny window of opportunity she has to build muscles around her new partial hip replacement and get back on her feet.

So we're at a critical moment, and it's a really good thing I'm here. Ma stuck in a wheelchair for good means figuring out what to do when she leaves here (or even if she'll *ever* be fit to leave).

Run Susan run, back to Ma, who's on a break and seems a little tired. We look for somewhere quiet to talk on the phone with AARP about the new coverage, something I can't do without Ma there to give permission. They tried conferencing her in when I was home yesterday, and I think we caught her just as a pain pill kicked in:

—Is this Marjorie von . . . Mouse-swizzler?

—No, it's not; it's Mother Brigid.

—Ma, it's about medical insurance, she needs your legal name.

—Oh. Let me see . . . mumph.

—Ma'am, I have your daughter on the line. Can you give me your social security number please?

—It's . . . um.

(Sounds of rustling around. Some snoring.)

—Hello? Ms. von Munk-schnitzler? Ms. BRIGID?

(Snoring.)

—MA!!!

—Oh! Yes . . .

(Rustle rustle, then the BONK BONK of Ma's phone receiver falling on the floor where she can't reach it. . . .)

Hopefully, Ma won't need the pain pills for too much longer.

The Kate Incident especially concerned me. Ma's friend Kate recently moved into a retirement community just outside Philadelphia. The other night, Ma woke up from a dream: Kate was visiting. When she looked around the room and couldn't find her, Ma decided Kate must have stepped into the bathroom. Ma waited politely for an hour or so, and then began to worry. She pressed her call button. It was almost midnight, and when the aides couldn't find Kate in the bathroom, Ma got really concerned. She sent everyone on a hunt through the whole place, looking under beds and in closets. Finally, she thought to call Kate's place in Philadelphia. And wake her old friend out of a sound sleep.

I wheel Ma past her room. The TV in there is blasting. Ma's roommate, Evelyn Sue, is sweet as can be. Even more deaf than Ma, Evelyn Sue likes to watch loud television all day long. She has MS and has been at Cloverfield for twenty-five years. Imagine twenty-five years of roommates filing through for rehab or dying or whatever; it boggles the mind. So TV is Evelyn Sue's comfort. I've been hearing it starts in the morning with the Latin Mass (*SO misguided, the Catholics*) and then *The Price Is Right*. (*My brain is turning to oatmeal. I can't read my prayers. I can't even hear myself think.*) And by afternoon, it's *that show about the people going west—you know, the one with the man with the battered hat and that thin woman with the scratchy voice.*

—*The Beverly Hillbillies, Ma?*

At the end of the hall is a little sitting room for private visits. When I close the door, suddenly the blare of Evelyn Sue's TV and the parakeet lady's shrieks stop cold. I'm so used to the noise, I've forgotten it was even happening. It's not till you get into an oasis like this, alone, that you realize how draining it is just to be in a bustling nursing facility. The unexpected quiet comes as a complete shock, like when you're on a train and everything's rattling like crazy for hours and then suddenly you go through a tunnel and there's this vacuum. Silence.

Such a relief to Ma, that she immediately falls fast asleep.

It's awful to have to wake her but there is not much time left. We phone AARP and get that sort of settled (famous last words). Then there's this pivotal therapy thing to discuss. Is she giving up the fight to get on her feet again?

—No. It's that therapist's voice, she speaks though her nose and it hurts my ears. She pushes my kneecap. Very ignorant.

Ma crosses herself a few times during my lecture telling her how crucial her cooperation is, and we agree it would be good to try a new person.

Passing the ecstatic lady with the parakeets, we go back to Ma's room. *Bonanza* is blasting. There is a sudden appearance in the doorway: an agitated occupational therapist, who has been hunting Ma and wants to show her how to get into bed with only one helper. I sort through Ma's drawers and listen.

—Please take off my skirt now, says Ma.

—Why? asks OT lady.

—This is when I go to bed.

I look at my watch. Three-thirty! It's past my chance to make it home before the boys. I REALLY have to go so I can get dinner on the table. But this three-thirty bedtime doesn't sound right.

The OT lady cocks her head at Ma.

—You have dinner in bed? Can't you sit up for dinner? It would be good for your circulation.

—Yes, I can sit up, but they never seem to take me to dinner, so I have it here.

I dart out into the hall and find *Frohn*ces.

—Who should I talk to to make sure Mother Brigid can have dinner sitting up in the dining room from now on?

—She wants to get up for dinner??!!

*Frohn*ces looks delighted—like she actually is interested. That's nice. It's amazing how much you can accomplish in a three-hour visit.

Okay, time to kiss Ma good-bye, wave to Evelyn Sue, power-walk down the hall and jump into the car. I can get on the highway just in time to beat rush hour traffic, zoom home and feed the boys. *Run Susan run.*

Colette will be so impressed: the fact that I'm doing the Dreaded Walk Down the Hall all the time now doesn't even register with me anymore. It's wonderful what a comfort Ma's church friends are and how happy she is to be near them—almost like this wasn't an accident after all.

Lola's belly-button tattoo would not be a good look for me. But still, something tells me we've got just enough lives left to make it. At least, to the next level of the game.

16.
Plug-Pulling for Dummies

ME (*on the phone to Colette*): Ma had Medicare with a state Medigap when she first got to the Nork. Then I switched her to an HMO. LTC worked out great once we proved her ADLs were messed up. Unfortunately, that nightmare Alf experiment was a total fiasco. So Ma had to go home and that's why we didn't want her to do the TATA. Now that the co-pays have gone up so much, I've decided to switch her out of ESD to Medicare with an Arp Medigap, which may help the Arnack at her Sniff to get her PT and OT paid for along with her OxyIR and the other Rxs. What we should be thankful for is that her mini-mental was almost perfect.

Colette: What?

I could never have rattled on like this a couple of years ago. Now I barely need all the notes I carry around. I can do it in my sleep; the people I talk to on the phone all day have taught me. I am very careful to write down everything they say, and I delight in showing off my new vocabulary to Colette when I give her my daily reports. Being mostly British puts her at a slight disadvantage, though. I'm thinking about making a little glossary so we can communicate more efficiently:

- *TATA:* The Wizard's miracle surgical procedure for rectal tumors.

- *Medicare:* Government-run health insurance for senior citizens. Ma quit traditional Medicare years ago for fiscal reasons, and now we want it back. Medicare pays doctor's bills, but there are limits so it's good to get a supplement.
- *Nork:* Naturally Occurring Retirement Community, like the senior-friendly Mills House apartments.
- *ADLs:* Activities of Daily Living. Eating, dressing, bathing, transferring (which is getting in and out of beds and chairs), and toileting. Those are the big five. You need to be really bad at two of them in order to get your LTC to pay for the Alf or the Sniff.
- *Alf:* Assisted-Living Facility, like Happy Hide-Away. One step up from a Sniff, meaning you have to be somewhat self-sufficient.
- *Sniff:* Skilled Nursing Facility. Like Cloverfield. This is where you go to recuperate from broken hips or if your ADLs are really out of control or something.
- *LTC:* Long-Term Care insurance. Pays for home health aides, Alfs, and Sniffs not covered by the HMO.
- *HMO:* Health Management Organization. With an HMO, you get marvelously low premiums in exchange for their right to poke their nose into your business all the time, looking for excuses to not pay for your treatment and generally rough you up. We now think they should be avoided like the plague they are. If you get anything out of this book, it would be to get the heck out of your HMO. Now. Just stop reading and do it.
- *ESD:* Eat Sh— and Die. From here on out, this is the pseudonym I'll be using for Ma's HMO.

When you go to the doctor, you hear people moaning about their insurance. They used to play Muzak in waiting rooms, now mostly you just hear the soft drone of voices telling their sad stories: They'll be switched out of this on that date; they *called the doctor; did the fax come through; Blue Cross blah blah deductible co-pay referral primary group number.*

Sort of like when you get caught behind someone with a lot of coupons and discount cards at the market. You're envious and slightly resentful of their determination to be thrifty, embarrassed that your business does not need to be as complicated as theirs—you feel like a slacker. But their life looks so tedious, and you sort of wish you didn't have to be in line behind them with their red tape all over the place. Mostly, you hope to God this is not going to have to be you someday. Well, Someday has arrived.

It has been a nuisance to have to follow ESD's rules about getting specialists referred by the primary doctor. Because the premiums are fixed and a lot cheaper, I've put up with ESD, but boy do they sock it to you when your medical needs intensify. Ma's hospital and skilled nursing daily co-pays increased dramatically this year. Now, the saving on premiums is so far outweighed by the maximum yearly output for co-pays that we've got a whole new set of worries.

- *Co-pays:* Your share of the bill after the HMO pays. This keeps you from making wasteful health decisions, supposedly.

It would have been better to switch out of ESD in between calamities. Last fall, we got notices about the co-pays going up, and I knew they had a special window of time when it'd be easy to revert to Medicare. But back then, the cancer was cured, the crisis was behind us, and it was just hard to imagine the soul-sucking cauldron of indescribable looking-glass bureaucracy we'd find ourselves in. Now that it's about a month after the accident, I've decided to tackle an insurance swap.

Ring. Ring.

(I get out my notepad every time the phone rings these days.)

—Hello?

—Is this Susan Morse?

—Yes?

—This is Maxine, the Arnack at Cloverfield?

- *Arnack:* Registered Nurse Assessment Coordinator at a Sniff. This is a sordid job some nurses opt for. As far as I can make out, they have no hands-on contact with patients.

Instead they spend their days on the phone with the HMOs trying to get them to agree to pay for things. These nurses get it from both ends: HMOs on one side and people like me on the other, each alternately screaming about their rights. I guess this job is a reasonable option if you're so burned out from nursing you can't bear the thought of it anymore.

—Yes, Maxine.

—I just wanted you to know that ESD has terminated your mother's coverage for room and board and rehabilitation therapy starting tomorrow.

—Oh my gosh. Why?

—They say she should have reached full weight-bearing status by now.

—Wait a minute, Maxine. PT and OT say that any day the doctor will approve full weight-bearing activities, and she'll be fully independent again in about a month.

- *Weight-bearing activities:* Exercises while standing on both feet, holding onto something for support at first.
- *PT and OT:* Physical Therapy, which should need no explanation, and Occupational Therapy, which helps you figure out how to do all those ADLs when you've been messed up with cancer and broken bones and things.

—You can appeal, Ms. Morse. ESD will be calling you.

Nausea. A high-pitched alarm is shrilling between my ears. My brain instantly contracts to the size and condition of a spider monkey on crack, making this next conversation somewhat hallucinatory. I think I may have swallowed my pen, too, so lord knows how I'll ever remember what was *really* said.

Ring. Ring.

—Hello?

—Ms. Morse?

—Yes.

—This is Bertie Walker. I am a heartless creep from ESD.

—So I gather.

—I'm calling to explain why we want to abandon your mother to molder in a rat-infested state home when she still has every chance of recovering. We plan to do this based on the technicality that the therapy for your mother's hip is not progressing according to our guidelines. It does not matter to us that her broken shoulder delayed her, and uninterrupted therapy could mean recovery in a matter of weeks. We definitely understand she is not yet able to change her own colostomy bag, and that if she has to go home right now it will be impossible for her to cope at all since she can't walk yet or even get out of bed unassisted. It is legal for us to do this to her because of our rigid and cleverly constructed rule system, which is designed not by medical professionals, but by money-grabbing fat-cats who got George Bush elected and would also like to kill your children.

—Got it, Bertie. How does the appeal process work?

—Basically, Ms. Morse, you try a series of appeals providing detailed letters from the many medical professionals caring for your mother now (who are justifiably appalled at our behavior) specifying why this decision is not just inexcusable but also seriously stupid. Through all these appeals, we will keep repeating the same denials until hopefully you will give up in exhaustion.

—I wouldn't count on my giving up, Bertie.

—You're welcome to try, Ms. Morse, but it's a little irksome to us that your mother has an advocate like you. We wrap things up so much more efficiently if the patient is old, doped up on OxyIR, can't write, is barely able to hold a phone, and is stuck alone to advocate on her own behalf. We have every confidence that you will fail miserably anyway, and come to regret that decision you made after your father died to save a little money on premiums by leaving Medicare, which treats patients a little more like humans and not statistics. You will curse yourself for switching your mother to an evil, stingy HMO like ESD.

- *OxyIR:* Tylenol with codeine. Ma's still on it. I may have to snitch a couple for myself if this keeps up.

—So you're telling me you won't pay for my mother's care until she is better?

—That's right! We do realize we are being total monsters, so we'd like to offer you a tiny consolation. We'll pay for your mother's therapy for *three* days a week instead of the medically prescribed *five*. This is what I'll tell you right now just to get you off our back. Hopefully, you will think it's okay to stop paying attention. Then, when her therapists submit this inadequate program for authorization, it will go to a department that has no clue what is going on. They will say your mother is out of network, since she will still be two hours from home, in Carlisle. They'll say we only cover patients so far outside their networks when the care is urgently needed. They'll claim since she no longer qualifies for room and board at a Sniff, she must be fit enough to go back to Philadelphia for her continued treatment.

—That's ridiculous. She's—

—Yes, you and I know that this will not be true. But still your mother's Arnack will have to spend hours on the phone trying to explain the mess to a series of completely new people who have been thoroughly trained to lie to her and block her every way they can by putting her on hold, disconnecting her accidentally, and so forth. Our hope is that the Arnack will give up, too, and her facility will think long and hard before admitting the next poor old lady who has the misfortune of being covered by ESD. The best outcome to all of this is if sometime soon, when people with HMOs like ESD need rehab, there will be no facilities willing to admit them at all. It will be a great savings all around. Don't you think it's really in all our best interest, yours included, if you just let your mother die as soon as possible?

—I'm sorry. It's actually your *job* to get me to give up on my mother?

—Come on, Ms. Morse; don't act like you haven't thought of this already.

—My God.

—Everyone thinks about giving up, Ms. Morse, even if they're so repressed they can't admit it to themselves. Most people harbor tremendous resentment for their aging parents. Did you have a perfect childhood, Ms. Morse?

—No, but—

—And how has your relationship been over the last several years?

—Not great. But I think it's been sort of getting better—

—That's your problem. Guilt.

—What?

—You pushed your mother to get the cancer treatment. You're trying to keep her alive as long as possible, right?

—Of course, I am.

—Have you ever wondered why?

—Why what?

—Why you keep trying to help her if she was such a disappointment to you. What is it that makes you keep doing that?

—This is not about guilt!

—You can tell yourself that. But everyone's been there, even if their parents were nothing but delightful—the fantasy about Dad dropping dead in the checkout line at the grocery store right after a perfect physical. Mom going to bed a month or so later, feeling fine, and drifting off in her sleep. Or how about a real timesaving two-fer: Both of them could give up the ghost together arm in arm, hit by a truck crossing the street! You'll feel much better if you just admit to these thoughts, Ms. Morse.

—This is sick.

—Yes, and that's the problem. You're repressing what you really want for your mother and driving yourself crazy trying to prove you're a good daughter. This behavior is bad for you, and quite frankly, it's bad for us. We have the misfortune of living in an era of such extreme medical advances that older parents are being cosseted and spoiled and kept alive far, far longer than they should be, Ms. Morse. It's not exactly rational of you to help your mother out of guilt, and it's incredibly expensive for us. The bottom line is, all this therapy and care is only putting off the inevitable. So that's where we come in. ESD is here for you in your time of need, to provide some much-needed tough love. We make the practical decisions people like you can't bring yourselves to consider.

—Wait a second. I thought it was supposed to be the Democrats who want to pull the plug on Grandma. Health care reform hasn't even been initiated yet and *this* is what you plan to do?

—This is our best-kept secret, Ms. Morse. We've never needed a Democrat in the White House to put little old ladies out of their misery. Just get them to break their hips out of network and we'll take it from there.

—Wow. I had no idea ESD's health management was so comprehensive.

—So, Ms. Morse. Have I satisfied your needs at this time?

—Thanks, Bertie. I think I'll stay in denial and work on that appeal.

The lions have slipped the latch of their pen at the zoo. The whole group is out on the prowl. They have just located a sign. It reads:

FRESH! TASTY! MONKEYS!
this-a-way➤➤

I was already deep into the labyrinth of figuring out how to get Ma the heck out of ESD, but for other reasons. It had seemed like a good plan, back in the 1990s, to pay less every month, especially because Ma was macrobiotic and wouldn't even take Advil at the time. She had made a living will and literally thought all doctors were fools. ESD paid for her cancer treatment last year without much fuss, and I got the hang of requesting all the approvals on time. But at the end of the eight-month process, we got a notice that Ma's co-pays were about to skyrocket. This meant that if she were hospitalized again, savings on premiums would be completely nullified by the cost of treatment for any future illnesses.

So I'd begun exploring a switch from ESD back to Medicare. The thing making me increasingly anxious was the chance that, because she had not finished her treatment for the Orthodox Christmas broken bones, Ma could fall into some crack between the two policies. ESD did seem to be assuring me that we were allowed to disenroll up until March 31. My last phone call to ESD, though, was with an obliging man with a very thick Spanish accent. The battery was running out on the phone because of all my time on hold, and I felt mistrustful:

—(on phone) Are you SURE I can disenroll my mother anytime before March 31?

—I theenk so.

—You THINK so.

—Well . . .

—Look, I need to know for sure.

—Lemme talk to my supervisore.

Click. Muzak Muzak fading dangerously in and out.

—Meesus Morse?

—Yes?

—You can.

—I CAN?

(I have to be sure. This is crucial. There's this Spanish tendency to drop the "t" sound after the "n" at the end of English words. . . .)

—I CAN or I CANNOT?

—No.

—No. I CAN'T disenroll my mother before March 31?

—You can.

—Got it. I can't.

—No . . . Meesus Morse, you . . . CAN.

(The phone is fading, please, phone, DON'T DIE NOW.)

—C-a-n, I CAN?

—Yes.

Once we disenrolled from ESD, they would no longer pay for anything. This was a little scary, and required checking back with Medicare to make sure they'd really take it all on when she changed over to them. Medicare said they would pay what they were responsible for, but they do have limits. This is why with Medicare it is important to get a Medigap.

- *Arp Medigap:* American Association of Retired People's Medicare supplemental policy. A common alternative to an HMO is Medicare with a Medigap: a supplemental to pick up what Medicare won't. Medicare premiums get taken out of your Social Security, but you have to pay for the Medigap yourself. It's not cheap, but it's worth it. You get your pick, and the one we're flirting with is from AARP, affectionately referred to by those in the know as Arp.

A couple of weeks ago, Ma and I had called Arp to start the ball rolling. Leaving ESD was not as easy as Arp made it sound. Having been jerked around enough by the system, I was deeply wary, and terrified to actually commit until I was sure I wouldn't inadvertently get Ma into a jam where *nobody* would pay for her care. What was freaky was that each time I called Arp, I got a new person with a different version of how things would go. One would say *yes, switch her any time and we will start paying for her rehab therapy from the day you switch.* Next day, I'd call just to double-check before disenrolling from ESD. A new, grumpier Arp doppelgänger would need to hear my story all over again before I could even get to any questions:

—Name.

—von Moschzisker.

—Spell it.

—Small-*v*-as-in-victor-*o*-*n*-as-in-Nancy. New word. Capitol-*m*-as-in-Mary-*o*-*s*-as-in-Sam-*c*-as-in-camera-*h*-*z*-as-in-zebra-*i*-*s*-as-in-Sam-*k*-*e*-*r*. It's pronounced von Mush-ISSker.

(Daddy had a brilliant spelling technique, but I was too grumpy myself to indulge in it:

v *as in wiener schnitzel*

o *as in eau de cologne*

n *as in encephalitis*

M *as in empire*

o *as in aubergine*

s *as in estuary*

c *as in seaside*

h *as in agency*

z *as in xenophobe*

i *as in eyesore*

s *as in escarole*

k *as in que sera sera*

e *as in eejit*

r *as in aardvark.* Or Arnack or Arp, come to think of it.)

The Arp doppelgänger would go on to say that even after the switch,

ESD would still be responsible for Ma's rehab. Then I'd call ESD and, of course, their position was pretty consistent: Once Ma disenrolled, they would not pay for a single thing. Meanwhile the express train was roaring though the stations on the way to the deadline for the switch, March 31.

Every time I called Arp, Medicare, or ESD, they would try to trick me into their automated phone system's deathtrap. Here's how to bypass their robot questions (maybe mark this page):

—Are you calling about a claim?

—Agent.

—I'm sorry; before we switch you to an agent, we need some information. Please enter your member number by pressing the touchtone buttons on your keypad, or if you have a rotary phone—

—Agent.

—I'm sorry, but that number is not in our system. Please—

—Agent.

—I realize you would like to speak to an agent. To assist us in directing your call, please spell your last name—

—Agent.

—Please hold for the next available agent.

Click.

Followed by forty minutes of sporadic, sputtering Muzak.

I've learned to use speakerphone so I can be hands-free to put away the laundry or check out Medicare websites for more information. On one of these sites, I notice a familiar name: an old neighbor whose photo keeps turning up on all the websites for Pennsylvania's senior citizens business, right under the state seal and Governor Ed Rendell's beaming Democrat face. Andrea, whose daughter Noni went to school with Eliza. So *Andrea* is Secretary of Aging? Our home intercom systems were so similar they used to interfere with each other. Occasionally, I'd be alone in my house and hear Andrea's clanking pots and pans and her voice crackling out of the intercom:

—*Noni?*

—*What?*

—I can't hear you. NONI?

—What?

—WHAT?

After the novelty wore off, we decided it'd be safer to use different channels. I think I have Andrea's home number in the school book. Hmmm . . .

Click.

Medicare's sputtering Muzak stops playing. I leap to attention, and snatch up the phone.

Foreboding silence.

Ring. Ring. Ring.

—If you'd like to make a call, please hang up and dial again.

If any of this seems familiar, you have my sympathy. You also probably know what comes next:

- *Medicaid:* Not to be confused with Medicare. Medicaid pays for the total health care needs of low-income people who can't afford drugs, or even things like co-pays. This is what people in Ma's situation can turn to if they still need to stay at their Sniff but Medicare won't pay the room and board any longer and their funds are running out, their children are not made of money and their grandchildren would like to go to college.

At this point, I am showing signs of wear and tear. David is still away doing *The Seafarer*, the Broadway play he's waited for eons to do. For ten years, David has nobly turned down every stage offer, Broadway or no, because the schedule had been too hard on the kids the last time he did a play. But for this show, I told him we were finally ready—it's fantastic. Now this *get-out-of-ESD-with-the-rats-and-move-into-Arp* thing is happening and I hate to regret our decision, but wow. The fear factor has catapulted me into a strained mental state for a couple of weeks now. Colette is busy drawing up fresh Operation Ma financial projections and trying to keep Felix up to speed on the spreadsheets, which is no mean feat. She's alternating between being unbelievably helpful and sort of scarily, cold-bloodedly efficient. She knows we can't commit to pay indefinitely for Ma's health care, and she tries really hard to give me the space to face facts and deal with them in my own way, but what it boils down to is that talking to Colette these days is like having a root canal in the middle of a tax audit.

Ma has agreed to close up the apartment, and we are confronting the possibility of literally hundreds of thousands of dollars needed to get her comfortably through to the end, which is looking less and less pretty.

Colette's waiting for me to say the word and she'll fly over here. She is like a rock, every morning on the phone and throughout the day, too. So is David, who's getting a little concerned because he's never heard me sound so utterly, hopelessly stumped. It feels like every ounce of energy is being used calling, calling, thinking I have a plan, then having some new insurance person on the phone shoot it down.

When the boys stayed home for a snow day recently, they carefully steered around me, pacing back and forth in my headset, on their way in and out from sledding. Sam impresses me. This morning on the way to school, he informed me that there is *something not right with this ESD stuff*. Either he's reached a breakthrough and is emerging from adolescent narcissism a little ahead of schedule, or my condition is looking bad, bad, bad.

And, I have lost the impulse to eat: It seems to make no sense to stop for breakfast or lunch, and then I'll suddenly realize it's time to make dinner. Because the boys need to be fed, I'll throw something together and sit there with them, but putting the food into my mouth feels as foreign and unthinkable as jamming it into my ear. I have shed twelve pounds in two weeks, which, I've decided, is not actually such a bad thing.

So, my old neighbor is Secretary of Aging for Pennsylvania. Wow, who knew? She sure looks like she's important. One night after not eating dinner, I call her at home, apologizing for taking advantage of our mutual schools and addresses to ask a favor. Not at all, Andrea says, this is her job. The pots and pans clattering in the background sound sort of normal and reassuring. Andrea tells me Noni is at Mount Holyoke now—hope her cell phone reception is better than their intercom was.

Next morning:

Ring. Ring.

—Jack Wasserman.

—Jack Wasserman? You answer your own phone?

—Yes?

—Wow, I mean, I'm sorry. This is Susan Morse. Andrea—

—Oh yes, Susan, Andrea's told me you'd be calling.

—You know who I am?

—Yes, I hear you're having some trouble. Tell me all about it.

Words cannot express my relief. For those of you out there in Pennsylvania who need a Jack Wasserman in your life, I'm sorry to say he has recently moved on to head a new department educating Pennsylvanians on Long-Term Care preparation. This is good, he'll do a great job and we clearly need educating. So here's what you do instead of talking to him: Just Google the number for the Apprise office in Harrisburg. All Jack's people are still there and they will help you (he says they're like pit bulls, and he is right). They'll answer the phone and everything. Not only that, they seem to know exactly what to do—it's their job and they are there for you no matter who your neighbors are, God bless them.

So if you end up in anything like our situation, hang in there and hip-hip-hooray for government funding. Medicaid can carry you through the lapse between the HMO's plug-pulling tendencies and your mother's hopefully full recovery. She can get out of her HMO and set up that Arp Medigap if you have the funds. Keep up the appeals, because chances are you will win.

Then, when a few of the ADLs are up and running, if she's lucky your mother (or mine) can go back off Medicaid, wave good-bye to the Arnack, pack up her stash of OxyIR and return to her Nork or her Alf. And you can start shopping for your own Long-Term Care policy.

17.
Driving Lesson

SATURDAY

BEN HAS TO GO to the dentist.

It's the day after Jack Wasserman rode in to the rescue. The monkey still hasn't eaten much. It's gasping limply in a corner of the cage, waiting for the next anvil to drop.

Ben wants to drive himself to the appointment. He needs a parent to sign a form testifying he has logged fifty hours behind the wheel in order to take his driving test, and it has been slow-going. Whenever Ben drives, we make him meticulously count his time down to the exact second; we seem to be the only parents *on earth* who don't fudge the driving log. Ben is highly motivated for the license—he has a girlfriend. But the unlucky boy turned sixteen and got his permit right after David's New York play started, and his father is the only really capable driving teacher.

I once tried going along in the backseat on one of David's scary night driving lessons with Eliza, but they kicked me out of the car because I was about to lose the contents of my stomach. So it does not come as a huge surprise to Ben that I won't let him drive today, claiming stress, and he's nice about it. I leave him at the dentist and head to the market for a few minutes.

This next part is a bit of a blur. Something about going up and down the aisles of the market (hiking up pants that have begun to fall off my shrunken fanny) and feeling a little—different. My hands are sweating and it's getting hard to breathe; my heart has sort of turned into a cement block in my chest.

At the checkout line, people begin to stare. I sit on a windowsill across the aisle from the register and put my head between my knees. The cashier offers to come over and take my money. When they ask their routine question about carryout service to the car, for the first time in my life I say *Gosh yes*.

Ben's dentist is a three-minute drive from the grocery store. I think I can make it if I rest a little.

I take it slow. The cement block sensation can't be good. I won't let David quit the play. What's going to happen to Ma? I pull over outside the dentist and call Ben on his cell phone, tell him sorry I can't walk inside and, he's going to have to come to the car, and, oh, by the way, *you're going to have to drive. I'm way too stressed.*

We have an interesting drive home in which I alternately remind him to put on his blinkers and watch out for traffic lights while sort of panting and squirming around in the seat trying to figure out how not to pass out, and groaning that if anything serious happens to me he has *to tell Papa to sue ESD; it's all their fault. ESD, don't forget.* Ben seems unusually quiet. Poor boy's finally got what he wants, and it's ruined because probably all he can think of is whether or not to pull over and try out some cockeyed *South Park* version of CPR on his freaked-out mother.

At home, I leave a message with Doctor Maxwell's weekend service and stretch out on the sofa to wait. I catch David on his cell.

—Hello?

—Hi, it's me. Where are you?

—Susan! On the way to the matinee. Hi!

—I just thought you should know—

—I don't know, there are a lot of them.

—What?

—I'm sorry; I'm talking to my wife.

(David has a Bluetooth. If I call him when he's walking through Times Square, all the people hoping to spot an actor see no reason to give him his space because it's hard to figure out that he's on the phone. David is tediously conscientious, torn between not wanting to ruin anyone's big moment of celebrity-spotting excitement and his awareness that I am trying unsuccessfully not to fume on the other end of the line.)

—Are you there, David?

—Uh, maybe *The Green Mile?*

(They usually have to ask him what his name is and the name of a few of his movies—it's a handy reminder that he may be recognizable, but he's not THAT famous, so don't get a swelled head or anything.)

—I may be having a heart attack, but I think I'll be okay.

(Clank clank. The Bluetooth on New York streets makes him sound like he's rummaging around in a Dumpster full of empty paint cans. There's a siren, and a woman is squealing in delight.)

—*What?!* I'm sorry I'm talking to my wife. *What*, Susan?!

—I'm all sweaty and Ben had to drive me home and the left side of my chest hurts, but I think it's probably anxiety. Maxwell's about to call back.

—My wife is on the phone, excuse me. Susan—how about I tell them to get the understudy, and come home?

—NO! Let's just wait and see. I'll probably be okay.

—Are you sure? God. Hi. I'm in *The Seafarer*. It was *16 Blocks*. With Bruce Willis. Sorry, Susan.

(I know what he's doing: He's freaking out trying to find somewhere to converse in private. Ducking into doorways on Seventh Avenue and Forty-fifth Street with people peeking around the corner at him and waving their camera phones.)

—Tell her it's not really a good time because your wife is about to die and this is your last chance to talk to her, so could she please just take a picture and move the heck on.

—Uh . . .

—David, I love you. I'll call you when I figure it out. Sorry I had to do this to you before the show.

—That's okay. I'll call you after the matinee. I'm David Morse.

(*David MORSE! IT'S DAVID MORSE! Omygod you were in that SHOW, what was it CALLED? OH MY GOD!*)

—Bye. Call Ben's cell if I don't answer.

—I love you, Susan. Not *ER*.

—No, I hope not but I will go in if I have to. I'll see what Maxwell says—

—It was *St. Elsewhere*, not *ER*. Thank you very much.

Something about just resting here a few minutes seems to have a good effect. I haven't spent much time lying down lately. I'm even a little bit hungry, which is a novelty. I quickly find some cheese and crackers.

A few hours go by during which I enjoy myself immensely on the phone, scaring the crap out of everyone I can think of and getting them all dancing around wringing their hands. (Felix and I locked horns recently in an email exchange, and we had planned a phone date today to air our differences. I am not too disoriented to relish taking the wind out of his sails by being at death's door.) The food, the rest, and the transfer of anxiety to the family acts like a shot in the arm, and I'm beginning to feel more like myself when Maxwell finally calls.

—Hello?

—Susan.

—Doctor Maxwell!

—Describe your symptoms, Susan.

—I feel a lot better now, but I was sweating and Ben drove me home and blah blah my chest, but now I'm eating again and I think it's okay, right?

—Susan Susan Susan. I want you to get your son to drive you to Abington's Emergency Room because women your age have heart attacks.

—But that's such a hassle, it'll take hours and I'm finally lying down now and eating and I feel so much better.

—Listen to me, Susan. You know that if I told you to drive one of your children or David or his mother or yours to the ER you would not pause.

—Yeah . . .

—Get your son and have him take you to the emergency room right away.

David's mother lives nearby. She'll come over to get dinner for Sam and stay in case I'm gone all night. Now Ben gets to have another relaxing driving lesson. Walking out to the car, I find I have to lean on him, so it's probably just as well we're going.

Ben's driving is heroic if understandably white-knuckled. He needs some practice parking—we take up several spaces and toss the keys to the valet (ER valets are a welcome perk of suburb living). They put me in a cubicle hooked up to a bunch of things. As Ben sits beside me and the beeping monitor, I realize I'm right back where everything started about a year ago. The casting has been subtly adjusted: Now I'm the incapacitated mother in the bed who may be facing a major health crisis, and Ben is the dutiful offspring wondering what the heck he's in for.

They ask Ben if I've seemed okay lately. This interests me. *Have* I seemed okay lately?

(*Are they going to send social services to protect my kids from me, what if I'm cracking up and Ben has to become the caretaker like I did, what's going to happen about the play. Oh God.*)

Yes, apparently I have seemed okay although pretty stressed. I have an x-ray and an EKG and some more sympathy. We go home with a prescription for something and strict instructions to breathe deeply and eat more.

It was an anxiety attack. My heart is okay. The show will go on.

How embarrassing. Do I have to tell Felix?

Apparently anxiety due to an "extreme but temporary period of stress" means you are not supposed to have to worry about becoming dependent on the highly addictive substance they give me. Famous last words, I think, and lock it up, to be used only if the symptoms come back (they haven't).

Amazing what happened to Ben's driving log today. It's this cool "unusually challenging conditions" loophole we spotted. When you have to drive your crazed hyperventilating and possibly dying mother around, you get to double your time.

18.
PPPPPPP!

QUICK, EVERYONE: Act like you know what you're doing. Colette's coming!!!

There's an old military saying (British in origin, or so she tells me):

PPPPPPP!

or:

Prior Planning and Preparation Prevents Piss-Poor Performance!

This was Colette's motto as head of marketing for a world-famous garden plant nursery in East Anglia. International clients, high stress. It means get all your ducks lined up or you'll be spinning your wheels, everything will go to hell in a handbasket, the sh— will hit the fan, and you will be your own worst enemy.

I think I am about to be whipped into shape. Actually, I can't wait. I've been bustling around putting papers into orderly piles and repotting my African violets (they seem to have thrived on my recent neglect and are conveniently bursting with blossoms). This will make me look really competent; I just know it.

Ma has announced that she's definitely decided to give up her apartment, so Colette has emailed me a strict agenda for Operation Ma over the next twelve days:

- Tour retirement places, both in the Philadelphia area and Carlisle.
- Interview moving and storage companies.
- Figure out what Ma can sell—bring in appraisers and auctioneers.
- Meet with the geriatric psychologist about all ramifications.
- Visit Ma to discuss.

So the calls have been made and we have appointments up the wazoo. I also know Colette's secret agenda (I'm no dummy):

- Figure out if Susie's about to totally crack up.
- If she is, come up with a way to handle it. Options:
  1. Stay indefinitely. (*I wish. Not going to happen.*)
  2. Try to make Susie laugh a lot.
  3. If that doesn't work, at least get Susie to take that medication they gave her. (*She wishes. Not going to happen.*)

FRIDAY

One-legged Hopper delivers Colette from the airport. Squeals and hugs, with Ben and Sam trying to decide whether to hang around or dive for cover. Colette looks great as always, but different somehow. We are the only two blondes in our generation. She's five years older than I, but in my late teens I grew taller. For years, people used to assume Colette was my little sister. She says I'm prettier, which is flattering, and that I dress more stylishly because she's really a country girl and I've had the L.A./New York exposure. But at the moment, I'm not so sure. I'm pretty slovenly these days, and Colette's got this groovy understated-rock-star look going. It's subtle, but there's something about the skinny black jeans, the flat brown jodhpur-type half boots and the way her loose black cashmere sweater drapes sort of effortlessly that inspires admiration, and, I must admit, a twinge of sister envy. This dissipates when she makes just the right amount of fuss over the African violets and oohs gratifyingly at all my piles of papers.

SATURDAY

Colette recovers from jet lag. Susan, Ben and Sam leave for New York. (Oops—months ago, when life was simpler, I bought theatre tickets for *Macbeth*. The boys are studying this play and a mother/sons field trip seemed like a good idea at the time. So Saturday is a bit of a wash.)

SUNDAY

We spend the day at Ma's apartment to get the lay of the land. An antiques dealer comes to make an offer on some furniture. Opening drawers and cupboards, we become increasingly dismayed by the layers of stuff everywhere—some useless, some possibly vital and precious. The walk-in hall closet is particularly disturbing, so we make an executive decision to keep that door shut. What will Ma want me to do with all the art supplies?

Eliza is home from college on break, working on her first résumé. She's got a chance for a great summer internship. I have no clue how to make a résumé, never had to do one other than for acting, so it's a challenge but we find a sample online and try to figure out a way to make a freshman who comes to work, cost-free for the summer, look like a catch.

Colette calls Ma, who is feeling neglected. It's been hard to describe what's going on around here, why Colette can't make the long drive up to see her until Wednesday and why I haven't been there for a couple of weeks. Even though there's nothing we can do about it, it's hard to revel in this rare gift of one-on-one sister time, knowing Ma is waiting.

MONDAY

Over breakfast, I whip out my collection of brochures for retirement places. During the last few weeks, Ma and I have narrowed it down to four in Philadelphia and two in Carlisle, with varying degrees of affordability. Ma's been torn about which area to settle in—lately, it's been Carlisle because of the spiritual nourishment. Her geriatric shrink says the rule of thumb is *keep the older parent near the family*, but in this case we have extenuating nun-circumstances. The place she's staying at now in Carlisle is working financially for the moment, but living with a roommate wears on her. Plus if she stays, there'd be less contact with me because of the two-hour commute. We're going to have to keep our options open.

It's like a college search—you look at what you've got and figure out your Likelies, your Targets, and your Reaches. Likelies are state schools or community colleges: definite fallbacks barring a fluky disaster. Targets are within range but require a little more effort and fingers crossed. Reaches are Oxford or Harvard or MIT—dream institutions that you try for fun if you have the nerve. It helps if you look at it like a game: Keep your cards close to your chest and see what kind of deal comes your way.

We're covering the Philadelphia places first, and this morning is Barnard, a Likely. It's a standard pay-by-the-week place with an assisted-living section and a nursing wing—you can move back and forth between the two, depending on your needs. Ma's not interested because she doesn't have any friends there, but it's the one we have the best shot at paying for, so we've got to consider it.

Barnard was founded by Lutherans. This is part of our criteria: I've figured out that nonprofit religious-based places may be willing to take more of a gamble financially. Most important, you can trust their hearts are in the right place; they generally care. Also, they often have an endowment of some kind, which means they won't kick you out if you beat the odds and outlive your savings account. (Ma doesn't have a savings account, but she has her children. This makes the process even more stressful because if we let her go through our money as well as her own, we won't have Barnard to watch our backs and our own retirement pots will be empty. It's something to consider.) Ma's Long-Term Care policy will count as an asset, but aside from her meager income, that's it. So we're hoping we can manage whatever else Barnard might want to count on for payment in the long run.

Knowing this need would come eventually, Colette and I tried to scout a few places when she came over last year. We do want to know more about Barnard, but there's one we won't bother to see again this time around: the Retreat, a sort of pasture for elderly Roman Catholic nuns. It's spoken of with reverence around here. We'd heard they sometimes take needy but connected lay people, which Ma was at the time. (This was in the pre-Mother Brigid period. Ma still has lots of friends from her Catholic phase.) The Retreat gave us the heebie-jeebies when we stopped there last year: a sterile high-rise building, very *1984*, plopped in the middle of a flat, barren field. You needed advance permission just to get past the front desk, we were told by the stern, bureaucratic woman who guarded it that day.

There are red flags you should watch for when you're checking out nursery schools for your kids, and the same rules apply for retirement places. If you can't drop in unexpectedly, who knows what might be going on in the cloistered back rooms of the Retreat? Mean nuns with giant rulers rapping helpless old ladies across the knuckles and making them write *Jesus only loves me when I don't wet the bed* a hundred times on a blackboard?

So the Retreat is out, but we did like Barnard when we slipped in last spring. The residents all live along a series of new-looking hallways that branch out from the original building, an old Victorian mansion now housing offices. We refer to Barnard as the *show-offs* place because when we first buzzed through, rounding a corner at a good clip, a voice hollered:

—*Show-offs!*

We stopped and turned. There was a feisty little dame with a gleam in her eye, all in purple, perched in a wheelchair in the hallway.

—*Excuse me?* I said.

—*Show-offs, that's what you are. Look at you, all young and walking and everything.*

On our return visit to Barnard today, Rose, their friendly head of admissions, settles us in her office for a chat, and we tell her the story.

—That's Gladys. She's the best. Ninety-seven now and still scrappy.

Barnard seems cheerful and welcoming, and Rose clearly cares about the residents. Colette sits back to let me tell our story. Then Rose looks over Ma's financial details and says she thinks there's a good chance they can figure something out. She takes us to see the dining room (very nice) and a room that might suit Ma.

It has a shared bathroom and one small window facing directly out on a brick wall that's close enough to touch. The wall is all you see.

I look at Colette. She has her poker face on. Years ago, determinedly proud of her independence after a divorce, Colette had to live in the only place she could afford: a miniscule mobile home across from the nursery where she worked. She now lives in the country with her husband, Badger, in a lovely old eighteenth-century barn they scrimped, saved, and sweated blood to convert from a wreck.

—Jolly good. Excellent closet space, Colette says.

We have agreed all along that we're going to have to face facts here, but I am speechless. *This* is what Ma can afford? Even here, most likely she will still need help from us financially as well as Medicaid, big-time, after the insurance runs out the third year. She would be *lucky* to be here in this sad little room? I can barely conceive of it. All I can think is *thank God Colette is here to give me courage.*

So *this* is what a Likely is like?

TUESDAY

Today's another full Philadelphia day. There's a Reach in the morning: a place started by Episcopalians many generations ago, called the Abbey. This is one of those Continuing Care Retirement Communities, which means it has all different levels of care from regular, independent homes through to full-time skilled nursing. Once you're in, you're guaranteed access to whatever help you need as you age, without having to pay extra fees or stress out too much.

The Abbey is not the most expensive of its kind, but it's no bargain, either. You put down a hefty entrance deposit and pay by the month. Ma can't afford it, but we can't assume they won't be willing to work with whatever we're able to scrape together. Ma and I talked about the Abbey years ago, after she sold the Florida house, but we never even got to the financial discussion because Ma was still active and painting, and she wanted the Mills House apartment. Now two good friends are here, Babbie and Olivia (they brought the bagels to the tonsure), as well as lots of people Ma knows. She has asked us to definitely consider it.

The thing we've figured out is that it's a terrible idea for a child to sign a contract for her parents at a CCRC, unless the child is incredibly wealthy and truly madly deeply generous. These places are set up so the entrance deposit is there to help with monthly expenses if the residents live long enough to go through all their savings. If a resident's *child's* name is on the contract, then as long as the child has any money, the deposit will never be touched. The CCRC bears very little risk this way, and the child could end up bankrupt if the parent lives a really long time. So this deal has got to be made with Ma's meager assets, or not at all. I don't believe a deal for Ma is possible at the Abbey if she is truly unsupported, but we're going to go through the motions anyway.

We also have another CCRC Reach in the afternoon, called the Crescent. This is where Ma's friend Kate lives. It's not church-affiliated, so I'm not really sure why we're going, but you never know. Ma would love to be near Kate.

And tonight, we have a treat: *John Adams* is having its first world screening at the Philadelphia Constitution Center. David McCullough, who wrote the book, will be there with Tom Hanks, who produced, the director Tom Hooper, and Paul Giamatti, the star. David can't come because of the play, but his mother and the kids and I are going, and Colette, too. I wonder what kind of shape we'll be in by then.

Georgia Brady is the admissions person at the Abbey, and our appointment is at ten. We pull into the long sweeping driveway past well-groomed landscaping. It's rather grand.

Colette snorts.

—Settle down, Coco.

There's something we siblings still grapple with individually: We really grew up sort of schizophrenic, with parents who were polar opposites in many ways. Daddy's childhood was privileged. His family went on holidays abroad and put him through Yale and the University of Pennsylvania's prestigious law school without much bother, but he had no problem turning his back on all of it. It's hard to say how much of his attitude stemmed from alcoholism or his passionate conversion to the Democratic Party in the 1950s. As a soldier boy Daddy reveled in the army's Spartan lifestyle, so much simpler than what he had enjoyed as a child. He did still play a lot of golf at an exclusive club for a long time after he quit law (we recently learned he had been quietly gambling there, and possibly losing a great deal of money for years). So it was complicated, but we all know that if he'd had his way, we'd have lived in low-income housing and all gone to public schools and state-run colleges.

This would not have been the end of the world, but Ma wouldn't hear of it. Even though she had been required to do without for most of her own early years, she'd had *proper schooling* and so would we. We somehow managed to live in *Social Register* neighborhoods and go to private schools, for the most part, with tennis and things. The tension was always there, though, because we were barely able to afford our way of life. And with that tension came the inevitable feeling of not really belonging. A sense of lesser-ness that made it easy for us children to slip defensively into a form of reverse snobbery, especially when we sensed any kind of entitlement or pretension by the more comfortable establishment people around us.

There's something about the name—the Abbey—combined with this exclusive-looking entrance that seems to set Colette off. The driveway's graceful curves get her the way the brick wall outside the window at Barnard got me. Both our impulses (Colette's to grin and bear it at Barnard and mine to wish and hope for the Abbey) probably stem from the same general source: the push and pull of parental indoctrination. Old childhood war wounds.

—Susie, we'll never be able to manage this; it'll cost a fortune!

—I know, but let's just see what they say. Ma wants us to give it a shot. You never know.

—You sound like Ma: *God will provide.* What if the market collapses and we suddenly can't pay for it? Remember: Prior Planning and Preparation—

—Coco, the market's not going to collapse *that* much. We've got Democrats in Congress, a lame duck president, and we'll get a new one to fix his mess before you know it. What can possibly go wrong that hasn't already? This place is not as expensive as the one we're seeing after lunch, at least. And Babbie and Olivia like it here.

So we park and walk into the lobby, renovated since the last time I toured. It's even nicer than I remember: lots of floor-to-ceiling windows that let in the natural light; marble and bronze sculptures here and there; antique sideboards; attractive, comfortable sitting areas sprinkled around a beautiful bleached wood spiral staircase that sweeps up to the dining area above. It's like a really classy ski lodge or a high-end spa.

—You're right, Coco. This is not going to happen.

We bump into Olivia at the concierge desk. Olivia's still pretty fit. She's wearing tennis whites and looks thrilled to see us. It's nice to see her too but I think *rats, later we're going to have to explain to her why Ma isn't coming.* I can't exactly picture Mother Brigid in tennis whites over her colostomy bag and her hip replacement—she probably couldn't pass the physical here even if we did get the financial bit figured out.

We give our names to the receptionist and sit down to wait for their head of admissions: Georgia Brady, a tall, striking woman dressed all in shades of fawn and cream—beautifully cut wool trousers and a graceful silk button-down shirt. She has strong features and a confident style; Georgia is a ringer for Allison Janney, the press secretary C.J. on *The West Wing.* With her is a smaller, dimply Kristin Chenoweth-type sidekick named Lily: blonde, young and all smiles.

They take us around the corner to some soft armchairs for a chat. Georgia has a laserlike focus and directness that's immediately reassuring. She wants to know first why Ma isn't with us. (Translate: *Does your mother want to move into a retirement community or are you just browsing?*) I decide to let it all hang out.

I start to explain Colette's here from England for the week to help me and blah blah our mother's convalescing from surgery out of town and can't come with us, and trying to decide blah. Georgia breaks in:

—What's she recuperating from?

I tell them about the visit to church and the candle-lighting incident—I don't know why I just keep babbling on, oversharing about Ma and our ridiculously convoluted story, how her insurance cut her off and we switched it, she's about to go on Medicaid, she's using a walker so she may need assisted living for a while but she's supposed to become independent but who knows—

Georgia narrows her eyes.

—Why assisted living?

I look at her.

—Well, that's what I'm wondering, too, I say. Frankly I'm a little uneasy about assisted living.

—It's not all it's cracked up to be, she says.

I blink. Does this person really work here?

—You're telling me, I say. I wish I'd understood that a long time ago. Assisted living totally sucked for us during radiation last year.

I kind of like Georgia. Too bad I didn't meet her a long time ago. Even if we can't afford the Abbey, her input could have saved us all that trouble at Happy Hide-Away.

—Well anyway, I tell her, our mother may decide to stay in Carlisle because her church is there and she's a nun. There are two retirement places we're interested in up there, but we thought we'd look around Philadelphia, too. We came to you because Olivia and Babbie are here, and we're going to the Crescent this afternoon because she has another friend there. But a big part of our decision depends on the finances. She's got a tiny fixed income and a limited amount of help from us, so I guess we're just kind of going through the motions with you here, for her sake.

—Your mother's a nun?

—Yes. An Orthodox Christian nun.

And I blather on a bit more, about how Ma came to it late in life but she's really serious about it, and the church means a lot to her, so it's not very likely she'll want to move home. Georgia puts her hand up and turns to Lily.

—She's a candidate.

Lily nods.

—Right, I say.

I back up to the part of the spiel I skipped, because they need to know her condition: the cancer, the treatment, the clean bill of health after surgery. I'm mostly just talking to hear the sound of my own voice, waiting for one of them to tell me to stuff it and order us to leave. Out of the corner of my eye, I sense Colette looking back and forth from Georgia to Lily—they seem to be having a silent tennis match with their eyes.

—Hold on a minute, says Georgia, rather sharply. Just stop.

I stop. I look at Georgia. She breaks into this kind of Cheshire Cat smile, long and luxurious and full of lingering meaning and mystery. Very Allison Janney.

—There's a foundation for the clergy.

I look at her blankly.

—The clergy?

—Right. For priests. For nuns.

—Oh, that's nice, I say. But sorry, I know there are Episcopalian nuns, not as many as Catholic. Our mother's not either of those. She's Orthodox. It's a totally different church not a lot of people have heard of, I know I didn't—

—The foundation is also for rabbis, says Georgia. And devoted church secretaries. It's nondenominational assistance for people who have gone above and beyond with their religious what-have-yous.

I look at her, baffled.

—What-have-yous, I repeat stupidly.

—You can stop looking for a place for your mother now, Georgia says. You've found us.

Colette takes my hand. She doesn't let go.

Georgia and Lily look at our hands. They smile.

I'm really tired all of a sudden. *Maybe I do need one of those pills. It sounded like she just said we—*

—I'm pretty sure they can accommodate a studio apartment, says Georgia. Don't worry about the shape she's in—she just needs to not have dementia. Your mother will pay what we all agree she can afford, once we've looked at her income and her health care premiums. It's good she's not with ESD because we won't put up with HMOs. You should take her off Medicaid now. You children can just help her with the little extras: trips to visit her church and so forth. We'll need her religious résumé and some bank statements to get the process rolling. Forget about the Crescent, they'll never help you. Now, we'd like to treat you to lunch here with your mother's friends. I'll go call Olivia and Babbie. Lily will take you for the tour.

Colette looks at me. I look back at her.

—May I quickly wash my hands first? asks Colette.

—Me, too, I say.

Lily points out the ladies' room, which is fancy with a beautiful door and marble floors, distressed iron fixtures. We shut the beautiful door and grab each other and jump up and down and silently squeal and burst into tears and laugh, and I have to do a quick soft-shoe dance, then we pinch each other and pee and wash our hands and straighten our hair and walk calmly back out to Lily for the tour.

We're like two Little Orphan Annies waltzing around to inspect Daddy Warbucks's mansion on the first day, or twin Eloises (one slightly taller and a little less hip) skibbling all over the Plaza: the glassed-in swimming pool with its cathedral ceiling, the art room with cubbies for supplies. The studio that has a balcony looking out at trees, *trees, not a brick wall, trees.* The library with a bunch of photocopies of the daily *New York Times* crossword puzzle for the puzzle junkies, the huge greenhouse, the College, where you can take classes on stuff like Shakespeare (the residents are retired professors and things and they teach one another). A croquet lawn, a putting green for lord's sake, and a French chef who made the lunch, and there are ten different flavors of ice cream for dessert if you don't want a fresh-baked chocolate chip cookie or a slice of cheesecake. Ma will put on weight!

Seems like Mother Brigid pretty much just nailed the local Reach.

Olivia and Babbie are sworn to secrecy till Ma gets a chance to think. (What on earth there is to think about is beside the point. She would be nuts to pass on the Abbey. She's really used to the Carlisle idea, but all of a sudden it's not looking anywhere near as good to me as it once had. However, this is Ma we're talking about, and it's her life. She has a right to make up her own mind.)

The *John Adams* thing goes by like a blur—I think it went well, but I may have overstepped at one point by offering to sleep with David McCullough if he would try to get HBO to cast David as George Washington again when they do his other book *1776*. Mr. McCullough is devastatingly charming, with his lovely, genteel wife of many decades, Rosalee, by his side. He is probably about seventy-five. Since today's theme seems to be you just never know what will happen, there's no harm in tossing ideas out there, that's what I say.

WEDNESDAY

Run Susan run (with Colette), run out to Carlisle to see Ma and deliver the news.

The two-hour drive is more fun with Colette. I get to show her my favorite donkey farm by the side of the highway, the wonderful silo painted with a faded 1950s Cadillac ad, and all the overpasses with the funny names of their roads: Swamp Bridge, Girl Scout, Wollups Hill, Pinch.

I drop Colette at Cloverfield with Ma, who is flabbergasted that the Abbey has morphed from a Reach to a Likely. I dash over to our Carlisle Target, Glen Eden for a quick tour. Glen Eden and Cloverfield are our only two Carlisle options, and I haven't seen this one yet because I've had such a hard time tearing myself away from Ma when I do get up here. This is my chance to get something done and give Colette and Ma a little time alone. Glen Eden is really nice—set in the farmlands with fields and woods everywhere, beautiful views Ma would love.

But they seem less and less interested the more I emphasize Ma's financial issues. If we try to make a deal here, they'll want our help big-time, which we're open to if that's what Ma really wants. But we already know Ma thinks Cloverfield would be fine, and it's closest to the church. So I don't really get into it too much, just scurry back to Cloverfield in time for lunch—I've asked if we can try the food in the assisted-living wing where Ma may be headed. Ma's had terrible trouble with the food here and we wanted to see for ourselves.

If Ma opts for Cloverfield, she may have to stay in the nursing wing and keep getting help from Medicaid. It's doubtful they have the kind of resources the Abbey has, but they really seem to want Ma. Shirley in Admissions has made a huge effort—we have a cheery little private dining area with a real server at a carefully laid table, and fish is the main course. Ma needs soft food because of her teeth, and she still never touches meat, which has been a problem up here.

Shirley is so glad we came on Fish Day.

Anyway, I think it's fish. I'd rather not describe it: a greyish shriveled blob sort of thing, swamped in something viscous. No wonder Ma's been losing so much weight. I can't believe how sweetly she of all people has tolerated this, for literally months. She is really brave, because this is truly awful.

Colette has that *I-lived-in-a-trailer-don't-mind-the-brick-wall-outside-the-window* poker face on again. She gamely forces down a bite or two, pretending not to gag.

—Yum, she says.

Meanwhile, Ma is dutifully gobbling everything on her plate, down to the last bite. I pick up a forkful.

The stench. Oh, please. How do people do this? Sorry, I'm sure they do, but seriously, how?

—So, Ma, will you please come live with Babbie and Olivia at the Abbey? For us?

Mother Brigid puts down her fork, crosses herself, and looks very serious. It's amazing that our mother, with all her standards and sensitivities, her linen napkins and candlesticks, would be so fully prepared to sentence herself to this kind of food for what's left of her life.

It's as if she has become a sort of modern-day hermit in the desert.

Orthodox Christianity claims to have kept closer than any religion to the original practices of the early followers of Christ. Among those early Christians were people who, in around the first century, found it difficult to keep their spiritual focus in ordinary society. So one by one they left and took to the wilderness like John the Baptist. They lived alone and fed themselves as best they could: locusts and honey, whatever. Just to be able to concentrate and avoid worldly distractions. It's not that they considered themselves more special or holy than others—a lot of them felt quite the opposite, and that was the issue. They knew they needed a quiet, simple life to keep their faith intact.

Eventually, other Christians followed, uninvited—those who needed a living example for inspiration. Then the John-the-Baptist types had to figure out what to do with the sheep types. So rules were made. This is how the first monasteries and convents came into existence.

I'm still not converting. But I'm definitely impressed.

I'm having the same otherworldly feeling I had at the tonsure ceremony. I have known this person my whole life. I would never have predicted she'd be willing to make this kind of sacrifice. For the Ma I know to ever consider staying here in Carlisle, living on this kind of food for the sake of her spiritual sustenance—the evolution of this fascinating, complex woman, her absolute determination is awe-inspiring. It just is.

—Ask Father Nectarios, says Ma. I'll do whatever he decides.

Ring. Ring.

—Yes, he says about the Abbey, but please bring her back for the High Holy Days if she's fit, God willing. We'll keep her away from candles.

Prior Planning and Preparation has truly Proven to Prevent Piss-Poor Performance. But let's give credit where it's due with another P-word: Ma was right. God *did* Provide.

THURSDAY

Well, the schedule today sure has changed. High on the list: Make a nun résumé quick and find Ma's bank statements before the Abbey changes their minds. Good thing Eliza sourced that résumé sample on the Internet, because we'll need it. But first I have a therapy appointment with Rita, who is supposedly helping me to cope this year without having to dump every thought I have on Colette and David.

In the morning, I'm jumping out of my skin, racing all over the house flapping my papers around. Colette pretty much has to shove me out the door—this appointment is happening not a moment too soon because I'm like some kind of geyser about to blow. When I get to Rita's, I do, gulping my heart out from under a towering pile of crumpled tissues. Leave it to me to conjure up the one negative in this happy fairy tale come to life—I am inconsolable.

—What if she DIES before she GETS HERE??????

Rita is kind about my condition. Her mother is installed in a modest but decent assisted-living place Ma would not even consider back during radiation, because she once visited a friend there and *it smelled like tinkle. Unacceptable.* Our sessions to date have been about teaching me to reconcile with the sad facts of life for the elderly, and they've been incredibly helpful. Now here I am paying this nice hardworking woman to listen to my despair over a miracle—it's like having a close friend whose kid settled for a city college downtown, making the best of things, and yours has just gotten a scholarship to MIT or wherever, and you expect *her* to comfort you because it's JUST TOO FAR FROM HOME!!!

Rita should really tell me to get over myself, but she listens to all my pathetic palavering. Only two weeks ago, she was hearing me coldly calculate how long Ma would live and the costs. The subtext was practically out of ESD's playbook: *Hopefully, she* will *pop off before the money runs out, because the cheapest route sucks.* Now I've got to seem like a spoiled baby:

—I WANT MY WONDERFUL DARLING PERFECT MOTHER TO LIVE, LIVE, LIVE!!!!!

I really should be ashamed.

Okay, that's enough of that. Even I am sick of myself.

19.
Departure

MARCH 27, 2008

HAS THE HAPPY ENDING started yet?

At one point during all the proceedings (the handing-in of the nun résumé, the submission of the financial particulars, the approval of the apartment), Georgia Brady explained the beauty of a CCRC: Kids get breathing room to sit back and enjoy their parents during the twilight years. When Lily showed me the apartment, she asked *what will you do with all your free time?*

—*I have something to write,* I said.

Ma will have her cataracts done this summer: no problem. The nurse at the Abbey will schedule visits, and appointment reminders will appear in Ma's mail slot. Aides will materialize on cue with eyedrops. The in-house doctor's office will be magically given all insurance information, and her transportation will be arranged, with a helper by Ma's side if she needs one. Follow-ups will snap into place, and all I'll have to do is share the excitement when Ma can see better. In Georgia Brady's words: *She'll be ours.*

Not quite yet. We're still waiting for medical approval, so the future feels almost real but not quite. She'll stay at Cloverfield for the rest of this spring at least, and I'll have plenty to do in the meantime. I have to pack up Ma's apartment soon; I've given them a move-out date.

Colette and I did a lot of sorting before she left; next Ma and I have to really go over what to sell, what to give away, what to store, what to toss, what to keep, and how to fit what she keeps into one small room and a storage closet down the hall.

But first, the boys and I get to have spring break.

Every year at winter's end, we take a week somewhere tropical with two other families. We're really good buddies, and it's become a tradition. Fishing and scuba diving for the men and boys; sunbathing and parading around in bikinis for the teenage girls; crossword puzzles for me and my lady friends, between long walks designing elaborate scavenger hunts and things for the group. David can't go this time, and neither can Eliza because her break doesn't overlap with ours. That's very sad, but not sad enough to skip our island getaway.

I've pushed myself to get ahead on paperwork this week. Monthly bills have been paid in advance. The latest appeal with evil ESD has been filed, in response to their most recent denial letter:

Dear Ms. Morse,

Our panel of experts has carefully reviewed Ms. von Morphschmuckster's case. It is our opinion, as professionals who know so much more about these things than you, that the decision to dump your mother was correct.

Isn't that miserable woman dead yet? Time for you to get a life, Ms. Morse.

Respectfully, ESD

Coming soon: A phone hearing with a judge. I can't wait.

The iPods have been updated; passports are at the ready. Sunscreen, bathing suits, sandals, and books for the beach are packed. Arrow the dog is suspiciously sniffing two bags of scuba gear in the front hall. The alarm clock is set for six a.m. tomorrow—we have an early flight.

I've said good-bye to Ma, who's enjoying her final few weeks of attention from the priests and all her friends at church before she leaves Carlisle. Last year in March, she was deep in radiation, and David was doing *John Adams*. I almost sent the kids off on break without us, but a friend stepped forward and offered to take over my job for a week. This year, I think Ma can go it alone.

My only issue is that our destination, Guana Island, doesn't have phones in the rooms, and my cell phone won't work outside the country. I could rent one there, but the idea is I'm taking a real break. Colette is right—she can handle it from overseas. She is my legal stand-in with the Medical Power of Attorney, and Cloverfield has her contact information. I sent her a detailed email with all the names and numbers I could think of—got it off just barely in time before her Internet went on the fritz. (This always happens.)

I had a long talk with Ma this afternoon to go over all her instructions (*Try to keep eating. Don't make any sudden movements. Don't go outside if it looks like rain. No field trips to church. Call Colette if you need anything, but don't forget about the time difference, and please DON'T DIE*). It feels nostalgic—one last flurry of anxious fussing. We're almost there.

Nine-thirty p.m.:

Ring. Ring.

—Hello?

—Susie.

—Ma! Why aren't you asleep yet?

—*C'est impossible.*

—What?

—*Je ne peux pas dormir du tout. Du tout!*

—You can't sleep at all at all?

—*Oui, c'est ça.* Yes.

—Ma, why are you speaking French?

—*Parce qu'elle est ici.*

—*She's* there? Who's she?

—*La nouvelle copine de*—

—Your new friend? What—

—*de CHAMBRE. Ma nouvelle copine de CHAMBRE.*

—Ohhhh, your new *roommate* is there and you don't want her to know what you're *saying?*

—*Exactement.* (That's French for *you betcha.*)

Ma is pretty much fluent in French. Her mother and Granjack took Ma and her sister Bobs to live in the south of France when they were teenagers in the late 1930s. They went to school and had all kinds of adventures, driving with their older half-sister Priscilla through the hills outside Cannes during blackouts at night with their car headlights painted blue. They were there for two years, making it back to the States just before the Nazis moved in up north and things got bleak.

I also went to school in France, for the last semester of boarding school. I double majored in theatre and French literature in college, so I can keep up. Sometimes I think I mainly went Gallic in order to be able to cope with moments like this, when Ma resorts to French.

The first time I can remember this happening was striking. It was shortly before we left for Ireland, so I was maybe about four. We were living in Penllyn. Daddy had probably been in the throes of hepatitis, or heart trouble, or career frustration, something. Ma was *beside herself,* as she put it, tipped over the edge by sinus pain—she'd been having fits of rage for days.

One morning, she woke us girls up with the Latest Answer To Everything: We had to *learn French immediately*; it was *essential* to our *upbringing.* She'd read somewhere that children thrive on language exposure the way plants need sun, for their very souls, and you have to start them at an early age or they'll miss the crucial developmental sweet spot when their brains are like sponges. She wanted to saturate us—we'd learn the same way a baby learns to speak, by being immersed. *Sink or swim.*

Her intentions may have been good, but I think this was the moment it occurred to me that our mother was a bit of a challenge.

That episode lasted just long enough to make a life-altering impression on four-year-old me. It was one thing to be ordered around and harangued in English—by the time you're four, it's possible to follow simple commands. But the sight of Ma clutching the bridge of her nose and screeching unintelligibly like a frantic Pepe Le Pew was unsettling.

So, in order to reduce Ma's frightening behavior to its usual, more familiar level of weirdness, I figured I had to somehow fix her nose. This seemed to hinge on my ability to learn French in, like, one day flat. I've often thought my hard-won facility for the language several years later may have been nothing more than a long-term survival project.

Good thing, because it seems now Ma has an urgent roommate problem, and it must be handled in French.

Ma recently put her foot down about her first roommate, Evelyn Sue. The nonstop TV-blasting was bad enough, but when Ma discovered Evelyn Sue's kids would be sending her a cuckoo clock for Easter, she put in an urgent request for a change. There are no private rooms at Cloverfield, and for most residents, television is a way to take their minds off the monotony. By a stroke of luck, they found her a new roommate who at least doesn't keep TV on from morning to night. The move was sudden, and I haven't been up to meet this new one yet.

Apparently, the adjustment's not going too well. What I get from Ma is that TV is not the issue this time. She can't even bring herself to articulate it in French, but apparently *The Beverly Hillbillies* at full volume would be a picnic compared to whatever's going on in the new room. Something about amputated legs and visits from a husband in the evening and crying for home inconsolably when he leaves. It's too much for Ma—she wants out, and it can't wait till I get back. It has to be *tout de suite*, like tomorrow. What complicates things further is that while the new living situation seems to literally terrify Ma, she is too immobilized, both physically and emotionally, to think of a way to talk privately to the right people at Cloverfield herself. And the right people won't be there until tomorrow morning at nine.

I can't be sure Colette will be able to reach Ma on the phone in the morning, or even if Ma will manage to get the problem across to her if she does. England is asleep right now. . . .

Here's the thing, in case it's not obvious: I've been a fierce mother, especially when my kids were little—one of those parents who mostly refused to spend weekends away from her children. I'd call on the way to dinner with extra pointers for babysitters as they occurred to me.

The twins were breastfed longer than most women consider seemly. Eliza's first bath was in bottled spring water; I warmed it on the stove. I once darted out onto the soccer field during a lull in a practice and reapplied sunscreen to a mortified eight-year-old Sam.

I could do a monkey about Ma's roommate problem. I could start hyperventilating and running around, and get the boys all on edge. It might be fun.

No. We really are leaving. The bags are packed. There is a way to deal with this, just let me think for a second.

Email!

Oh, nuts, that's right: Coco's email's down.

Okay, then I'll email Felix, explain what's up and ask him to call Colette in the morning. Simple.

Actually, not simple.

Felix is extremely smart. Yale-grad smart. He's a whiz with computers. He's read every *New Yorker* from cover to cover for decades, and he clobbers me easily at Scrabble. But he likes things to be very very very *clear*. When something's not *clear* right away, he'll be the first to admit that his initial impulse is usually to behave like an asshole. He always gets over it; he's happy to help. But he likes to throw his weight around a little bit while he's getting revved up to step to the plate. He also is easily distracted, which means conversations tend to veer off in many directions. Whenever you must approach Felix, it's a good thing to make sure you have your wits about you. If you get anything even slightly wrong, you will definitely pay for it.

And then, of course, there's me. Beleaguered, put-upon me: the *Special* Daughter Standing by her Poor Old Mum. Carrying the world on her shoulders. The *Special* Daughter just wants to know that everything is in order, so she can get a good night's sleep and escape at the crack of dawn for a second or two to her luxury island retreat with the piña coladas and massages with mango body wraps in a breezy spa tent with billowing white curtains on the beach. This can't be too much to ask. . . .

Emailing won't do the trick. Felix will read, but he also likes to call and *clarify* everything, and I won't be available for that. If I can't email, then I have to call and *talk*. And that's an accident waiting to happen.

Felix will want to know why Ma will only speak French right now (this could veer off into why Felix hated Latin and Greek not to mention French) and why I can't email Colette (time for a sidetrack about how useless Colette is with technology). I just have to get him to agree to call Colette in the morning and tell her to call the nursing home and get the manager on the phone (another sidetrack about why he can't just call the home himself and how I misuse the term Power of Attorney—*Suse. Listen carefully. You can't BE the Power of Attorney—you HAVE the Power of Attorney*). I'll only feel able to go once he understands Colette needs to tell the manager to wheel Ma to a conference room where she can privately explain what the problem is with the roommate (more sidetracks about what's going on with the Abbey, and what's all this about crying over your amputated legs and don't you think Ma's doing this on purpose just to keep you here and why can't you do it yourself when you get there and what on earth kind of island is this you're going to for chrissake?).

We children scattered like buckshot when we left home. Felix skedaddled to New York, but that wasn't far enough so he detoured to Vermont. Colette went to England for a semester abroad and basically never came back, and I escaped to L.A. It all seemed circumstantial, but it was awfully convenient. For each of us, there have been long periods of time when we've lived our lives without talking much to one another.

There has been speculation about why I'm the one who decided to move back home and then was nuts enough to ask Ma to join us here. There's Colette's imprinting idea. It could have something to do with horoscopes or past lives. Maybe Ma has simply put me under a spell. Most likely, it's my caretaking habit, the result of the gardener incident in Ireland. By the time I invited Ma here, I hoped all the work I'd done on that episode in therapy had paid off enough so we could find a new way of dealing with one another.

I don't want to think there's any such thing as *Special*, it seems terribly wrong to see things that way, but maybe, being the youngest, I am just the least damaged of all of us.

Back during the cancer, I asked Ma once if she had any thoughts on how her illness figured into God's Great Plan—if there was any benefit to be found in the challenge she was facing. Her answer was immediate: This ordeal would help to heal the family and bring us together. In our worst moments of despair, I've tried to hold onto this thought. More and more, I feel we're almost there. I can't wait for Ma to move to the Abbey where I'll be closer, and finally maybe calm enough to help her cope. I can't wait to see how things turn out, when the whole family has a chance to discover they can enjoy this lovely person she's becoming.

First things first: Happy ending or no happy ending, I'm going to call Felix. Then I'm going to get on that plane, and take my boys to Guana.

20.
Keep

—A BASKET OF CORKS with something stuck to them.

—What?

—A basket of corks.

—What do they look like?

—They've got something stuck to them.

—Something's stuffed in them?

—No, Ma, STUCK.

—What's stuck?

—CORKS.

—Forks?

I'm standing on a chair in Ma's walk-in closet in the Mills House, working my way through her top shelves. I'm determined to include Ma in this process as much as is humanly possible. Colette and I got rid of the top layer of obvious dumpables last month, and now it's down to the nitty-gritty. What does Ma want to keep? This means describing every item to her so she can be the one to make decisions. It's going okay. The current roommate is so out of it she wouldn't know a TV if it jumped up and bit her, so it's much easier for Ma to talk on the phone now. I still think she needs that new hearing aid. The good news is I finally got a Bluetooth gadget for my cell phone—this is not the kind of thing you want to do with wires attached to you, if you can avoid it.

—These corks, Ma. What do you want to do with them?

—Let's give them to somebody.

—Who?

—Who might like to have them?

—Not me, thanks.

—The great-grandchildren?

—Ma, these are corks with some kind of gross red stuff sort of stuck to them. I don't think your great-grandchildren would want them. I just wasn't sure if they were some necessary art thing or other.

—Oh. Well, I don't know. . . .

—I'm throwing them away. If you don't know what they are and I think they're disgusting, then they can't be important. Here I go throwing them away. Walking to the trash bag. Bye-bye, corks.

We've already done her books. She's giving a ton of them to Father Nectarios for the church library. There's not much room in the new place, so Ma's mostly keeping vital personal items and whatever is particularly essential to her spiritual health.

—*What about* God's Fools: The Lives of the Holy Fools For Christ?

—*Very important. Keep.*

—*Thought so. What about* How to Behave and Why?

—*I thought I gave that to you.*

—*You did, for the kids for Easter. A book on manners was so very thoughtful. This must be your copy. And here's the one by Bill O'Reilly you gave us for Christmas.*

—*What's the title?*

—*It's called* The Nasty Hypocrite's Guide for Little Old Ladies Who Want to Insult Their Grandchildren.

—*Susie!*

—*Sorry.* The O'Reilly Factor for Kids: A Survival Guide for America's Families.

—*Keep.*

—*Here's one called* Orthodox Faith and Life in Christ *by Justin*

Popovich, translated by Asterios Somebodyorother et al. I can't pronounce it.

—What does the cover look like?

—It's got an old guy with a long white beard and glasses. He looks like he's falling asleep at his desk.

—Keep.

—This one's called The Elder Somebodyelse of the Aegina.

—Who is on the cover?

—Another old guy with a beard and a hat.

—Oh, he's fabulous. Yes.

—Saint Arsenios the Cappodocian. Old guy with a beard, no hat. It's a drawing, not a photo. He's wearing a blanket on his head.

—For Father Nectarios. No, wait. Keep.

—Saint John of Kronstadt. Keep, I know. Oh . . . wow, this is from another life . . .

—What?

—I wonder if you ever read this book I just found on your top shelf.

—Which?

*—*Srebrenica: Record of a War Crime.

—What on earth is that?

—This is the one I gave to you for perspective, after you gave us that O'Reilly book. It's about the war in Bosnia when these Orthodox Christian Serbs rounded up thousands of Muslims and murdered them. What should I do with it?

—Well . . .

I used to take such offense at Ma's righteousness, how she insists Muslims hold the monopoly on depravity—as if all Christians are perfect. My seething indignation is gone now, melted away. I guess I needed to learn tolerance as much as I felt she did. It's kind of sweet that she actually kept this book.

—I'll give it to the Episcopal church, it's more their thing anyway. Ma?

—Yes?

—I love you no matter what you believe.
—That's good.
—Yes, it is.

There were some fabulous finds among the books: Ma's journals from the south of France before the Second World War, with a long account of a reckless teenage adventure she and Bobs had featuring a suspicious amount of schnapps, and a ski trip to the mountains with older friends all mixed up in a tempestuous love triangle. There was a gun involved and a car accident, and Bobs ended up in a hospital before they could escape. Wow—keep.

And, there's a curious, crumbly old volume belonging to Ma's mother, the adultering bolter: *King's Daughters' Journal.* The King's Daughters was a ladies' group devoted to good works at the turn of the century. It seems they put out this diary-type book with space for personal entries on all the days of the year. Each blank page is headed with a virtuous quote, like:

So let our lips and lives express
The holy gospel we profess;
So let our works and virtues shine
To prove the doctrine all divine.
—Rev. I. Watts

Granny must have been spiritually tone-deaf at the time. It is on these pages that she saw fit to meticulously hand-copy reams of love letters from Grandsir the flyer during their affair. Very odd letters to read, full of romantic nicknames and sappy declarations of eternal devotion. Perhaps Ma and I have a shared inclination to differ ideologically with our mothers.

Tucked between the pages is a picture of the dashing couple on horseback together near the polo field at Penllyn, posing on exactly the same spot as David and the children in their swimsuits, in that wonderful painting Ma gave me. The tree whose branch I know and love in the foreground of my painting is just a sapling in this old 1919 photograph. *Keep.*

—Ma, let's talk about the art.

—Yes.

—Felix noticed there's a gallery area near the dining room at the Abbey. He thinks you could have a little show if you like.

—Oh no.

—Why not? I'll bet people would love to see your paintings, and your place is so small. You want to sell some things, right?

—Yes, but not like that. Just for friends. I'm Mother Brigid now—this and the black clothes will be confusing enough for everyone at the Abbey. I'm trying to simplify. I don't want to arrive there and be *Mother-Brigid-who-used-to-be-Marjorie-von-Moschzisker-and-would-you-like-to-buy-some-pictures.*

—Got it. Ma. Can I ask you something?

—Of course.

—When did you realize you wanted to be a nun?

—Years ago.

—After Daddy died?

—No, I started thinking about it long before that. When I was little.

—Wow.

—Yes. Father Basil says my whole life has been a pilgrimage. Now I've arrived.

Our parents' marriage was harsh for quite a while. When I was in boarding school, Daddy felt so desperate over their inability to compromise on his budgets that he moved out and sold the antiques from his side of the family to clear their debts. The formal separation lasted two years. Daddy still took care of Ma, paying her an allowance and the rent of our family home, from a distance and with firm rules. She's acknowledged that her satisfying career as a portrait painter might never have flourished without that forced incentive.

Daddy had his second heart attack just after he left her. He went to live in a small run-down dump of a hotel near our house. When I was home for vacations, I used to meet him at a local pub for dinner and watch him numb himself with martinis. He'd ask questions about school and my life, and then forget my answers and ask the same questions again. One balmy summer evening, he invited me back to his place—he had a cassette tape I'd never heard, of Martin Luther King's "I Have a Dream" speech. His little room was a shock: so sad, with his undershirts and socks drying on the edge of the bathtub. He perched on the bed so I could sit in his only chair, and we listened to Reverend King in rapt silence.

Years later, just when David and I had first moved back to Philadelphia with the children, I ran into an older couple who used to do things with my parents before they separated. I was glad to see these old friends after so many years, but that night I called Daddy in Florida to tell him I couldn't figure out why they'd seemed a little cold. He explained that after he'd left Ma, this couple had invited him to dinner.

—*We've picked you instead of Marjorie*, they said.

He was so affronted on Ma's behalf (and well-oiled cocktail-wise,

I'm guessing) that he told them both off and stalked out before they could serve the main course.

Corporate law was too dull for Daddy's taste. He had a varied legal career as a prosecutor and defense lawyer. He wrote, too, and still deserves some credit for a historic period of rejuvenation in Philadelphia under the Democrats. He so respected Ma's conviction about the necessity for art in all our lives that he eventually dreamed up the "One Percent for Fine Arts" program: One percent of public money spent on any building project must be used for fine arts—sculptures, frescoes, murals, and fountains, whatever. Whenever I go in the city, I'm bumping into reminders of Daddy—Claes Oldenburg's *Giant Clothespin* by City Hall, or Ralph Helmick and Stuart Schechter's pewter birds suspended in patterned flocks above my head at a ticketing lobby in the airport—and I'm thinking about his relationship with Ma.

They got back together when he joined AA, to all our amazement. They still had their moments, like when she backed her car over his shih tzu. (*Your father left the front door open, and Dusty wandered out and fell asleep in the driveway. I told him he had to be careful about the door, but he doesn't pay attention!*) Daddy was extremely sentimental about his pets.

Anyway.

—What should we do with the Chinese barrel?

—That could go to Margaret—it's in her portrait, she might like to have it.

—There are a few more books here I must have missed.

—Oh, what?

—There's one called *The White Stallions of Vienna.*

—That's for Colette. She loves the Lipizzaners.

—What about *The Birds of North America*?

—Keep. Birds are very important.

—*A Stranger in Spain.*

—Strangers on a train?

—One stranger. In Spain.

—Oh. I mumph . . .

—Ma?

—Yumph . . .

—Ma, do you need to go to sleep now or can we go on?

—No, I'm all right. What did you say about *strange brains*?

—A STRANGER. In SPAIN.

—Why would I have that?

—I don't know; it's your book. Do you want to learn Spanish?

—Give it to your cousin Christine. She's taking her daughter to Spain.

—Okay. Christine. Now, *Gut Instinct: What Your Stomach Is Trying to Tell You.*

—Definitely keep.

—Strong's *Exhaustive Concordance of the Bible*? It's an updated edition. Sounds exhausting to me.

—Ha-ha. Keep.

As Ma became more and more religious, Daddy had to find ways to keep up with her on his own terms. They went to church together. He embarked on a column for the local Florida paper, earnestly exploring the key aspects of a given religion each week—Buddhism, Judaism, Lutheran, what have you. Ma was his editor.

I stop for a minute to look at a framed photograph—a real treasure.

Colette took this picture. We all have our copies. Ma and Daddy in Sarasota, probably taken a year or two before he died. Sparkling water, bleached wood. A faded sky.

It's a picnic on a dock; Ma is holding a paper plate. She has a little cross around her neck. They're both wearing beautiful turquoise button-down shirts that almost match—Daddy's is cotton, and Ma's is definitely linen. Daddy has a jaunty straw hat to keep his freckles out of the sun, and Ma's adjusting the brim for him. His eyes are closed, and he's patiently dipping his head so she can reach, with dignified acquiescence. And they're smiling; it seems like he's just teased her about something that made them both laugh. Daddy did love to make Ma laugh.

This is a picture I hold in my heart. *Keep, yes, keep.*

I was furious at Daddy for quite a while after he died, even before I heard the rumors about his gambling at the golf club. He had made some effort to warn us that Ma would need financial help. But the closer I looked into their affairs, the more clear it became that his children (who had not much of a sibling bond at that point) had been left with a colossal, time-consuming, emotionally draining, and expensive mess. Given the circumstances, it was mostly going to be *my* mess, and could end very badly for Ma. The most disappointing thing was that if the two of them had been more practical, the job I'd volunteered for could have been so much less stressful. I kept wondering what he was thinking would happen. I'd look at that picture of them in their matching shirts, smiling and fiddling away while Rome burned around them, and just think *Phooey.*

There was a night that first year after Daddy died when despair really kicked in: I was in the middle of selling their Florida house and apartment hunting for Ma and dealing with the accountant I'd had to hire to sort out the three years of tax mistakes Daddy seemed to have overlooked, and somehow trying to convince Ma she couldn't afford to keep racking up bills with her icon video project no matter how much she thought all humankind needed it, and figuring out how to set the boundaries so there wouldn't be any unfortunate episodes with Ma and the kids.

That night, I got the kids to bed and went outside to stew on the back steps. I was so focused on my anger at Daddy, I wished more than anything he hadn't gone and died so I could tell him to his face how *stupid* he was, and ask him *why, why* did he do this, and, this *terrible* job of his that I'd somehow inherited SUCKED and he was *really bad at it.* WHAT did he think the end of Ma's life would be like, or mine and David's and our children's for that matter? And WHY did he even marry her and *create* this problem if he couldn't solve it before he had to go and DIE? I mentally shook my fist at the night sky in the general direction of where he might be right then, and thought *Daddy! What am I going to DO???*

Then I emptied my mind for a minute and listened. I'm not psychic and I don't even like the idea of communicating with spirits; whether that's possible or not is beside the point. But I was so desperate; I sat there on the steps, looked up at the stars, and waited.

I waited, and then I heard something that I've puzzled about a lot over the years. Even now, I think I'm only just beginning to understand and appreciate what I heard that night after I'd railed at my recently deceased father and demanded he come back right away and explain himself, or help, or *do something for lord's sake*.

He laughed. I really heard him laugh.

The laughter went on for a while, and it grew, and sort of embraced me. It's hard to explain. It was so so real.

Daddy had a great laugh, warm and intelligent and full of compassion. His laugh was never at anyone's expense; it always included us. When he took me for driving lessons in his eager little orange VW bug, I'd regularly stall out on this one hill on a quiet road behind the golf course and start to roll backward, feverishly trying to get back in first gear, squeaking in monkey panic:

—*Ohmygodohmygodhelpohmygoddaddyhelpdaddyhelp!*

He always kept his cool on that hill. He didn't barrage me with rapid-fire instructions. He'd sit back and wait till I figured it out. And he'd laugh, like we were both having the most jolly time rolling backward down the hill by the sixth fairway. As if we were sharing the most wonderful joke.

That used to really piss me off.

So here we are some three decades later, Ma and I: We're on the sun-faded dock in our matching shirts. She'll be adjusting my jaunty straw hat from now on, and I'm working on my humility and patience. Rome's not burning anymore, and we both really know how to laugh.

Toward the end of his life, Daddy told me he was hoping he'd be the first to die, because life would be just too dull without Ma. She kept him amused, he said.

I think I kind of know how he felt.

Sarasota, 1995

21.
Sisyphus

LIFE IS GOOD. Why can't I enjoy it?

The apartment at the Abbey is all painted and carpeted. I'm moving Ma's stuff in tomorrow, right after the twins head out for their Latin final. Then I'll have a couple of weeks to make things ready before I pick her up. I'll spend the night in Carlisle so we can get an early start in the morning, and Ma can stop briefly at the church for a big bash they're having that weekend. The Bishop (that hottie with the long black braid and the *Harry Potter* sorting hat) will be there, and she doesn't want to miss him.

David's home right now, but he's taking off again soon. Ma's move to the Abbey is timed for a weekend when the boys are staying with friends at the shore (we're not dumb enough to leave teenagers alone in the house overnight). She'd like to stay a little longer and go to a special service the following week when the Bishop's in town, but I've explained this is my only free block of time. Ma offered to find a friend to drive her, but I won't hear of it. There's nobody else I trust to get her here safely.

—*You're very overprotective, Susie.*

—*This is nonnegotiable, Ma. You're barely over the last accident. You are not going anywhere,* especially *that church, with anyone but me.*

The other day, I realized what this two-year crisis has been like: Sisyphus. He couldn't stand it that everyone had to die. So he went against the gods and imprisoned Death. Death escaped, because you can't defy fate, and when it was time for Sisyphus to go to the underworld, *he* tried to escape as well. Sisyphus was very persistent, but the gods finally caught him and they were pissed. They decided that for all eternity, Sisyphus would have to push a rock all the way up to the top of a mountain. At the top, the rock would always roll down. So Sisyphus would have to start over. And over. And over again. A bit like those driving lessons in Daddy's orange bug car out behind the golf course.

As for me, I've really been in trouble, because I've had not just one huge boulder, but two. I've had the mother, and I've had the children—I've been running back and forth, trying to keep them all rolling at once. No wonder I'm such a wreck.

They call us the Sandwich Generation: people with school-age children and aging parents, stuck in the middle, everyone depending on us. Seems normal, right? Families are families, what's the big deal? Ever since cavemen there have been parents and grandparents and children. But what's getting people's attention these days is that my generation decided to wait a little to have our babies. So we're older than we used to be with children still in the home. And, with advances in medicine, our parents are living longer than cavemen's parents did.

I know what a sandwich cavewoman like Mrs. Ugh, say, would do if she was busy with baby Wugh Ugh when her elderly, toothless father needed someone to mash up his mastodon burger for him (with the shortened life span, Grandpa Ugh would be elderly and toothless by maybe age thirty). Mrs. Ugh could simply shout across the campfire if she needed help with Grandpa Ugh. Then her sister, Mrs. Mugh, would hop to it right away. Mrs. Mugh could let her teenage son, Lugh Mugh, handle the firewood chopping for a few minutes, so she could lumber over and chew up Grandpa Ugh's burger for him. (Oh, that lucky, carefree Mrs. Mugh—no worries about Lugh's Latin grades for her!)

And Mrs. Ugh's husband wouldn't have to travel all over the

continent looking for mastodon meat, either. He'd just go out with his friends for the day every once in a while, and they'd all bring it back together, no problem. That way, Mrs. Ugh wouldn't be thinking about how maybe it might not be such a good idea to have Grandpa Ugh stay in their cave with them. She wouldn't be worried about who'd be around to help chew Grandpa Ugh's burgers when Wugh and all the other little Ughs went clambering out of the cave to start their own families.

In fact, Mrs. Ugh wouldn't be feeling the urge to explore some new interests once the little Ughs were grown, and maybe even travel around keeping Mr. Ugh company on all his long-distance mastodon hunts, and looking out, say, for all those filthy foreign cave sluts that have been flinging themselves at him all these years.

Mrs. Ugh's marriage must have been a smashing success.

Start saving now for your own CCRC like the Abbey. The numbers of Sandwich people are supposed to quadruple by the time our generation's little Ughs are all grown up. Either that or you could join the clergy.

Ma's actually right; I am overprotective, I know it. Maybe I should just let her get a ride down from Carlisle if she wants more time with the priests so badly, but the thought of her falling again and being stuck up there is unacceptable. I won't chance it.

—*Wretched girl, woe on you! What life remains for you? Who will now approach you? To whom will you seem beautiful? Whom will you now love? Whose will you be?*

—That's not quite right, Sam. It's *whose will you be said to be.*

—God.

—Sam. Start over.

—*Wretchedgirlwoeonyou. Whatliferemainsforyou. Whowillnow approachyou. Towhomwillyouseembeauiful. Whomwillyounowlove. Whose. Will. You. Be. Said. To be.*

—Perfect.

—*Whom will you kiss? To whom will you bite the lips?*

—Good lord. Bite the lips?

—Mama. Stop.

—Tell me again, why are we doing this?

—Because you are making me, Mama. Because you are obsessed and insane.

—Hush. I know that, but why *this* stupid thing? Why not just memorize verbs?

—Because. This is the only part of the exam I have any chance of getting right. If I can't memorize this, I'll flunk Latin.

—Is he going to give you the Latin version of this *bite the lips* poem printed in the exam tomorrow?

—Yes, but—

—So you're only supposed to translate it? Why don't you just sit here with the Latin version and practice translating it?

—It won't work that way.

—What do you mean? Why won't translating it work?

—I can't.

—Why not? This is stupid, Sam; it's a Latin exam.

—I don't know any Latin.

—Of course, you do. You've been studying it for four years.

—I don't.

—You mean the only way for you to pass this Latin class is to ignore the Latin completely and simply cram a bunch of pointless English gibberish into your brain and vomit it out onto the page tomorrow?

—Yeah, pretty much.

—*Man*, Sam . . .

Sam's not a fool. He gets along great with the English department; I think they share his anarchic inclinations. I keep telling him he could be a lawyer if that garbage collector idea of his falls through. You'd think Latin would be a good idea for someone whose mother thinks he should go to law school. But if Sam doesn't understand something, he doesn't like to bother.

Ben's managing, but even he and the other boys can't keep up with the smarty-pants girls in their class. He and Sam sit in the back, trying to crack each other up without getting caught. The year has been one long, miserable hate-fest with students acting out nonstop, and Mr. Goodfellow, the Latin teacher, at the end of his rope.

Sam hates Latin. He has tried all year to get the hang of it. I stayed out of this as much as I could; a friend in the math department told David I've got a bit of a reputation. (Who *me*?) So when Sam told me he couldn't for the life of him figure out how to do translations, I offered outside tutoring and suggested he talk to his teacher. Sam did try, but he hasn't had much success getting through to Mr. Goodfellow, and at this point he's exasperated.

And here we are on the night before the final. Sam's average is D minus. This is the last year of the high school language requirement. After the exam tomorrow, Sam can forget all the Latin he knows (this should not take long). Mr. Goodfellow has sent a courtesy email warning about Sam's shaky average. Okay: Sam has convinced me that everything hinges on his being able to perfectly spout this word-for-word English translation of Catullus, a first-century Roman poet, whining pathetically to his heartless ex-mistress Lesbia.

Memorizing the English and not even looking at the Latin is obviously ridiculous. This can't possibly be what Mr. Goodfellow has in mind, but it's clearly too late now for Sam to learn any Latin. Ben's not studying this way, but I've somehow ended up sitting here enabling Sam in a truly pointless exercise. How do I talk myself into things like this? What kind of parent would encourage such a blatant rejection of learning?

I guess our predicament could be worse. What if I were helping Sam write the verses out on his wrist or something, letting him practice sneak peeks? At least, he won't be breaking the honor code.

I think I hate Latin, too. I've never studied it, but I definitely, definitely hate it.

Mr. Goodfellow insists he doesn't hate Sam, but I'm skeptical. Sam says he doesn't hate Mr. Goodfellow, but I wouldn't blame either of them for having their moments. I have moments like this where I'm not overly fond of Sam *or* Mr. Goodfellow. What's the point of teaching if your students make you despair every day? It's not like he gave birth to them or anything.

Actually, I wouldn't blame Mr. Goodfellow if he decided to hate me, too. Poor Mr. Goodfellow, he's simply trying to manage like the rest of us. *I* could despair just thinking about it.

I had to beg Sam to let me help. Usually, he refuses. He let me give him some tips for his *Macbeth* paper recently, because I got him to laugh by pointing out the running theme of Macbeth's sexual complexity:

—Listen, Sam, here's Lady Macbeth: *"When you durst do it, then you were a man, and to be more than what you were you would be so much more the man"—she's saying he can't get it up!*

—*All right, all right. Okay, I get it.*

—*And here's Macbeth himself: ". . . and put a barren scepter in my gripe, thence to be wrenched by an unlineal hand, no son of mine succeeding"—think about it, Sam. It's masturbation!*

—*Mama. I get it. Shut up.*

Maybe Sam's letting me work with him tonight because he's hoping for more entertainment.

—What is this guy Catullus' problem, Sam?

—He's a loser. He's all hung up on Lesbia, and she's DTF for the entire city of Rome.

—DTF? What's that?

—Down to F—. You know, she's a skank. The town whore.

—That's interesting. Lesbia's not the first name you'd think of for a town whore. What does her name mean in English?

—Mama. I *told* you. I don't *know.* They were together basically one time and then she dumped him and he couldn't get over her. And she was a whore anyway, sleeping with everyone she could get her hands on while he wrote all these stupid love poems about their tragically doomed romance. Catullus was a tool, but now everybody thinks he's this genius poet. All the other people's decent poems got blown up by volcanoes or burnt by barbarians, and we're stuck memorizing Catullus.

—Try the next one, Sam.

—*Unhappy Catullus may you cease being a fool.*

—*To BE a fool.* Does this have to be exactly perfect?

—I think so. *Unhappy Catullus may you cease being a fool.*

—No, Sam. *Cease TO BE a fool. Unhappy Catullus may you cease to be a fool.*

—Dammit.

When I got the email from Mr. Goodfellow, I took it as an opening. I called him to sympathize over how awful the class must have been for him this year. We tried to sort out what to do for Sam. It was a reasonable conversation. He suggested Sam take the exam later in the week, on makeup day, so he'd have a little extra time to study. But Sam wants to get the final over with on-schedule so he can then focus on chemistry. Sam is convinced his brain will be more receptive to this memorization now than it will be the day after chemistry. I'm not so sure.

—I'm going to call him.

—No, Mama, don't. You said you'd stop calling teachers.

—We have to call, Sam. Let's just warn him that you're studying really hard and you may not be ready in the morning, so you may want to take him up on the extension, but you don't know yet, all right?

So I leave Mr. Goodfellow a message.

—*There when those many playful things happened, which you were wanting and the girl was not wanting—*

—Hold it, Sam. *Not not wanting.*

—What is it then?

—That's what it is, Sam: *not not wanting.*

Mutual sigh.

Ring. Ring.

It's Mr. Goodfellow. Turns out you need to give twenty-four hours' notice if you want an extension for an exam.

—Oh, Mr. Goodfellow . . . gosh.

Mr. Goodfellow says he doesn't have the authority to waive the twenty-four-hour rule for Sam, but the head of the upper school, Mr.

Hollins, does. If Mr. Hollins says it's okay, it will be okay with Mr. Goodfellow.

—Do you think he'll say it's okay? Is that typical?

Mr. Goodfellow doesn't know. It's nine-thirty at night. I'm sure the head of the upper school understands how much more important Sam's Latin grade is than anything he himself might be doing, like sleeping. I get Hollins's machine, of course. I leave a message.

—Sam, you'll have to keep cramming till we get him on the phone. Where were we?

—*Now nevertheless meanwhile these things which have been handed over . . .*

Sheesh.

We never hear from Mr. Hollins, so I call his office at the crack of dawn on the morning of Ma's furniture delivery and Sam's exam. He says he'll call Mr. Goodfellow and get right back to us with his answer.

Time passes. Wait. Wait. Wait.

I feel old this morning. There's a huge, growing knot down around my coccyx that's sort of throbbing. Not a good feeling on a moving day.

Mr. Hollins never calls. Maybe this means the answer is no? It's time for Sam to leave for the exam.

—Sam, you'll just have to find out when you get there.

—This is stupid. I'm going to take the stupid thing. I'll be fine.

—No, you need more time. You have a D minus. I'll be at Granny's meeting the movers, so call Papa if they give you the extension and he'll come pick you up. Good luck.

—Please don't call anyone else at school, Mama. Sometimes you're completely delusional about reality. You're just trying to fix your own delusion.

—Sam. I do what I do. I can't help it.

I drive over to the Abbey and sit in Ma's apartment waiting for the movers. Just as I see the truck pulling up outside:

Ring. Ring.

It's my cell phone: Mr. Goodfellow with another courtesy call. There has been no word from Mr. Hollins either way. He's waited as long as he can. It's time to hand out the exams. I'm standing on Ma's balcony flagging down the movers and pointing them toward the elevator.

Beep. Beep.

—Okay, that's that then. Someone's beeping in now—thanks, Mr. Goodfellow, for trying.

Beep.

—Hello?

It's David, to say that Mr. Hollins has just called the house and said it's fine with him if Sam wants an extension.

And *rrrrip,* just like that, right out from between the two hip pockets of my jeans busts my long hairy tail. How is it that I never noticed *that* before? And, my free hand, the one not holding the phone, is hanging down so low I can reach my ankles without even bending my knees. Was it always like this? Well, if that's how things are, why bother to control this urge I've been feeling all morning?

I grab the railing of the balcony and swing myself up the post on the side to hang from the awning pipe and from there I take a flying, jabbering leap—I'm running amok, zigzagging all over Mother Brigid's spanking new studio, tearing out fistfuls of my own fur and scattering it around on her brand-new wall-to-wall carpet. Almost on all fours (one hand still clutching the phone), I streak through Ma's kitchenette into the bathroom, and fling myself around in there using her handicap grab bars. I stamp around in a circle on the little bench in her shower.

—WHY DIDN'T HE TELL MR. GOODFELLOW?!!!!!

—Ouch. Too loud, Susan.

—Oh my GOSH, David. Is he going to tell him? It's too late!

—Susan, calm down.

—Okay, that's it. I'm calling the headmaster. I can't sit back and watch Sam flunk Latin on a technicality.

I dial the main number at the school and ask the operator to put me through to Mr. Zane. While the phone is ringing, what seems like fifty moving men with about five hundred thousand boxes arrive at the door of Ma's tiny studio. Peeping over the boxes is Olivia in her tennis clothes, big welcoming smile on her face, stopping by to see how things are going. I climb up on top of a big pile of boxes and vigorously pound my chest, wave at Olivia, scratch my armpits, and point at the phone clamped to my ear. She takes one look at me and ducks out of sight.

—Hello?

I roar out my story to Mr. Zane, who gets it right away. Mr. Zane is reliably calm, cool, collected, and decisive. The perfect guy to have to deal with nut-job parents like me. He says he'll head over to Mr. Goodfellow's classroom at the girls' school and take care of everything.

Okay, deep breath. Stuff the tail back in the pants.

Why does this keep happening? I thought this happy ending we're having meant I was saved from the fate of being a piece of salami terminally squished between two pieces of Wonder Bread. Maybe Sam's right: Do I run around trying to fix my own delusions all the time? Some kind of need to be needed? You figure it out, and when you do, I don't want to know. I'm busy.

Wretched girl, woe on you!

At dinner that night, Sam describes his morning:

Sam was sitting at his desk in the Latin room taking his exam with all the other students. The grammar section was a wash, as expected. But the Catullus and Lesbia *section—that he could do. He was rolling along writing out verbatim all the gibberish about biting the lips etc., and the door to the classroom opened. Everyone in the room looked up. The headmaster of his school walked in, along with the headmistress of the girls' school. They conferred quietly with Mr. Goodfellow, then all three approached Sam's desk and ordered him sternly to step outside.*

Was Sam Morse in trouble? Everyone watched in fascination and horror as Sam, appalled, got up in the middle of his tenth-grade Latin exam and made the long walk out to the hall with the heads of the two schools.

—How are you doing, Sam? asked Mr. Zane.

—Fine, said Sam.

—How's the exam going?

—Uh . . . fine.

—We want you to know that you can take it on another day if you like.

—Oh.

—Would you like to go home and take it on another day?

—Uh, no thanks. I'm, uh. I'm fine.

Every once in a while, Colette and I speculate on how Ma's death will affect us when the time comes. At the height of my exasperation, I was sure I'd feel nothing but relief when this job is over. Colette has always thought otherwise, and these days I'm beginning to grasp that she's right. I don't like to think about Ma's death too much, but the image I have is from the Coyote/Road Runner cartoons—they've been on one of their classic chases along dusty desert trails, and the Road Runner veers off just before they get to a cliff. The Coyote doesn't react fast enough, and he keeps running several yards off the edge of the precipice.

When he loses momentum, there's a pause, suspended midair, still in running position. He turns his head, looks blankly at the camera. He blinks once or twice. Then gravity takes over and he plummets (leaving his blinking eyes behind for a second or something), splats face down, limbs akimbo, stamping a permanent Coyote-shaped snow angel on the floor of the canyon thousands of feet below. Whatever the emotional equivalent is of his suspended blinking moment followed by that surprise free-fall, there's no way around it: That's what I'll be going through when Ma meets her maker.

And this I know: When I stumble cursing to answer the phone much too early in the morning, and I don't see Ma's phone number on caller ID after all, a fist will clamp around my heart. When I find myself keening mawkishly in the condiments aisle at the supermarket, clutching a bottle of *plain olive oil* to my breast, I will be profoundly grateful. Because all I've ever really wanted is to feel this way about my mother.

When I studied French, we read *The Myth of Sisyphus* by the philosopher Albert Camus. Camus had his own take on the situation. He likened Sisyphus to a drone in an office or factory, working a pointless job. He imagined what Sisyphus was thinking each time he had to trudge back down the mountain after his runaway rock and start over. The hopelessness. But Camus also decided that once Sisyphus could actually own up to how ridiculous his activity was, he would find peace. If he could acknowledge this truth, he could learn to live with it.

So here I am, acknowledging my truth.

Okay, I don't really remember all that from my college French classes—I reviewed it on Wikipedia this morning. But the point is there is nothing wrong with me for having this urge to push rocks up hills. Even if it's true that where the rocks end up doesn't always make much difference in life, what's the harm in trying, if I feel inclined?

Shoot me. I'm a rock roller.

And honestly, a simian attitude just happens to come with this territory; it's even fun to hang by your tail on occasion. The key is self-awareness. As long as my conscience can cop to what I'm really doing, I'll have acceptance and peace whenever I need it.

Fine: I'm a *monkey* rock roller. A *monkey coyote* rock roller. On rye, easy on the mustard, pickle on the side.

Sam got his Latin grade up to a C for the year. Don't ask me how.

Just get Ma to the Abbey. If that happens, I promise: I'll keep my tail in my pants.

And I will never meddle in my children's schooling again.

I promise.

22.
The Four Seasons

I KEEP THINKING about something that happened to David and me once, in Santa Monica.

It was about fifteen years ago. We were there for an event with just enough time for a quick walk on the beach. The Santa Monica beach is freaky any day of the week. It's like a sideshow: boom boxes and baby strollers, musclemen with tattoos, lots of fake breasts and addicts asleep under cardboard boxes. It's all so weird that nothing really surprises you.

But we were both struck by a group of men walking toward us: three young guys with perfect *GQ* haircuts, very tall and fit, identical black T-shirts carefully tucked into tailored, belted black dress pants. Even their matching dark sunglasses seemed out of place. Was this a fashion shoot? They were all wearing shoes. There was something just off about them.

Then suddenly: those eyes. Vivid blue and alert. Creased smile lines crisscrossing old, well-tended skin. Wallabee shoes, khaki pants. A Mister Rogers-style beige cashmere cardigan sweater buttoned all the way. A baseball cap slightly askew.

He looked right at us, and his face lit up as if we were friends, but he didn't stop moving. The *GQ* guys swept him along—one on either side of him and one a little behind. He turned from side to side to wave with delight at everyone they passed.

Nobody else stopped their kite flying or sunscreen applying or overdosing to look, which was extraordinary.

Ronald Reagan in retirement. Out for a walk with the Secret Service.

I wasn't particularly political in the 1980s. We lived in L.A. then and volunteered regularly at a food giveaway program at our church. We saw the lines grow longer during each year of Reagan's presidency. We had friends dying of AIDS, a disease nobody in power seemed to take seriously—it was just a gay man's predicament, and not worth the trouble. We listened to poetry readings—firsthand stories of murders in El Salvador, committed by the rebels our government openly encouraged. David followed the news more than I, and was particularly disgusted by the Iran-Contra scandal. Reagan emerged so unscathed.

Many disagree about what kind of president he was. It's a matter of perspective. This was our perspective.

Until we had children and the economy began to fall apart in the early 1990s, I didn't think about policy. Selfishly, it didn't concern me until I sensed my own little world was affected. But the entertainment industry began to suffer, it got hard for many actors to find work, and that's when I roused. I took an uncharacteristically intense satisfaction voting Democrat in 1992. I blamed Reagan and his malfunctioning trickle-down economic theories, and wished I could give him a piece of my mind for endangering all of us, especially my children. I'm known to hold a grudge.

Now, here was the man who did not help our dying friends, the man who said homeless people were homeless by choice as he cut programs and their numbers ballooned out of control. Ketchup became a *vegetable*. This was our moment, a chance to tell off a supposed villain. Instead, David and I watched him melt into the beach crowd. Then we looked at each other, eyes brimming.

David thinks what got him so moved was mostly the unexpected jolt of that poignant proof of mortality—this man who had once seemed so powerful and destructive, was all of a sudden just a little boy out for a walk on the beach.

As for me, I just think it will be so lovely if we *all* end up on the beach.

The Abbey has turned out to be more than good; it's excellent.

There was a robin's nest in full production right outside Ma's front door when she arrived late last spring. Her cozy studio now has all the icons hung, by David, the master picture hanger. She's on the second floor with a balcony that looks out on trees and a children's playground. After being wrenched from the lovely gardens she created in Philadelphia and Florida, followed by over a decade on the tenth floor at the Mills House with windows that only opened a crack, then finally enduring that six-month incarceration upstate, Ma's enjoying the open air.

She passed her scooter test and has a shiny blue one with a basket and MOTHER BRIGID tacked to the bumper. Now she can zip around the grounds, a sporty version of *Whistler's Mother*, always in black with her long white hair flying behind like a banner: down to the library to check out the *Wall Street Journal*, over to the dining room for lunch with old and new friends. There's the greenhouse and gardens and sunning herself on the patio by the pool on bright summer days. Movie nights. A spacious art studio with plenty of natural light and easy-to-reach cubbies for all Ma's supplies. Father Basil came for a visit, and Ma went to Carlisle for an overnight in the fall, with everything carefully planned down to the last detail. She keeps talking about how grateful and happy she is.

Sam is learning to drive. He lucked into a great crop of teachers this year, and he's getting all As and Bs. He aced his PSATs. Ben is squiring his girl around in a little blue Camry. Eliza has a job taking pictures for the college paper, and David is at home. Our house is a hive of writers: homework and history papers. David's novel. We confer daily to exchange thoughts, and Colette is just a click away.

I've been reading my chapters to Ma as soon as the printer spits them out. She alternately shouts with laughter, marvels at how much I remember, and blusters in almost-mock indignation at my tendency to dwell on disgusting and personal details. (*Really, Susie. It needs polish; your edges are dreadfully rough!*)

The helpers at the Abbey are called "companions." Long-Term Care still covers them. They come as needed to give a hand with anything you require, so Ma is treated like a queen by people of all shapes, sizes, and ethnicities. She appreciates every one of them and it's clear the admiration is mutual. I hear things like "your mother is a lovely lady. . . ." Some of the former aides who used to come around before the Carlisle escapade have even tracked her down to make sure everything's all right. Ma is flattered.

And now, Barack Obama is in like Flynn.

That part didn't sit too well with Ma. For a minute or two during the financial crash, it looked like she was leaning his way. But I hooked up her TV just in time for the Republican Convention, unfortunately. She must have gotten mixed up about that suspicious middle name they kept repeating. She seemed a little agitated for a few days after the election, but we'll cut her some slack. He's in, he's in, he's in.

Oh, and ESD. *Heh-heh-heh.*

I stuck it out through all the levels of appeal by phone and by mail, and refused to give up when the final one was denied on the same basis. (*Ms. von Mopfister was not progressing. She needed to be put out of her misery posthaste. Please let us know if you need any further assistance with this matter. Warmest regards, ESD.*)

When we got an appointment for a September phone hearing, I sent all the papers in with weeks to spare. Everything was copied as directed to everyone involved, including ESD: letters of support from the surgeon and the therapists at Cloverfield, letters of lack of support from ESD, the works. By Certified Mail. Signature Required on Delivery. Return Receipt Requested.

The judge's office reminded us repeatedly that Ma could use a lawyer for the hearing, but I kept my fingers crossed and braved it alone. The Friday before the big day, Cloverfield called to warn me that ESD had just piped up with a request for medical records, but their fax machine didn't seem to be working.

The day of the hearing I was on the edge of my seat.

—Ring. Ring.

—*Hello?*

—*This is Judge Bobby Jameson's office calling. Is this Susan Morse?*

—*Yes, indeed, it is!*

The judge gave me a chance to help him pull out the most crucial page of evidence from the pile of stuff I had sent. Then we conferenced in with a medical director from ESD, who tried to spring their favorite trick on us, claiming they had only received the records that morning. I managed to keep my voice level:

—*Would you like me to fax you the signed receipt showing that the information was sent to ESD over a month ago, Judge?*

—*I think we can go ahead for now, Ms. Morse.*

Score one for Mother Brigid.

ESD's medical director got plenty of opportunities to give their version. The man did his characteristically ESD-ish best to make their side of the case crystal clear, with brilliant, irrefutable arguments, like:

—*Uh . . .*

My closing statement was cathartic. I got to say that despite ESD insisting a full-scale rehabilitation would be futile, indeed Ms. von Moschzisker *had* recovered quite adequately and was currently living independently—no thanks at all to her travesty of a so-called Health Management Organization. Not only that, but also ESD had abandoned my mother much too soon, when her doctors and therapists were adamant she could only recover with their support and treatment. All her bills for the last, crucial few weeks of rehabilitation in skilled nursing had been paid by other means. This was not about money. This was about the principles of respect, and human decency. So there.

ESD's closing statement:

—*Uh . . .*

The judge signed off to do some thinking. Three weeks later, a notice came in the mail:

ESD was responsible for Ma's room, board, and therapy until the exact date her therapists at Cloverfield officially declared her "independent." ESD must pay for an extra twenty-seven days.

Heh-heh-heh.

NOVEMBER 26, 2008

Ma's birthday falls the day before Thanksgiving this year. We'll have turkey together tomorrow at our house. So today, in the interest of variety, I'm taking her to Center City for birthday lunch at the Four Seasons Hotel. The kids want to come!

I've turned in the minivan from my old days as a chauffeur, and leased a new toy in deference to Daddy and the oil crisis: a nice little VW Passat sedan. Sam's had one driving lesson in it, but I'm possessive. This is our first chance to see if we really can fit five people in, three of whom are giants and will have to sit in the back.

We have parcels: bottles of organic honey Ma wants to dole out to friends for Christmas gifts, some of her special yogurt, and a variety of cheeses for entertaining. Tiny plastic stands to prop up the smaller icons on her bookshelf. She's been hinting about a black cashmere cardigan I have and how *it's exactly the kind that would be perfect* for her. Knowing I'd never be able to find this exact one, I got mine dry-cleaned on impulse and wrapped it for her as a gift. I finally found the Liberty fabric she likes (*it's the only thing that doesn't scratch!*) and made her some pillowcases by hand to match the fancy terra-cotta sponge paint she'd just commissioned on the wall behind her bed.

The paint took a little adjusting after she moved in. Ma decided on colors while she was still in Carlisle, using paint chips I sent her. I expressed some concern about her choice for the bathroom.

—*This yellow is pretty sharp, Ma.*

—*That's fine; I want it to have some bite.*

You don't argue with an artist about colors. I sent Felix pictures before she arrived:

—*Wow, that's pretty sharp, Suse . . .*

Ma seemed happy enough when she got there though, and we hung her original blue and green towels. In August, she had her cataracts done, and true to Georgia Brady's word, I didn't have to lift a finger or even make one phone call except to ask Ma how it went. Everything, I mean *everything* was done for us.

But as soon as the first eye was done and Ma went into her bathroom:

—*Heavens, this yellow is TOO SHARP!*

So the bathroom needed a layer of white glaze. Mark, our wonderful painter, enjoyed the artistic stimulation of working with Ma, after he got over the horror himself.

—*That* was *a pretty sharp yellow in that bathroom, Susan.*

And for her birthday, Ma has a new set of towels in sophisticated Golden Wheat, and some jolly pink cyclamen, because she says the air will be dry in winter with the heat on and the windows closed. There's a book about British rooks and crows from Colette (*We all have to read this right now, Susie, it's very important!*). Funds have been pooled for a luxurious full-length cashmere blanket (*Essential!*). From Felix: a brick doorstop she's wanted with a needlepoint frog on the cover, to replace the old cast-iron rooster she's too weak to lift herself (*Look! I can just kick it across the floor!*).

The worries about the future are a past life nightmare. We get to spoil Ma now, and this feels really, really good.

So the kids and I have made a special effort to dress, and I carefully bring up Table Manners in advance. This is new. Having been obsessively scolded all my life about elbows on the table and such by Ma, I have issues. In the first place, she's a hypocrite. We were not supposed to call from room to room, but Ma hollered like a banshee when she wanted to, and I'm sorry to say she sometimes chews with her mouth open and picks things off serving plates with her fingers. The irony is not lost on me: Ma got a degree to teach Montessori. She was one of the founders of Philadelphia's Please Touch Museum in the 1970s, a wonderful place that paved the way for a much-needed new philosophy that made it possible for kids to actually *want* to visit museums. But she was like a harpy with my siblings and me about manners.

When we had children, I vowed not to repeat her mistakes. It has been an interesting experiment with mixed results—the kids have had to pretty much figure manners out for themselves. I've always done my best to shield them from her disapproval, but she chafed under my vigilance and was quick to make up for lost time on the handful of occasions she managed to get them to herself. There was a traumatic Grandparents' Day at the boys' school that still festers, when Ben cried in the car on the way home. The other boys had doting grandparents admiring all their industrious work, and Ben spent the day being barked at by Ma about fetching proper chairs and putting away coats.

But today is Ma's birthday and this year I want things perfect for her, so in the car on the way over, I break my self-imposed gag order and gently ask them to keep their elbows off the table at lunch.

—*What did she say about our elbows?*

—*It doesn't matter, you know I don't care about your elbows, but Granny does. There are some situations where elbows are important, and you're going to have to suck it up because this is one of them. It's her birthday; let your elbows be your present. I don't want you guys to feel bad about Granny today, so please get over it—she's a lot of fun to be with now, she really is nice. . . .*

They get that. They've noticed how nice Ma is, I don't really have to tell them, but I want so much for this to be happy for everyone. Mending is tricky, but everyone's game and we're all in pretty good spirits. I send them up ahead with the packages while I park.

The kids are a surprise—Ma thought it would be just the two of us. She loves having everyone together, so she is thrilled, showing off her new digs and getting them to put everything away where it belongs and take the iron rooster out to the balcony (*you have a rooster??*) and find her hearing aid, which has fallen under the bedside table where she can't reach.

So we go downstairs and everyone gets to see how Granny works her scooter—she has to face the back of the elevator and back out carefully—and she barely crashes into anything. We leave the scooter at the curb, and Ma slowly slowly slowly walkers to the car and *eeeeeases* herself into the front seat without falling in a heap and breaking every bone in her body before we can celebrate her birthday. *Thank God that's done.* I'm impressed at the difference between the ways she handles herself at home and abroad. Ma can ricochet around her studio like a marble in a life-size 3-D Christian-themed pinball game, because it's set up so well and she knows where everything is. But when she goes out, she's savvy enough to think before she moves.

I stow the walker in the trunk. The children stuff themselves in the back, grumbling about seatbelts and knees. Ma laughs, offering to move her seat forward and they say *no thanks.* I am in HEAVEN.

Ma remembers to put her seat belt on. This was a little passive-aggressive game we played for most of my years as Ma's driver. She would start talking the minute we got in the car, *forgetting* to buckle up. I would refuse to start the car until she did buckle. Sometimes we'd sit there for a full fifteen minutes till she paused for a breath. Then when I'd ask her to buckle, Ma would reach for it and I'd start the car. But as soon as we were rolling, she'd have all this *trouble* figuring out how to work the thing (*this is* very *poorly designed—so unnecessary!*), and I'd have to pull over again so I could reach all the way over to fix it. Ma always remembers her seat belt now.

I make sure to take Henry Avenue, not because it's faster but because it's prettier while still being smooth. *Pretty* is very important to Ma, but not quite as much as *smooth.* This way, we go past the special public school with the farm—that's a really *pretty* part and Ma tells us the history and points out the cows, and children having a riding lesson in the ring.

We go along the Schuylkill past the boathouses, with Ma reminding us how lucky we are to live in such a beautiful place. I horrify everyone by pointing out the route I'll take in June when I swim in a wet suit down the river as part of a triathlon team in honor of my fiftieth birthday, and show them where David will meet me on the other side to continue the race on his bike. Ben and Sam have a team, too. Ma's so impressed she wants to be there. That would take some doing, but you never know.

At Rocky's steps by the front of the art museum, everything stops. There's a roadblock up ahead, and traffic is dead as a doornail waiting to funnel into a tiny one-lane detour. Well, sorry, this is just not going to spoil our fun. The boys sing songs and I do PG-rated cursing, which makes Ma hoot. The boys are getting hot. I start to fuss about Ma when they open the windows but she says *I'm fine, we can put on my seat warmer, this is such a wonderful car.* Eliza calls for the number of the Four Seasons to warn them, and is connected to some dry-cleaning establishment instead, but who cares? Just try, try again.

We valet park, of course. The little ramp cut into the curb in front of the hotel is like Mount Everest. I glue myself to Ma's back as she walkers up. When we get through the front door, I send Ma with the kids on the handicap route and sprint up the steps to tell the restaurant we're almost there.

—Yes, Mother Brigid's eighty-seventh birthday! We have her special flowers on the table and the cake is ready, everything's fine, no rush.

Five million years later, Ma comes inching one careful step at a time around the corner flanked by the kids, with a small bottleneck of guests behind who don't dare try to pass. Excited to be out somewhere new and different with eyes that can see, she's moving slowly so she gets to really milk each second for what it's worth. She's asking about everything as she creeps along: *Children, look at that chandelier! Where did they get this marble? Who made that jacket in the glass case? What kind of flowers are those? Are they real?*

There's an odd piece of art on display, a giant-size lady's old-fashioned green velvet boot with buttons, which has to be examined and clucked over for several hours. People everywhere are smiling at this ancient little bent-over old lady in black with her long wispy white hair, her Old World accent and charming curiosity, her intriguingly commanding presence, and I think *if you only knew,* but yes, it's BLISS.

We arrive at the restaurant. Every worker in the place seems to drop everything to leap to her side and Ma graciously doles out tasks—*pillows for the chair if you please, the purse can go here and the walker there, yes, thank you.*

Eliza has decided to major in art. This doesn't surprise Ma, who reminds us she identified the talent years ago at a middle school art show when the only thing of note was a print she spotted across a crowded room. She made a point of moving in to identify the artist's name: Eliza Morse. She had it framed, and it's one of the few things besides icons and family photographs Ma asked David to hang in her tiny new place.

The first course arrives. Ma has only ordered a main dish, crab cakes. When she sees my butternut squash soup, I have to order her some, minus the confit of duck.

I look around and notice a small miracle: Nobody's elbows are anywhere near the table.

When the main course arrives, Ma eyes my tuna sashimi salad and wants to know where it was on the menu. But she eats her crab, every last bit. This was a big component of our years of struggle, I realize. I'm sure it's common, when a mother wants what her daughter has, and who wouldn't wish for a cashmere sweater and three funny children, a happy marriage, squash soup? I'm not sure I really know how we've been blessed with this new peace between us. It could be Ma's many months in Carlisle with little to do but pray, talk to priests, and try to get strong. For me, it's partly the Abbey giving me space by taking some of the hard stuff over, of course. That support has given me a chance to stand back and admire this process of aging, and mellowing, and surrender, and grace.

—You can do this too someday, children, says Ma, when I sign the slip.

—What? asks Ben

—Take your mother to the Four Seasons on her eighty-seventh birthday.

Sam snorts.

—When she gets that old, this hotel will definitely be a Walmart—

—What? Oh, poppydop, says Ma, and everyone smiles. Poppy*dop*?

They pack up the rest of the cake and perch the boxed vase of flowers on the seat of Ma's walker, with some special Belgian chocolates for everyone on the house. We make the long voyage back to valet parking with a pit stop at the ladies' room. When we reach the door, we stop again to check whether anything has changed in the big flower display since our arrival.

I take one more mental snap shot of Ma: flanked by her three tall grandchildren, bravely soldiering along through the crowd in the lobby. I think of the blue-eyed man-child with his agents in black on that beach in Santa Monica.

There's a mishmash of holiday families waiting outside the hotel for their cars, a baby sleeping in its stroller. We ease the walker down the front sidewalk's flume ramp again. I'm so busy trying to make myself into a human shield around Ma that I can't reach the vase when it tumbles, box and all, off her walker during the steep descent. *Crash*, everything lands on the cobblestones, and the vase Doesn't Break. A miracle, but also the first sign of Trouble Ahead.

The kids jam themselves into the back again. My Passat has a fancy new trick for valet parking: a little key you can pop out to lock the glove compartment. We discuss all the other features, the knob for the sunroof, and the special compartment in the backseat that accesses the trunk, which somehow I haven't figured out yet.

I decide we'll skip the mess at the art museum and take the non-scenic expressway home on the other side of the river, but we find ourselves in another inexplicable jam. It's three forty-five on a Wednesday, for heaven's sake. Somewhere across from Boathouse Row, stranded in a sea of cars, Eliza starts to speculate about the location of the nearest bathroom. Too much coffee after lunch.

This is an interesting problem, because really there isn't a decent place between here and the Abbey, and if we go out of our way, the extra time including all the traffic will probably mean that Ma will need the bathroom, too, before we get her home. There is definitely not a suitable place for Ma between here and there, even if we do take a longer route.

—Oh dear, says Eliza.

—Can you make it?

—I sure hope I can. . . .

—This is so great, I say. We are having so much fun!

—What? says Ma.

Everyone laughs uneasily. Quite a while later, we have gotten pretty much nowhere and Eliza has begun to squirm. Ma mentions quietly that she has a thing or two to take care of when she gets home involving some very personal supplies she didn't think she would need until at least late in the afternoon, well after four, and she sort of needs them right now actually. It's that cursed *bag*.

We are completely hemmed in. We start to speculate about Ben requisitioning someone's motorcycle. How about we tie Ma's walker to it, strap Ma to the seat, and dodge all the cars to get her home a little quicker? Eliza looks sweaty. I begin to wonder if there's a smell coming from Ma.

This continues till we get off the expressway and into another jam on Henry Avenue. Nobody's upset, we're still having fun, sort of, and I'm kind of tactfully muttering at the people in the other cars that I know it's not their fault but they are all still pretty much a bunch of idiots. Sam points out a knee-high bush with no leaves that might make an okay screen if Eliza hopped out onto the median strip. Eliza's asking us not to make her laugh, which is good, but the conversation has shifted to the medical implications of her situation.

We crawl past the school with the farm and there definitely is a faint smell, but it might be the horses. I keep saying we're almost there and Ben says *Eliza just get out of the car and run for it, it's right over there at the next traffic light.* She's actually thinking about it, but it's really about to get better and we finally finally screech to a halt in the driveway outside the Abbey's main entrance—*Eliza, the ladies' room's right through there, behind the stairs, quick, get out and RUN!*

Ma's another story. I say to Ben *wait right here and don't move.*

—What? says Ma.

—*I can drive,* says Ben.

—*Oh no, you don't,* I say. *You don't know how to work my new car yet. Don't move,* and I take the keys with me, which seem to be a little messed up because the tiny valet glove compartment key thingy is popping out like I haven't clicked it in quite right or something, but there's no time to think. I launch Ma on her way across the lobby and run ahead to make sure this bathroom is the one with handicap bars and things. Yes it is, and there's Eliza coming out of a stall looking restored.

I get to take a minute and tell Eliza *this is the fancy bathroom where Aunt Colette and I went after they made the wonderful offer and we were alone for a second and jumped up and down and silently squealed and hugged each other and bawled, isn't it gorgeous?* I send her off and tell her to wait in Ma's place for the boys. Just when we open the beautiful door, there's Ma—like a cuckoo clock.

I watch her maneuver into the stall, and say *wait right here and don't move, I'll be right back with your supplies.* She tells me where the stuff is in her bathroom. I go back out and Eliza is still in the lobby, rolling her eyes. The boys seem to be locked in the car. It's honking rhythmically with lights flashing because the alarm has been going off the whole time we were all in the restroom.

So I go out to rescue Sam and Ben, who are full of pent-up boy energy from the car ride and all that time with their elbows off the table. I think *oh, what the heck* and give Ben a crash course on how to work the freaky newfangled parking brake and get the weird key out. I ask him to park, unload the cake, and take the flowers and stuff to Ma's apartment where we'll all meet up in a few minutes, because I've decided to run over, collect Ma's equipment, and bring it back in the scooter so she can ride to her apartment without having to stagger along with the walker (she must be exhausted by now) or get in and out of the car.

Ben's got a gleam in his eye as he slides behind the wheel. When Sam takes the passenger seat beside him, they exchange a secret twins' smile. I think *this will not end well.* But fingers crossed, off I go at a sprint. Dashing to Ma's place, grabbing everything that looks colostomy-related (sanitary wipes, a weird sort of pouch that looks like a flesh-colored ziplock Baggie with a large hole cut in the side, some kind of plastic disk that might be an attachment for the Dirt Devil vacuum but it could be vital, and, if all else fails, several pairs of disposable briefs). I try to shoehorn her paraphernalia into my huge purse, no need to broadcast to everyone at the Abbey. Then I rush downstairs, leap on Ma's scooter, and make for the lobby like a bat out of hell.

I'm not as good as Ma with the scooter. There are a few elderly eyebrows raised along the way, but I manage to park it somewhere sort of appropriate, near the mailboxes. I race-walk past a small herd of fragile old souls doddering unsteadily through the lobby and then at last I lurch into the bathroom and lean, panting, against the beautiful door.

—*Is everything okay, Ma?*

Yes, it is! And thank God, I brought all the right stuff. We live a charmed life these days.

The truth is a little messy public spectacle wouldn't have mattered. Everyone at this extraordinarily lovely place is winding up the journey, making the best of it. There is comradeship, and absolute tolerance. Safety in numbers. I pray we're all lucky enough to end up like this.

When we get back to the studio, Eliza is there, enjoying the huge flower arrangement that has arrived from an admiring out-of-town cousin. She's still laughing about a sideshow in the parking lot below Ma's balcony window: My white Passat appears to have given birth to Ben, who was experimenting with that secret passageway in the backseat and has emerged magically out of the trunk headfirst. He is now chasing Sam around all the trees to get his jacket back.

—*What?* says Ma.

Ring. Ring. It's David at home, wondering what on earth happened to everybody.

Ben, Ma, Eliza, and Sam, November 2008

POSTSCRIPT

Ma approves of Michelle Obama. She thinks the new vegetable garden at the White House is going to finally wean us all off processed foods.

She broke her other hip about nine months after she got to the Abbey. Ma's not complaining. She also has new hearing aids. The guy who fitted her for them said she was long overdue for an upgrade, and he could not believe she'd been able to function at all with her old pair.

Of course, I had to read Ma this book from start to finish. She likes it, but there's something Ma thinks everyone needs to know:

—*It's very important.*

—*Go ahead, Ma. You can tell them yourself.*

—*How?*

—*They're reading this. Just say what you want them to hear.*

—*Oh. Well. It's about the opening sentence.*

—*Nobody dies at the end of this book?*

—*Of course they don't.*

—*No, Ma, I mean that's the opening sentence.*

—*But they don't.*

—*Well, actually, Ma, someone did.*

—*No, they didn't.*

—*Yes, Ma. Marbles did. Last summer.*

—*That's a cat. That's different. They don't even know about Marbles.*

—*Yes they do. Chapter Two: Marbles the cat "has been with us since the earthquake and is now hanging on by a thread."*

—*Well, that doesn't matter.*

—*Excuse me, but tell that to Eliza. Marbles was* her cat.

—*Can I tell them what's important or not?*

—*Go ahead.*

—*Nobody dies.*

—*Except Marbles.*

—*Susie!*

—*Sorry. Go ahead.*

—*You spent all that time trying to keep me alive, and your efforts are much appreciated, but I think they should know about Grandsir and me.*

—*They do: Chapter Six. You saw his soul go up through the ceiling.*

—*Right. That's what they all need to know. And you, too. Nobody dies.*

Thanks. I think we got it, Ma.

Philadelphia, 2009

ACKNOWLEDGMENTS

First thanks go to Colette, fellow fair-hair, muse. You asked for this book, gave me the best ideas, and your hand is on every page.

To bus companion, amateur EMT, and godfather Michael Bamberger: for giving me courage, a title, and a publisher.

To Brendan Cahill and everyone at Open Road for believing in this book, and for giving me dream editors: Andrea Colvin, blessed with a valuable combination of discipline, perception, and wit, and Marjorie Braman, who somehow managed to get right inside my head. I suspect she has magical powers.

To David Sedaris, for setting the standard: you don't know me, but when you come to Philadelphia my friend Ellen and I are the ones screaming like Elvis fans. You signed Ellen's book, and now she believes you are her boyfriend. You are not. You are mine.

To Amy Banse, Barbara Ziv, Ellen Hass, Liz Tyson, and all the whip-smart members of Academentia, past and present: you have taught me to recognize good writing. And, to so many other equally challenging, sensitive readers who kindly took time to give valuable feedback, especially Becky Sinkler, Court van Rooten, David Stern, Perri Kipperman, Marion Rosenberg, Joe Dworetzky, Joan Cooke, Chris Van Melzen, Kate Schwarz, Priscilla Baker, Pebble Brooks,

Courtney Kapp, Ruthie Ferraro, Anne Price (who has never let me forget that marinated salmon), Diane Fleming (we will always have Paris), Betsy Down, Mr. Badger (I believe I owe you several thousand ink cartridges), and Felix von Moschzisker.

To our supporters during the crisis: friends, family, clergy, doctors, nurses, therapists, health care administrators, and to those overworked, undercompensated aides and caregivers who show gentle consideration to elderly people in need.

To Michael von Moschzisker, greatly missed, who taught us to believe in the Golden Rule *and* the federal government, and had a disarming way with words.

To the rest of the family tree—those we know now, and those who came before—particularly Ma's cherished brother, Sidney, and her four captivating sisters, Virginia, Rebecca, Priscilla, and Barbara, all sadly no longer with us, each of them every bit as exceptional as our mother.

To Ma: you are loved. You are *Special*.

To Eliza, Ben, and Sam: Thank you for keeping me laughing, and for not freaking out. If any one of you ever writes a book about me, fine. Don't forget there's plenty of embarrassing stuff I could have included in mine and did not.

To my husband, David: For your steadfast patience, faith, generosity, and insight. For insisting I find each chapter's heart, and for always cooking dinner. (I was just kidding about David Sedaris; Ellen can have him. I'm pretty sure you are a better cook than he is anyway.)

PHOTO AND ART CREDITS

Williamstown, 1980	Robert Baker-White
California, 1984	Scott Clarke
Sarasota, 1995	Colette Barrere
Philadelphia, 2009	Colette Barrere
final photo	David Morse

All paintings and sculptures reproduced throughout the book are by Marjorie von Moschzisker

Copyright © 2011 by Susan Morse

Cover design by Jim Tierney
Interior design by Danielle Young

ISBN: 978-1-4532-5818-7

AUTHOR'S NOTE

Many names of people, places, facilities, and churches have been changed. Some family members who were involved in our story have not been included at their request, and out of respect for their privacy.

Questions regarding long-term care planning and medical insurance options should be addressed to the competent members of those professional areas. I see through my own narrow lens.

Published in 2011 by Open Road Integrated Media
180 Varick Street
New York, NY 10014
www.openroadmedia.com

OPEN ROAD

INTEGRATED MEDIA

Videos, Archival Documents, and New Releases

Sign up for the Open Road Media newsletter and get news delivered straight to your inbox.

FOLLOW US:
@openroadmedia and
Facebook.com/OpenRoadMedia

CPSIA information can be obtained at www.ICGtesting.com
Printed in the USA
BVOW061448080412

287103BV00001B/2/P